Wisdom, Science, and the Scriptures

Wisdom, Science, and the Scriptures

Essays in Honor of Ernest Lucas

Edited by

Stephen Finamore and John Weaver

PICKWICK Publications · Eugene, Oregon

WISDOM, SCIENCE, AND THE SCRIPTURES
Essays in Honor of Ernest Lucas

Copyright © 2014 Wipf and Stock Publishers. All rights reserved. Except for brief quotations in critical publications or reviews, no part of this book may be reproduced in any manner without prior written permission from the publisher. Write: Permissions, Wipf and Stock Publishers, 199 W. 8th Ave., Suite 3, Eugene, OR 97401.

First published in 2012 in the UK by The Centre for Baptist History and Heritage, Regent's Park College, Pusey Street, Oxford, OX1 2LB 2012.

Pickwick Publications
An Imprint of Wipf and Stock Publishers
199 W. 8th Ave., Suite 3
Eugene, OR 97401

www.wipfandstock.com

ISBN 13: 978-1-62032-966-5

Cataloging-in-Publication data:

Wisdom, science, and the Scriptures : essays in honor of Ernest Lucas / edited by Stephen Finamore and John Weaver.

xiv + 264 p. ; 23 cm. Includes bibliographical references.

ISBN 13: 978-1-62032-966-5

1. Lucas, Ernest. 2. Wisdom literature—Criticism, interpretation, etc. 3. Religion and science. 4. Bible—Hermeneutics. I. Finamore, Stephen. II. Weaver, John. III. Title.

BS476 F563 2014

Manufactured in the U.S.A.
Typeset by Hilary Soper

Contents

Acknowledgements		ix
List of Contributors		xi
Introduction by Stephen Finamore with Hazel Lucas		xiii

Part One	**Wisdom in the Bible**	1
1. Gordon Wenham	Creation in the Psalms	3
2. John Bimson	Fierce Beasts and Free Processes: A Proposed Reading of God's Speeches in the Book of Job	16
3. Hillary Nyika	The Traditional Israelite Legal Settings: Social Contexts in Proverbs?	34
4. Knut M. Heim	Personified Wisdom in Early Judaism	56

Part Two	**Science and Christian Faith**	73
5. Paul S. Fiddes	Ancient and Modern Wisdom: The Intersection of Clinical and Theological Understanding of Health	75
6. Brian Haymes	The Way of Practical Modesty	99
7. Elaine Storkey	The Environment and the Developing World	118
8. John Weaver	Hopeful Disciples in a Time of Climate Change	134
9. Robert S. White	Take Ten: Scientists and their Religious Beliefs	157

Part Three	**The Scriptures**	181
10. Simon Woodman	The Evolving Agenda of Biblical Studies	183
11. Mike Pears	Moving Towards a Theological Perspective on 'Place' in Mark's Gospel	197
12. Stephen Finamore	'Not Made with Hands': the Heavenly Temple in Hebrews and Revelation	223
Part Four	**... and Cricket**	241
13. Robert Ellis	'Play Up! Play Up! And Play the Game!' Cricket and Our Place in the World	243
Select Bibliography of Works by Ernest Lucas		263

The prayers that follow each contribution are by Sian Murray Williams

Acknowledgements

The editors would like to express their thanks to a number of people whose work has made it possible for this book to be produced. First there are the authors whose essays are included. Secondly we are grateful for the work on the project carried out by Trisha Dale and Hilary Soper. Then there is the work of Anthony R. Cross, formerly of Regent's Park College. Next there are the colleagues who made significant contributions and we are especially grateful for the administrative support offered by Fran Brealey and for the advice on Ernest's publications given by Shirley Shire. Finally, we are thankful to the Whitley committee who have have helped with funding and to the trustees of the Bristol Baptist College who committed staff time and financial resources to the work.

Contributors

John Bimson
Tutor in Old Testament at Trinity College, Bristol.

Robert Ellis
Baptist minister, Principal of Regent's Park College, Oxford.

Paul Fiddes
Baptist minister, Professor of Systematic Theology in the University of Oxford and formerly Principal of Regent's Park College and Chairman of the Theology Faculty.

Stephen Finamore
Baptist minister, Principal of the Bristol Baptist College.

Brian Haymes
Baptist minister, formerly principal of two Baptist colleges: Northern Baptist College, Manchester, and Bristol Baptist College, and Minister of Bloomsbury Central Baptist Church.

Knut Heim
Methodist presbyter, Vice-Principal and Academic Dean at Trinity College, Bristol.

Hazel Lucas
Teacher of physics and design technology, and freelance writer.

Sian Murray Williams
Baptist minister, Tutor in Worship Studies at Bristol Baptist College.

Hillary Nyika
Baptist minister based at the Guy Chester Centre, Methodist Regional Oversight Tutor and Lecturer in Biblical Studies at the Eastern Region Ministry Course and South East Institute for Theological Education, and occasional tutor at Wesley House, Cambridge.

Mike Pears
Baptist minister, Co-ordinator of Urban Expression, Bristol, Director of re:Source Bristol, and Tutor in Urban Mission at Bristol Baptist College.

Elaine Storkey
Theologian, writer and international speaker. Since 1997 she has been President of Tearfund, the Christian relief and development charity, involved in monitoring aid, relief and advocacy work in countries of the Global South.

John Weaver
Baptist minister, Chair of the John Ray Initiative, connecting environment, science and Christianity, formerly Principal of the South Wales Baptist College and Dean of the Faculty of Theology, Cardiff University.

Gordon Wenham
Professor Emeritus of the University of Gloucestershire and Tutor in Old Testament at Trinity College, Bristol.

Robert S. White
Professor of Geophysics, University of Cambridge, Associate Director of the Faraday Institute for Science and Religion and a fellow of the Royal Society.

Simon Woodman
Baptist minister, formerly Lecturer in the School of Religious and Theological Studies, Cardiff University, and Tutor in Biblical Studies at South Wales Baptist College, Cardiff.

Introduction

This collection of essays is offered in admiration of and in gratitude for the work of Ernest Charles Lucas and in appreciation of his friendship. It has been produced to mark his retirement in 2012. The title of the volume acknowledges Ernest's particular areas of interest and expertise.

The word *wisdom* comes first for two reasons; first because the Bible's wisdom literature is a particular love about which Ernest has published a number of books, and second because wisdom is a characteristic of the man. He offers his insights with a quiet, gentle humility which has endeared him to generations of students and to all his colleagues. Several of the contributions to this volume pick up the theme of biblical wisdom while others touch on the practical application of a wisdom shaped by the Scriptures to vital contemporary issues. Once again, this reflects some of Ernest's especial concerns. He has been committed to helping Christians work out how to be disciples in the workplace and has written on questions of health and healing.

The second word of the title, *science*, reflects both Ernest's first career as a research biochemist and his interest as a theologian in exploring the relationship between science and faith. Many of his publications have been of enormous help to others as they have worked through the issues involved. This area of interest is reflected in a number of the contributions to this collection including Ernest's passionate interest in and concern about climate change.

The final words of the title are *and the Scriptures.* Ernest has specialized in Old Testament and in particular parts of it. Nevertheless, at one time or another he has taught every part of the Bible and retained a keen interest in the discipline of Biblical Studies. Once again, this is reflected in some of the contributions.

Of course, we have not managed to find a contribution for every area of Ernest's extensive academic interests. The select bibliography will show that he has written on other areas, especially the *New Age* movement, that are not touched on here. However, it did not seem right to restrict the collection to Ernest's academic interests alone. There are other aspects to the man and among them is a love of sport, especially cricket. And so the collection ends with a reflection on this wonderful pastime. It helps make this an even more appropriate and personal gift to our friend.

Each of the essays is followed by a prayer which draws together some of the thoughts expressed and offers them to God. This is our way of acknowledging that all Ernest's endeavours, like those of the contributors when at our best, have been shaped by his Christian spirituality and discipleship.

Most of the contributors are colleagues and former colleagues of Ernest's. A couple are former students. All are friends. We hope that many of Ernest's other friends will be among the readers of this book and that you will be reminded of him as you enjoy the contents.

Ernest was born on 20 May 1945 in Bangalore in India, the third of his parents' four children. His father was a soldier and his mother was the daughter of a missionary family. They were Brethren. When India became independent the family moved to the UK though his mother had never been there before except for a short visit in 1937 when Ernest's father's regiment went to England to take part in the coronation of King George VI. His father became a Scripture Reader with the Soldiers' and Airmen's Scripture Readers Association. It was a financially precarious existence but the aware-ness of God's involvement in the family's life through the experience of answered prayer played a large part in convincing Ernest of the truths of Christianity. He became involved in the young people's group at Wellington Road Gospel Hall, Hounslow and then at Dean Hall Brethren Assembly in Ealing, West London. The family's faith helped them to cope with the loss of Ernest's mother to cancer when he was fifteen years old.

Ernest attended Grove Road Primary School, Hounslow, from 1950 to 1956 and then Isleworth Grammar School between 1956 and 1963 where he ran the Christian Union and which he left with A levels in pure mathematics, applied mathematics, physics, and chemistry. He gained a place at Lincoln College, Oxford, and read chemistry from 1963 to 1967, the only one of his brothers and sisters to attend university. He was actively involved in both the College and the Inter-Collegiate Christian Unions, becoming Vice-President of the latter (known as OICCU) and being co-opted onto the National Executive of the Inter-Varsity Fellowship. He wrote apologetics leaflets, which led to his becoming known to the Humanist Society as the 'OICCU Pamphleteer'. It is an interest which has never left him. Ernest's fourth year at Lincoln College involved a project and this helped convince him that scientific research should be his career.

In 1967 Ernest took up the offer of a place at the University of Kent at Canterbury to undertake research into enzyme chemistry. While researching he met Hazel Craddock who was studying physics at the university and they were married in April 1969. As a couple they supported the work of the student Christian Union and helped to found the University Sceptics Society, which discussed controversial subjects, including religion, with the aim of bringing discussion of important issues, including the claims of Christianity, into the Senior Common Room. Ernest gained his doctorate in 1970.

Next came a post-doctoral research fellowship at the University of North

Carolina in the United States of America. He continued his work on enzyme chemistry. While living in America he ran the student Sunday-school class at Cresset Baptist Church in Durham, North Carolina, which grew from four to 34 over the two years. During this period he received many opportunities to speak on issues of science and apologetics and his ministry had a significant impact on friends and neighbors. In 1972 Ernest and Hazel returned to England and Ernest took up a one-year post-doctoral fellowship at the University of Oxford. While there they joined Headington Baptist Church and Ernest decided that he was being prompted to apply for theological training and to consider, though he was unsure at this stage, the possibility that God was calling him to the Christian ministry.

So from 1973 to 1976 Ernest, without a grant, and living without a regular income, and with a son, Craig Charles, who was born at the end of 1972, read theology at Regent's Park College, a Baptist foundation within the University of Oxford. He earned small amounts from offering lectures at what was then the Oxford Polytechnic and he and Hazel received generous support from friends in the USA. In 1976 Ernest gained the top first in the university. The years at Regent's had confirmed the call to ministry and Ernest was called to the pastorate of Durham City Baptist Church. Ernest and Hazel's second son, Stuart James, was born in the December of their first year there and the family remained till 1978 when Ernest was called to Liverpool Bible College, to membership with Laird Street Church and to the pastorate of Cottenham Street Baptist Church in inner-city Liverpool. In 1986 the family moved to Southport where they joined Norwood Avenue Baptist Church.

In 1984 Ernest began work on his second doctorate, this time on the book of Daniel and under the supervision of Professor Alan Millard of the Department of Oriental Studies at the University of Liverpool. In 1988 the family moved to Bromley and Ernest took up a position as Director of Studies, and later as Associate Director, at the London Institute of Contemporary Christianity under the leadership of John Stott. Ernest continued to work part-time on his thesis and was awarded the PhD in 1989. He enjoyed the institute as it played to his particular interests and strengths in exploring the relevance of Christianity to the whole of people's lives, especially to their work. He had a particular ministry among the institute's overseas students. The family settled at West Wickham and Shirley Baptist Church while Ernest found himself in demand as a speaker in churches up and down the country.

In 1994 Ernest and Hazel moved again, this time so that Ernest could take up the position of Tutor in Biblical Studies at the Bristol Baptist College. He taught widely, covering Old Testament, science and religion, biblical interpretation and biblical languages. He was a key part of the team which revived the fortunes of the college and helped it to thrive. His contribution was formally acknowledged when he was appointed Vice-Principal. While serving at Bristol, Ernest and Hazel were at first in membership with Chipping Sodbury but in 2001 they moved to Wales where they are involved in the life and mission of the Magor and Penhow Baptist Churches.

Underlying all of Ernest's character and achievement is his deep faith in the God revealed through Jesus of Nazareth. He constantly impresses us with the way in which his convictions integrate every aspect of his life and learning. In particular he enjoys a spirituality of the aesthetic within the natural world; microscopic, visible to the naked eye, and macroscopic. His experience of the utter beauty of things which are invisible to the unaided human eye, a beauty which seems to be gratuitous, to serve no apparent purpose but to give joy, feeds his appreciation of the work and character of the One who made all things. The stunning photograph on the cover of this book has been chosen with these thoughts in mind. It was taken by NASA's Hubble Space Telescope and is of the Quintuplet Cluster of stars in the Milky Way. So, while this book is for Ernest, it is, like all our best endeavours, more truly for the God whom Ernest loves.

Stephen Finamore with Hazel Lucas

PART ONE

Wisdom in the Bible

1

Creation in the Psalms

Gordon Wenham

It has been a pleasure working with Ernest Lucas these last few years. He is both congenial and efficient, as well as being an excellent teacher. But in the wider world he is probably best known for his work on the opening chapters of Genesis and their relationship to ancient Near Eastern mythology on the one hand and modern scientific theory on the other. To see Genesis 1–11 as a revolutionary theological revamping of what were to the ancients familiar accounts of the origins of the universe and the human race in particular is probably the most helpful way to read the opening chapters of the Bible.[1] More recently he has contributed a volume on the Psalms and Wisdom literature in the *Exploring the Old Testament* series (Lucas, 2003). It therefore seems appropriate in a volume dedicated to Ernest to devote an essay to the teaching of the Psalms about creation.

It is remarkable how much there is in the Psalter on the topic. Psalm 104 by itself is longer than Genesis 1, and there are mentions or fuller statements on the topic in at least 32 other psalms.[2] There are many paths we could follow in this discussion. Do the psalms know the Genesis accounts? If they do, how do the psalms interpret Genesis? Are they indebted to ancient Near Eastern sources? Do different groups of psalms categorized by genre or by title differ in their approach to creation theology? In what situations is creation mentioned? Are there recurrent situations that prompt the psalmist to invoke the Creator's activity? Is there a coherent theology of creation running through the Psalter?

We start by examining the terms used to describe creation in the Psalter. Though the psalms often mention God's creative deeds, they rarely use the term for creation typically used in Genesis and Isaiah, *bārā'*, a term that occurs 11 times[3] in Genesis 1—6, usually of the creation of man,[4] and 20 times[5] in Isaiah 40—66. But in the Psalms it occurs only three times in the qal:

Create in me a clean heart,
O God, and renew a right spirit within me. (Ps. 51:10)[6]

The north and the south, you have created them;

Tabor and Hermon joyously praise your name. (Ps. 89:12)

Remember how short my time is!
For what vanity you have created all the children of man! (Ps. 89:47)

and three times in the niphal:

Let this be recorded for a generation to come,
so that a people yet to be created may praise the LORD. (Ps. 102:18)

When you send forth your Spirit, they are created,
and you renew the face of the ground. (Ps. 104:30)

Let them [= heavenly bodies] praise the name of the LORD!
For he commanded and they were created. (Ps. 148:5)

bārā' 'create' is thus used of God's creating the heavens and the earth (Pss 104:30; 89:12) and mankind (89:47; 102:18). It is used of God's past actions (89:12; 148:5), his ongoing present activity (104:30) and his future deeds (51:10; 102:18).

On the other hand *yāṣar* 'mould', 'form', used but three times in Genesis 2:7,8,19, and 21 times in Isaiah, is used five times in the Psalms in connection with creation. God is the Creator of the human heart: 'He ... fashions the hearts of them all' (Ps. 33:15) and the human eye (94:9). He shapes the seasons 'summer and winter', the 'dry land' and 'Leviathan'[7] to play in the seas (74:17; 95:5; 104:26). Here allusions to Genesis are particularly clear (cf. Gen. 1:9,10; 8:11; cf. 1:21). But once again this term is not restricted to God's past deeds: rather it seems to describe God's ongoing activity in maintaining life.

But much the commonest term to describe God's creative activity is the quite ordinary term *"āśāh*, 'make'. In Genesis God makes 'the firmament' (1:7, RSV), 'fruit trees' (1:11–12), the 'two great lights' (1:16), wild animals (1:25; 3:1), and 'man' (1:26, 5:1; 6:6–7; 9:6), 'a helper' for the man (2:18). In the Psalms God makes 'all the nations' (86:9), 'the sea' (95:5), 'his people' (95:6; 100:3), 'the moon' (104:19), all his works (104:24), the psalmist (119:73), and 'lightning' (135:7). As with the term 'create', *bārā'*, so the term *"āśāh* is used of divine creative acts both in the past and in the present.

Less common, but more obviously figurative, terms drawn from the field of building include 'build' (Ps. 78:69), 'lay a foundation, found' (24:2; 78:69; 89:11, 102:25; 104:5), 'establish' (24:2; 65:6; 93:1; 96:10; 119:90), 'spread out like a tent'(19:4; 104:2). This imagery, likening the creation of the world to building a house, is nowhere explicitly used in the Genesis accounts, but it may reflect Near Eastern views of creation. In them the creation of the cosmos is linked to temple-building, so that it is natural to use the language of the one to illuminate the other (see Walton, 2009: 72–92).

If one looks at the way creation language is used in different categories of psalms, no clear pattern emerges. Though creation is mentioned in proportionately fewer Davidic psalms than say in the psalms of Asaph or the so-called enthronement psalms (93–100), two of the Davidic psalms (Pss 8 and 19) are among the most beautiful of all creation-oriented psalms. Creation is also a frequent theme of the anonymous psalms in books 4 and 5 of the Psalter (e.g., Pss 104, 136 and 148). So whether one views the titles of the psalms as indicating their real authors or merely the sources from which they have been drawn, it would be unwise to claim that a psalm's use of creation motifs is a mark of authorship or source.

Form-critical categories also appear to be irrelevant in discussing creation: hymns and laments both often include reflections on creation. Psalm 33,

> the earth is full of the steadfast love of the LORD.
> By the word of the LORD the heavens were made,
> and by the breath of his mouth all their host (Ps. 33:5–6)

is typical of hymns in appealing to creation as ground for the praise of God (cf. Pss 8:1–8; 19:1; 100:3; 104:1–35; 135:6–7). In lament, by contrast, reflection on creation gives psalmists hope that God is able to act and remedy their distress. As Psalm 75 puts it:

> When the earth totters, and all its inhabitants,
> it is I who keep steady its pillars. *Selah* (Psalm 75:3)

But references to creation are also found in royal psalms (e.g., 72:5; 89:8–14[8]), psalms of confidence (91:13), thanksgiving (65:6–10) and entrance liturgies (15:1; 24:1). Thus form criticism also seems to be a blind alley in illuminating the psalms' use of creation theology. Maybe straightforward exegesis will prove more helpful.

Psalm 8

Psalm 8 is the first hymn in the Psalter, a beam of light, after a string of laments. Although on first sight it looks like an interloper, it is carefully placed. Psalm 7 ends:

> I will give to the LORD the thanks due to his righteousness,
> and I will sing praise to the name of the LORD, the Most High. (Ps. 7:17)

and Psalm 9 begins:

> I will give thanks to the LORD with my whole heart;

> I will recount all of your wonderful deeds.
> I will be glad and exult in you;
> I will sing praise to your name, O Most High. (Ps. 9:1–2)

Thus both psalms declare the psalmist's intention to sing praise to the name of the Lord, and Psalm 8, which opens and closes with 'O LORD, our Lord, how majestic is your name in all the earth!' (Ps. 8:1,9) shows the psalmist fulfilling his vow. More precisely it is a response to his plight set out in Psalm 7. There he describes himself as pursued by false accusers. He prays that God will arise and vindicate him (vv. 1–11). He then reflects on the inevitability of divine judgment on the wicked (vv. 12–16), which prompts his vow to thank and praise the name of the Lord (v. 17). Then comes Psalm 8 which declares:

> Out of the mouth of babes and infants,
> you have established strength because of your foes,
> to still the enemy and the avenger. (Ps. 8:2)

God's ability to still the enemy is reinforced by reflection on his power to create.

> When I look at your heavens, the work of your fingers,
> the moon and the stars, which you have set in place,
> what is man that you are mindful of him,
> and the son of man that you care for him? (Ps. 8:3–4)

The logic of the sequence, that the enemy will be judged by the Creator, is that it is impossible for man to resist divine judgment. But that is not the conclusion that the psalmist draws. Reflection on the creation account in Genesis 1 reminds him that the climax of creation is the making of man in the divine image to rule the rest of the created order:

> So God created man in his own image,
> in the image of God he created him;
> male and female he created them.
>
> And God blessed them. And God said to them, 'Be fruitful and multiply and fill the earth and subdue it, and have dominion over the fish of the sea and over the birds of the heavens and over every living thing that moves on the earth.' (Gen. 1:27–28)

In Near Eastern thought, kings were often seen as God's image, or representative, on Earth. Genesis however democratizes this idea by declaring all human beings are images of the divine, i.e., God's representatives. These ideas are expressed even more vividly in the psalm:

> Yet you have made him a little lower than the heavenly beings
> and crowned him with glory and honor.
> You have given him dominion over the works of your hands;
> you have put all things under his feet. (Ps. 8:5–6)

That creation is both the basis for hope in ultimate divine vindication and the proof of God's benevolence are regular themes in the Psalter. So too is the emphasis on the consequences of creation as opposed to the act of creation itself. Hence Psalm 8 seems to reflect Genesis 1's approach to the creation of mankind rather than Genesis 2's version, where Adam is made from the dust of the Earth and has the divine breath breathed into him.[9]

Psalm 19 reflects on the witness of the created world to its Creator, 'The heavens declare the glory of God and the sky above proclaims his handiwork' (19:1). But it is a silent witness: 'there is no speech, nor are there words' (19:3). Here the glory of God is compared to the sun, filling the sky with light and heat, from which no one can hide. The sun's penetrating power is akin to the law, which embraces the whole of existence and this reminds the psalmist of his own failings, so that he prays:

> Who can discern his errors?
> Declare me innocent from hidden faults.
> Keep back your servant also from presumptuous sins;
> let them not have dominion over me!
> Then I shall be blameless,
> and innocent of great transgression. (Ps. 19:12–13)

Here we have the corollary of the assurance that the Creator's insight will ensure the punishment of the wicked (cf. Ps. 94:8–10): it also implies he knows the hidden faults of the relatively righteous, as Psalm 139 puts it:

> My frame was not hidden from you,
> when I was being made in secret,
> intricately woven in the depths of the earth.
> Your eyes saw my unformed substance;
> in your book were written, every one of them,
> the days that were formed for me,
> when as yet there was none of them ...
> Search me, O God, and know my heart!
> Try me and know my thoughts!
> And see if there be any grievous way in me,
> and lead me in the way everlasting! (Ps. 139:15–16, 23–24)

Psalm 33

Psalm 33 is one of the few psalms in book 1 which is not ascribed to David, but it contains one of the clearest comments on Genesis 1:

> By the word of the LORD the heavens were made,
> and by the breath of his mouth all their host.
> He gathers the waters of the sea as a heap;
> he puts the deeps in storehouses.
> Let all the earth fear the LORD;
> let all the inhabitants of the world stand in awe of him!
> For he spoke, and it came to be;
> he commanded, and it stood firm. (Ps. 33:6–9)

This passage bears little obvious relationship to the preceding context, which says:

> He loves righteousness and justice;
> the earth is full of the steadfast love of the LORD. (Ps. 33:5)

but verse 4 links with verses 6 to 9:

> For the word of the LORD is upright,
> and all his work is done in faithfulness.

Verse 4 states that God's word is reliable: it achieves what it says. (One might compare Isa. 55:11: 'my word ... shall not return to me empty, but it shall accomplish that which I purpose'). The psalm then cites Genesis 1 as proof of the irresistible power of the divine word. The heavens were created at his word and the seas and deeps, symbolic of chaos and anti-God forces, were confined to their proper limits. God's power in creation is thus an assurance that what he says happens. This reinforces the message of verse 4. But clearly the divine word in verse 4 is different from the word in verse 6. Can we identify the former?

It is not obvious what is the divine word that verse 4 is alluding to. No divine words are mentioned in verses 1 to 3. But if one looks back to the previous psalm, Psalm 32, certain possibilities arise. The two psalms are closely connected: for example[10] the first verse of Psalm 33 repeats most of the terms in the last verse of Psalm 32.

> Be glad in the LORD, and rejoice, O righteous,
> and shout for joy, all you upright in heart!
> Shout for joy in the LORD, O you righteous!
> Praise befits the upright. (Pss 32:11—33:1)

Psalm 32 has given several reasons why the righteous should rejoice: the forgiveness of sin (vv. 1,5), the hearing of his prayer (vv. 5–6), the promise of future guidance and protection (vv. 7–9). These blessings are all summed up in verse 10: 'steadfast love surrounds the one who trusts in the LORD.' But what is the divine word or words that Psalm 33:4 is alluding to? There is only one[11] directly quoted in verses 8 to 9:

> I will instruct you and teach you in the way you should go;
> I will counsel you with my eye upon you.
> Be not like a horse or a mule, without understanding,
> which must be curbed with bit and bridle,
> or it will not stay near you. (Ps. 32:8–9)

This promise of divine guidance is reassuring and indeed a reason for praise, but it does not seem as key as the assurance of forgiveness which forms the heart of the psalm. Indeed the terminology of 'sin', 'transgression', 'iniquity', 'steadfast love', and 'forgiveness' in verses 1, 2, 5, and 10 aligns this psalm closely with Psalm 51, the greatest of the penitential psalms, identified as David's confession after he had been rebuked by the prophet Nathan. These terms are drawn from the account of Israel's greatest sin, the worship of the golden calf, in Exodus 32–34. So we should perhaps look to these stories to see if we can identify a divine word that should prompt such an outburst of praise.

Exodus 34:6–7 is God's disclosure of his character to Moses after the latter has successfully pleaded for the nation to be spared annihilation in punishment for their sin.

> The LORD passed before him and proclaimed, 'The LORD, the LORD, a God merciful and gracious, slow to anger, and abounding in steadfast love and faithfulness, keeping steadfast love for thousands, forgiving iniquity and transgression and sin, but who will by no means clear the guilty, visiting the iniquity of the fathers on the children and the children's children, to the third and the fourth generation.' (Exod. 34:6–7)

This summary of God's character is seen as central in the Old Testament, being quoted by psalmists and prophets alike (see Wenham, 2011: 169–81). Not only does it fit thematically with Psalm 32; its terminology—'steadfast love', 'forgiving', 'iniquity', 'transgression', 'sin'—is taken up in the psalms. So could it be the divine word that 32: 5 alludes to?

But if we take the title of the psalm, 'A Maskil of David', seriously, or at least as an indicator of how the Psalter's compilers understood the psalm, then Nathan's declaration to David: 'The LORD . . . has put away your sin; you shall not die' (2 Sam. 12:13) is the more likely candidate. This is not to say that the Exodus passage is irrelevant: its language is so evident in Psalm 51, the psalm most associated with David's sin and his penitence. As that terminology is present too in Psalm 32, we should not write it off. But the primary reference is to God's absolution of David through the mediation of the prophet Nathan.

The striking thing about Psalm 33 is that it compares a declaration of forgiveness to the divine word that brought creation into being. The created order demonstrates God's faithfulness, his righteousness and steadfast love. That is why the righteous should shout for joy.

Psalm 104

The longest psalm dealing with creation is Psalm 104. It is one of a group of four which sum up and reflect on the history of Israel told in the Pentateuch. Psalm 103 introduces the God of grace, 'who forgives all your iniquity, who heals all your diseases' (Ps. 103:3). Then comes our Psalm 104 which retells Genesis 1, with a few glimpses of Genesis 2 and 3, focusing on the present blessings bestowed by a loving Creator. Psalm 105 tells the story of Israel from the patriarchs to the conquest. Psalm 106 focuses on Israel's propensity to sin particularly in the wilderness and conquest. But despite their rebelliousness:

> For their sake he remembered his covenant,
> and relented according to the abundance of his steadfast love (Ps. 106:45)

and this gives them hope that he will bring them back from exile:

> Save us, O LORD our God,
> and gather us from among the nations,
> that we may give thanks to your holy name
> and glory in your praise. (Ps. 106:47)

Psalm 104 is thus sandwiched between psalms whose dominant note is the steadfast love of God, a note which characterizes Psalm 104's approach to creation. It displays in all sorts of ways God's care for his creatures. The psalm is more interested in extolling God's continuing providential care than describing the original creation decrees as set out in Genesis 1.

If we examine Table 1, setting the creative acts of Genesis 1 against those of Psalm 104, certain differences are immediately obvious. There is no creation of the firmament in the psalm, unless verse 2 is an allusion to it. The land and plants are mentioned before the sun and moon, and the fish after man and the animals.

The second great difference is in language. While Genesis 1 may be described as elevated prose, Psalm 104 is vivid poetry. Compare the emergence of the land in the two versions:

Table 1

Genesis 1	Psalm 104
Light v. 3 DAY 1	Light v. 2
The deep v. 2	The deep v. 6
The firmament vv. 6–8 DAY 2	The heavens like a tent v. 2
Dry land v. 9 DAY 3	The land vv. 7–9
Plants vv. 11–13 DAY 3	[Plants v. 14]
Birds vv. 20–3 DAY 5	Birds v. 17
Sun and moon vv.14–19 DAY 4	Moon and sun v. 19
Animals/man vv. 24–31 DAY 6	[Man and animals vv. 21–3]
Fish vv. 20–2 DAY 5	Sea creatures vv. 25–6

And God said, 'Let the waters under the heavens be gathered together into one place, and let the dry land appear.' And it was so. God called the dry land Earth, and the waters that were gathered together he called Seas. And God saw that it was good. (Gen. 1:9–10)

And

> You covered it with the deep as with a garment;
> the waters stood above the mountains.
> At your rebuke they fled;
> at the sound of your thunder they took to flight.
> The mountains rose, the valleys sank down
> to the place that you appointed for them.
> You set a boundary that they may not pass,
> so that they might not again cover the earth. (Ps. 104:6–9)

The third difference between the psalm and Genesis is that in several instances the parallel between the psalm and Genesis is between God's initial act of creation in Genesis and his ongoing provision in Psalm 104. For example whereas Genesis 1:11 says 'Let the earth sprout vegetation', Psalm 104 says:

> You cause the grass to grow for the livestock
> and plants for man to cultivate,
> that he may bring forth food from the earth. (Ps. 104:14)

Similarly while Genesis 1:24–31 focuses on the initial creation of animals and humans, Psalm 104:21–3 concentrates on their present role in the divine scheme. There are references in the psalm to God's initial acts, e.g., putting the waters in their place (vv. 7–9) or making the moon to mark the seasons (v. 19), but these are but illustrations of God's abiding concern for the welfare of his creation. The ultimate origin of the world and its creatures is quite secondary to the experience of divine benevolence in the present.

This divine benevolence is particularly seen in God's transformation of the waters. Having curbed the waters of chaos by assigning them to their place, God makes these waters the source of life. Springs in the valley refresh every beast of the field (v. 11), make the grass grow, trees flourish and allow man to cultivate the ground (vv. 14–16). Even the seas are filled with living things both small and great (v. 25). God does not just supply water to drink but also food to eat. Man is enabled to bring forth food, wine, oil and bread to strengthen his heart (vv. 14–15):

> The young lions roar for their prey,
> seeking their food from God. (Ps. 104:21)

> All creatures . . .
>   look to you,
>   to give them their food in due season.
>   When you give it to them, they gather it up;
>   when you open your hand, they are filled with good things. (Ps. 104:27–8)

God, declares Psalm 104, is the great life-giver, who continues to sustain his creatures by providing them with water to drink and food to eat. But it is not God's past deeds that prove his steadfast love so much as his continuing providential care. This psalm is a paean of praise to the God who sustains his creatures by giving them an abundance of water and food.

> O LORD, how manifold are your works!
> In wisdom have you made them all;
> the earth is full of your creatures . . .
> These all look to you,
> to give them their food in due season . . .
> When you send forth your Spirit, they are created,
> and you renew the face of the ground. (Ps. 104:24,27,30)

That Psalm 104 knows Genesis 1 is generally acknowledged, so we may regard it as the earliest interpretation of that chapter, an interpretation that is rather different from those of some of its modern interpreters. We note that the psalm sits very light to the sequence[12] of creative acts in Genesis 1. The sun and moon are created after the birds, while the fish and sea creatures are created after man and the land animals. Indeed the fact of an initial creation seems less important to the psalmist than God's ongoing providential support of life. God's goodness is demonstrated by present experience of it rather than its historic beginnings. The birds acknowledge it by their singing (Ps. 104:12), while the young lions seek their food from God. It is not the process of creation that elicits the psalmist's praise, but the fact. It is through divine power that the cosmos is sustained and the powers of chaos are turned to benefit all living creatures, especially man. The message of this psalm and the many others dealing with creation is this: 'the earth is full of the steadfast love of the LORD' (Ps. 33:5).

Notes

1 His study *Can We Believe Genesis Today?* (IVP, 2005) is now in its third edition.
2 These passages mention creation either explicitly or implicitly: Pss 8:3–8; 18:15; 19:1; 24:1–2; 29:10; 33:5–15; 36:6–8; 50:10–11; 65:6–10; 72:5; 74:12–17; 75:3; 77:16; 78:69; 89:8–14; 90:1–4; 93:1–4; 95:3–5; 96:10; 98:7–9; 100:3; 102:25–28; 104:1–32; 114:7–8; 119:90; 121:2; 124:8; 134:3; 135:6–7; 136:4–9; 146:5–7; 147:4–5,8–9; 148:3–6.
3 Nine times in the qal and twice in the niphal.
4 Gen. 1:27 (3x); 5:1,2; 6:7; heaven and earth, 1:1; great sea creatures 1:21; everything 2:3.
5 Nineteen times in qal and once in niphal. Of the stars (40:26), the ends of the earth (40:28), deserts into watered land (41:21), the heavens (42:5; 45:18), Israel (43:1,15), God's children (43:7), light and darkness (45:7), rain and fertility (45:8) mankind (45:12), blacksmith (54:16), destroyer (54:16) new heaven and earth (65:17), Jerusalem (65:18).
6 Bible quotations are from the ESV, unless otherwise indicated.
7 It is notable that the psalms (e. g. 74:14; 104:26) are quite happy to use the language of myth about sea monsters and Leviathan. Whereas when Genesis 1:21 uses the same Hebrew term *tannin* 'sea monster', it has according to C. Westermann (1984: 137–8), less mythological overtones, cf. ESV's translation, 'great sea creatures'. Similarly the psalms are happy to talk about God creating the sun, moon and stars, whereas Genesis avoids such language and speaks of the 'greater and lesser lights', lest sun and moon be misinterpreted as sun god and moon god, cf. Wenham (1987: 9).
8 If Ps. 89 is to be categorized as royal rather than as a lament.
9 Echoes of Genesis 2 and 3 may be heard in Ps. 90:3 (ESV)

You return man to dust
and say, 'Return, O children of man!'

and Ps. 104:29 (ESV)

When you hide your face, they are dismayed;
when you take away their breath, they die
and return to their dust.

10 For other links between the two psalms see Vesco (2006: 307–8).
11 The speaker in the last four verses of the psalm is hard to identify. If vv. 8–9 are not spoken by God, they could be the psalmist's: he could be telling others what he has learned from his experience (so Clifford, 2002: 167–8; Seybold, 1996: 134).

Compare Vesco (2006: 306) as David promises to do in Ps. 51:13. On the other hand vv. 10–11 look like the speech of the psalmist, but they could be God's words.

12 It is often observed that the sequence of acts in Genesis is governed more by structural considerations than by chronological, that days 1 to 3 create the framework while days 4 to 6 create the objects to fill the framework, e.g., light day 1/sun and moon day 4. See Blocher (1984: 49–59); Wenham (1987: 6–7).

Bibliography

Blocher, H. *In the Beginning* (Leicester: IVP, 1984).
Clifford, R.J. *Psalms 1—72* (Nashville: Abingdon, 2002)
Lucas, Ernest. *Can We Believe Genesis Today?* (Leicester: IVP, 2005).
———. *The Psalms and Wisdom Literature* (London: SPCK, 2003).
Seybold, K. *Die Psalmen* (Tübingen: Mohr, 1996).
Vesco, J.-L. *Le psautier de David traduit et commenté* (Paris: du Cerf, 2006).
Walton, John H. *The Lost World of Genesis 1* (Downers Grove: IVP, 2009).
Wenham, G.J. *Genesis 1–15* (Waco: Word, 1987).
———. 'The Golden Calf in the Psalms'. Pages 169–81 in *A God of Faithfulness: Essays in Honour of J. G. McConville* (eds. J. A. Grant, A. Lo and G. J. Wenham; London: T. & T. Clark, 2011).
Westermann, C. *Genesis 1—11: A Commentary*. (Minneapolis: Augsburg, 1984).

Creator God
    such an explosion of color
    a profusion of texture
    an abundance of sound
    a smorgasbord of taste
    an inhaling of heaven's fragrance
    here on earth
    a soaking of the senses
    in your summoned cosmos.

    Overwhelmed and awestruck
    we find gratitude liberated from us
    before we even know it,
    wild and beautiful, to you and you alone

    In all your gift, in all your sustaining,
    in all your provision, in all your proclaiming,
    we are flattened before you
    in praise and adoration
    for your faithfulness, justice and steadfast

2

Fierce Beasts and Free Processes: A Proposed Reading of God's Speeches in the Book of Job

John J. Bimson

'As a mere argument there's something lacking perhaps, in saying to a man who's lost his money and his house and his family and is sitting on the dustbin, all over boils, "Look at the hippopotamus."'
'Job seemed to be impressed,' the Archdeacon said mildly.
'Yes,' Mornington admitted. 'He was certainly a perfect fool, in one meaning or other of the words.'

Charles Williams, *War in Heaven*

I don't believe the splendor of hippos is any sort of answer to the suffering of humans. Where do I even begin? The Lisbon earthquake? The London plague? Malignant melanoma?

James Morrow, *Towing Jehovah*

The interpretation of Yahweh's speeches in the book of Job (Job 38–41) is notoriously contentious. Gowan (1986) evaluates six points of view and offers a seventh, and the list has since extended considerably (cf. Dell, 1991: 29–56; Fyall, 2002: 21–3; Newsom, 2003: 234–58; Schifferdecker, 2008: 63–132).

Recurring issues include: do the divine speeches answer Job's complaints about suffering and injustice, or does God avoid those issues altogether and simply tell Job that he cannot hope to understand the divine purpose? Does God overwhelm Job (as Job had feared he would, 9:13–20), or is God's appearance in the whirlwind the very comfort Job most needed? Even among scholars who find in these speeches a coherent reply to Job, there is no consensus as to what that reply might be. To take one extreme case of disagreement: are we to understand that God 'has placed justice at the center of the world's structure' (Hartley, 1988: 515; cf. Gordis, 1978), or that the order on which the world is founded cannot be defined in terms of justice at all (Tsevat, 1980)?

Central to the hermeneutical problem is the significance of the two creatures Behemoth and Leviathan, on which so many words are lavished in the second speech. It is the second speech which finally brings Job to a new orientation, so a proper understanding of Behemoth and Leviathan seems likely to be the key to understanding the message of the divine speeches. This paper will therefore focus on the interpretation of the second speech, with only brief comments on the first to suggest how the two divine speeches cohere.

The significance of Behemoth and Leviathan

Not surprisingly, there is considerable debate over the nature and significance of Behemoth and Leviathan. The main views that have emerged among commentators can be grouped under three headings.

Naturalistic

Many commentators take the view that Behemoth and Leviathan are ordinary earthly creatures, like those referred to in chapters 38—39, albeit described with an extravagant degree of poetic hyperbole not found in the first speech. Several identifications have been proposed: Aquinas thought Behemoth was an elephant and Leviathan a whale (for the latter see also Milton, *Paradise Lost* I, 200–8; also Herman Melville, *Moby Dick, passim*). Others have suggested some kind of bovine for Behemoth. However, in the most popular interpretation, which dates back at least to Samuel Bochart's *Hierozoicon* of 1663, Behemoth is a hippopotamus and Leviathan a crocodile (thus RSV marg.; NRSV marg. retains this identification for Leviathan but offers none for Behemoth). This view was widely accepted among twentieth-century commentators (e.g., Dhorme, 1926, ET 1967: 619; Andersen, 1976: 289; cf. Driver and Gray, 1921: 352–53), its most trenchant defender being Gordis (1978: 570–71).

Naturalistic but symbolic

Clines is happy with the consensus when it comes to identifications (i.e., hippopotamus and crocodile), but in his early commentaries on Job (1979, 1989, 1994) he proposes a rhetorical significance for these creatures which is quite different from that of the animals and birds in the first speech. The point, he suggests, is that these creatures, although repulsive, incomprehensible and (at least in the case of Leviathan) dangerous, were made by God and have a place in his overall design. 'Suffering is a crocodile, a hippopotamus, terrifying and mysterious, yet part of God's world and possessed of a peculiar splendour of its own' (Clines, 1979: 590; cf. 1989: xlvi; 1994: 483). He has also proposed a further level of meaning: 'They are also symbolic of chaos, and the fact that God has created them shows he controls any chaotic powers that may threaten his universe' (1994: 483; cf. 1979: 589).[1]

Hartley also adopts what we might call a 'split-level' reading, though the lesson he draws from it is somewhat different. Accepting that a hippopotamus and a crocodile lie behind the descriptions of Behemoth and Leviathan, he adds: 'Nevertheless, into the factual description the author skillfully blends fanciful metaphors drawn from mythic accounts of monsters in order that these beasts may represent both mighty terrestrial creatures and cosmic forces. In this way the author addresses the cosmic dimensions of Job's affliction' (Hartley 1988: 521–22).

Mythological

A mythological understanding of Behemoth and Leviathan is in fact the oldest, with roots in Jewish apocalyptic and rabbinic literature. However, modern scholars adopting a mythological interpretation were in a minority until the 1980s. In 1985 John Day's study *God's Conflict with the Dragon and the Sea* (which devotes a lengthy chapter to Job 40–41), and the commentaries of Habel and Gibson all put forward a mythological view. Since then several commentators have espoused the mythological interpretation, though without necessarily finding the same message in Yahweh's second speech (e.g., Good, 1990; Dell, 2002; Fyall, 2002; Newsom, 2003; Schifferdecker, 2008). A view common to such interpretations (though not found in all the aforementioned) is that Behemoth and Leviathan are mythical chaos monsters representing cosmic forces hostile to God's purposes and inimical to human welfare. Such entities are well-attested elsewhere in the Old Testament and in ancient Near Eastern texts (Wakeman, 1973; Day, 1985; Beal, 2002: 13–22, 25–33).

Of these three options the mythological interpretation has the strongest support, as the following paragraphs will seek to demonstrate.

Behemoth, Job 40:15–24

The word Behemoth is the plural of the feminine noun $b^e hemah$ (beast), and elsewhere means simply cattle (but see Clines 2011: 1187 on Ps. 73:22). Here, where verbs, pronouns and pronominal suffixes are masculine singular, it is best understood as an intensive plural signifying the Beast *par excellence* (Clines 2011: 1149). While hippo-like characteristics undoubtedly feature strongly in the portrait of Behemoth, several scholars have identified mythological elements as well (Lang, 1980; Habel, 1985: 557–9, 564–68;

Good, 1990: 358–63; Day, 1985: 75–82; Gibson, 1988; Fyall, 2002: 129–37; for the opposite view see Alter, 1984: 40). Perhaps Behemoth is best understood as an amalgam of features, a portmanteau monster.

Even if hippo-like characteristics are held to be the dominant ingredients in the portrait of Behemoth, this does not rule out a mythological significance. In Egyptian mythology Seth, god of the desert, darkness and chaos, takes the form of a hippopotamus in his battle with Horus (Keel, 1978a; Lang, 1980; Habel, 1985: 557; Ahuis, 2011: 75). Some scarabs from Egypt's Middle Kingdom (c.2080–1755 BC) depict a male figure harpooning a hippopotamus. This scene was 'originally associated with the king as victor over the forces of chaos', though it was later appropriated by high-ranking private individuals (Ben-Tor, 2007: 35; cf. Keel, 1996: 123–5). On one example the king is dwarfed by a hippopotamus of enormous proportions (Ben-Tor, 2007, Plate 20:7), a clear indication of the latter's mythological significance.

Western readers may find it counterintuitive to think of the herbivorous hippopotamus as a symbol (or even one descriptive ingredient among others) for a chaos monster, but Dell makes the important point that 'the hippopotamus is a creature of great power that causes more human deaths in Africa today than any other animal' (Dell, 2002: 237).[2] The original readers of the book of Job presumably needed no reminder of the danger the animal posed. This side of the hippopotamus' character is overlooked by Clines when he writes that it 'is not so much dangerous as beyond being a danger: no one entertains thoughts of hunting it, so in a way it is no threat' (2011: 1184).

In fact Behemoth is an altogether ambiguous beast. On the one hand it is explicitly said to be part of God's creation: 'Behold, Behemoth, which I made as I made [or along with] you' (40:15, ESV). The further statement in 40:19a that Behemoth is 'the first of the ways of God' (ESV marg.) may signify either temporal priority ('a primordial production of God', Pope, 1973) or qualitative superiority ('the crown of the animal creation', Hartley, 1988). But then in 40:19b we meet the cryptic line: 'his maker may bring near his sword' (thus Pope, 1973, being 'as literal as possible'); 'its Maker can approach it with his sword' (Hartley, 1988); 'his maker brings out his sword!' (Good, 1990). Gibson finds here 'an undoubted suggestion that the Creator has to be more than usually wary of this particular creature of his', and offers the paraphrase: 'Let him that made him keep his sword unsheathed!' (1985: 254). Pope thinks the text 'suggests that the maker of Behemoth is also its slayer or conqueror' (1973: 324), but the idea of God *slaying* Behemoth is going too far: 'The image here is apparently not of El slaying The Beast as a chaos monster, but of threatening or intimidating it to keep it under control' (Habel, 1985: 567). Even so, the image conjured up by 40:19b does carry resonance with the long-running ancient Near Eastern motif of god versus chaos monster. For some scholars the emphasis on Behemoth as God's own creation undermines any such connection (cf. Beal, 2002: 50; Clines, 2011: 1188–9), but I will argue that this tension is in fact an important aspect of Behemoth's significance for the author of Job.

Leviathan, Job 41:1–34 (Hebrew 40:25—41:26)

The clearest evidence for a mythological interpretation can be found in connection with Leviathan. Outside Job 41 we find biblical references to Leviathan in Job 3:8–9; Psalms 74:14; 104:26 and Isaiah 27:1. In at least three, and perhaps all four, of these cases a mythological monster is envisaged.[3] However, there is great flexibility in the way the Leviathan motif is used by the biblical authors. In Psalm 74:13–14 Leviathan's defeat by Yahweh is said to have occurred in the primeval past:

> You divided the sea by your might;
> you broke the heads of the dragons in the waters.
> You crushed the heads of Leviathan;
> you gave him as food for the creatures of the wilderness.[4]

In Isaiah 27:1 Yahweh's victory over Leviathan is projected forward into the eschatological future:

> On that day the LORD with his cruel and great and strong sword will punish Leviathan the fleeing serpent, Leviathan the twisting serpent, and he will kill the dragon that is in the sea.

The biblical Leviathan has its equivalent in Ugaritic texts. In one text Mot (Death) addresses Baal in the words:

> Because you smote Leviathan (*ltn*) the twisting serpent,
> [and] made an end of the crooked serpent,
> the tyrant with seven heads,
> the skies will become hot [and] will shine.[5]

Elsewhere Baal's consort Anat boasts of having dispatched an assortment of monsters that had opposed Baal, including what seems to be the same seven-headed serpent:

> Surely I smote
> Yam, beloved of El, surely I made an end of River, the mighty god.
> Surely I lifted up the dragon, I . . .
> [and] smote the crooked serpent,
> the tyrant with the seven heads.[6]

Lambert (2003) has questioned whether the lines that speak of 'the tyrant (*šlyt*) with (the) seven heads' should be understood as describing Leviathan in these texts. The word *šlyt* is of uncertain etymology and some scholars prefer to take it as a proper name, in which case (unless it is a second name for Leviathan) a different monster may well be indicated. This would remove the evidence for Leviathan in the Baal texts having seven heads. Lambert adopts this line of reasoning and sees Leviathan described here in mundane terms as simply a 'twisting snake'. He then suggests that Leviathan should be identified with the snake which Baal holds (or spears) in the iconography on certain cylinder seals from the second millennium BC. The reference to 'the heads of Leviathan' in Psalm 74:14 is sometimes seen as support for reading '*šlyt* of seven heads' as part of the description of Leviathan in the Baal texts, but Lambert is cautious about a straightforward reading of this biblical verse. He points out that the apparent plural *r'šy lwytn* 'depends entirely on a mater lectionis, and the Dead Sea Scrolls have shown that great liberties were taken with these vowel letters before the fixed text was adopted, late in the 1st century B.C.E. Thus "head of Leviathan" *r'š lwytn* is entirely possible' (Lambert, 2003: 154).

Leaving aside the number of heads possessed by the Leviathan of Ugarit, it remains possible, even probable, that Psalm 74 speaks of a multi-headed Leviathan, even if other biblical passages do not. In ancient Near Eastern art, deities are depicted in combat with four-legged, seven-headed monsters (Pritchard, 1954: illus. 691; Kahler, 2008), as well as with single-headed serpentine opponents (Pritchard, 1954: illus.670; Keel, 1978b: 107–8 with illus. 142; Lambert, 2003). It may be of course that not all these monsters were thought of as Leviathan, but it is equally possible that the name had different referents at different times (Lambert, 2003: 147).

To the biblical passages which mention Leviathan we may add those that speak of the monster Rahab, for Day is surely right to suggest that Rahab is 'probably an alternative name for Leviathan' (1985: 39). These passages are:

The helpers of Rahab bowed beneath him [God]. (Job 9:13)
By his power he stilled the Sea;
   by his understanding he struck down Rahab.

By his wind the heavens were made fair;
   his hand pierced the fleeing serpent. (Job 26:12–13)
You rule the raging of the sea;
   when its waves rise, you still them.
You crushed Rahab like a carcass;
   you scattered your enemies with your mighty arm. (Ps. 89:9–10)

Was it not you who cut Rahab in pieces,
   who pierced the dragon? (Isa. 51:9)

The anonymous dragon (*tannin*) of Job 7:12 can also be included here, as this term is used in parallel with both Rahab and Leviathan:

> Am I the Sea, or the Dragon,
> that you set a guard over me? (Job 7:12)

But even if it is granted that Leviathan is a mythological monster in the foregoing texts, might it still be possible to defend a naturalistic interpretation of the description in Job 41? Some commentators think it is. Andersen, for example, accepts that elsewhere the name refers to a mythical sea-dragon, but thinks the 'extravagant picture' in Job 41 'fits the crocodile well enough' (Andersen, 1976: 289). This view is hardly convincing. The references to 'the deep' in vv. 31–2 (Hebrew 23–4: m^esulah and t^ehom) make it unlikely that 'the sea' (yam, v. 31) could be the Nile (as suggested by Driver and Gray, 1921: 371). Clines rightly points out that 'none of these [m^esulah, yam and t^ehom] refers unambiguously to oceans, and each is attested in reference to smaller bodies of water such as lakes or rivers' (2011: 1200); but their combination imparts a tenor to these verses which is distinctly oceanic.

> It makes the deep (m^esulah) boil like a pot;
> it makes the sea (yam) like a pot of ointment.
> It leaves a shining wake behind it;
> one would think the deep (t^ehom) to be white-haired.

The reference in v. 30 (Hebrew 22) to Leviathan spread 'like a threshing-sledge on the mire' does not necessarily indicate an animal that lies around on riverside mud, for mire (tit) also occurs at the bottom of the sea (cf. Isa. 57:20). In short, the impression strongly conveyed by these verses is that Leviathan's habitat is the open ocean, whose depths reach to the murky base of the world. Such is his bulk and power that even these vast watery expanses are churned into foam by his thrashings (Habel, 1985: 573).[7]

There are other clues that Job 41 describes a mythological entity. Leviathan breathes out flames and smoke (vv. 19–21, Hebrew 11–13). Attempts to apply these verses to a crocodile by treating them as poetic exaggeration fail to convince (Schifferdecker 2008: 180–81). Even Clines admits that 'the Leviathan of the poem appears to possess some of the characteristics of a fire-breathing dragon' (2011: 1191). He also accepts that in v. 18 (Hebrew 10) 'we have ... an embroidering of the picture of the real crocodile with fanciful or mythological material about a dragon' (2011: 1196). Further, he sees in v. 6 (Hebrew 40:30) an 'absurd picture ... of the guild of fishers (not "traders" as RSV) who have been out hunting for the larger-than-life Leviathan, who is at this moment at least not simply the down-to-earth crocodile' (Clines, 2011: 1194). Indeed, 41:1–2 (Hebrew 40:25–26) imply that Leviathan could not be captured at all, whereas crocodiles were successfully hunted in ancient times (cf. Herodotus, Bk 2, 70).

Then there is the phrase in v. 25 (Hebrew 17): 'When it raises itself up the gods ('elim) are afraid; at the crashing they are beside themselves' (thus NRSV;

Day translates the second half of the verse: 'the waves of the sea pass away from him'). While the word *'elim* could be translated 'mighty ones', Pope draws attention to a parallel in an Ugaritic text which lends weight to the reading 'gods' (Pope, 1973: 344; also Habel, 1985: 572–73), and also uses this to support an emendation of v. 9 (Hebrew 1) which is adopted by the NRSV: 'Were not even the gods overwhelmed at the sight of it?' (Pope, 1973: 336–37).

Finally, the name Leviathan itself ('twisting one', from *lwh*, 'coiled', 'twisted' or 'wrapped around') suggests something other than a crocodile, 'which has vertebrae shaped in such a way that it has great difficulty in turning its body rapidly' (Day,1985: 66, 68).

This is not to deny that crocodile-like elements have entered into the depiction of Leviathan in Job 41, just as reptilian features form part of many a monster in modern fantasy and science fiction. But those elements alone should not be allowed to define the nature of Leviathan. The overall impression is of something much more massive, an ocean-going, fire-spouting serpent or dragon, quite unlike any other creature. T. K. Beal brings out well how the imagery is probably intended to work:

> The description overwhelms the imagination, piling feature upon feature to create an impossible image, thereby conceiving an inconceivable monstrosity . . . Its descriptive language combines different elements that are categorically exclusive of one another, and thereby jams the imagination's ability to form a complete picture of the monster. (Beal, 2002: 52)

It is important to note that Yahweh speaks of Leviathan as his creation (41:33, Hebrew 25). As Habel rightly observes, 'The fact that Leviathan is "made" (*'sy*) indicates that ultimately he too is a creature like Behemoth' (1985: 574; cf. Fyall, 2002: 168; Beal, 2002: 50). This can easily be missed in English translations, where 'creature' too readily loses its force and may be taken simply as a synonym for 'animal'.

In conclusion, the argument for understanding Behemoth and Leviathan as mythological monsters rests on firm foundations.[8]

What is the message of the divine speeches?

The foregoing conclusion does not by itself solve the hermeneutical problem posed by Yahweh's speeches. Even when scholars agree that Behemoth and Leviathan are mythological creatures, there is no agreement as to their significance in the Job author's argument (cf. Day, 1985; Habel, 1985; Good, 1990; Fyall, 2002). However, there are some common observations which I believe take us close to the heart of the second speech.

Habel, discussing the ambiguities in the portrayal of Behemoth, concludes (1985: 567): 'Thus Yahweh announces that chaos, and presumably its evil effects, are part of the world he designed. He does not eliminate chaos or evil; his Lordship involves controlling the balance between the forces of chaos and order.' Perdue (1991: 196-238) widens the context of interpretation to take in metaphors used elsewhere in the divine speeches, and concludes: 'The metaphors indicate that God has created and continues to sustain a reality in which both chaos as a threat to life, and the wicked, the perverters of order, are limited in their destructive actions' (p. 210).

The following connections must suffice to illustrate this theme:

- In the first speech God sets limits to the sea (38:8-11), sea here, as elsewhere in the Old Testament, being primordial chaos (Beal, 2002: 48–49).
- In the Old Testament's mythological imagery, the sea is closely linked with the monster Leviathan or Rahab (Pss 74:13–14; 89:9–10; Job 7:12; 26:12; 41:31; Isa. 27:1; 51:9b–10), just as in Ugaritic texts Leviathan/Lotan is 'the dragon typifying Yam, the defeated sea-god' (Driver, 1956: 103).
- This limiting of the sea in Job 38:8–11 is paralleled in 38:12-15 by the limiting of the time of darkness ('that temporal vestige of primeval chaos', Perdue, 1991: 208), thereby also setting limits to human wickedness (for this flourishes in the dark, Job 24:13–17).
- The reference to the proud (*ge'e*) and the wicked in 40:12 is echoed by Leviathan's lordship over 'all the proud' (*gaboah*) in 41:34 (Habel, 1985: 574; Newsom, 2003: 249; but cf. Clines, 2011: 1201).

The metaphors in Job 38–41 invite comparison with other biblical texts, but also evoke tension with those texts. In Pss 74:12–17; 89:10–13, etc., the sea/the dragon/Leviathan/Rahab have been decisively defeated and destroyed, but in Job they are merely restrained: 'God limits, but does not eliminate, chaos from reality' (Perdue, 1991: 226; cf. Habel above on Behemoth). In the section of God's first speech which deals with his acts at creation (Job 38:4–11) there is no mention of a battle with Leviathan (compare Job's words concerning Rahab in 26:12–13). This raises the question, to which we will return below, of whether it is strictly accurate to speak of Behemoth and Leviathan in Job 40–41 as chaos monsters.

The same tension is evoked by the resonances Behemoth and Leviathan have with extrabiblical traditions. As Newsom points out, an allusion to the Horus and Seth tradition in the description of Behemoth 'might create an expectation of divine enmity toward the creature. ... Such expectations, however, are not fulfilled by what is actually said about Behemoth. Here the stress is on Behemoth as a creature of God, one described with evident pride for his size and strength' (Newsom, 2003: 249). Likewise the description of Leviathan: 'The shock of this passage is that it runs counter to the expectations of those who think of Leviathan in terms of the *Chaoskampf* (Newsom, 2003:

251). In short the author of the book of Job is employing these images in non-conventional ways, subverting the meaning attached to them in extrabiblical tradition and (in the case of Leviathan) in other biblical texts. The reader is forced to reassess their significance.

Tension is heightened by the ambiguity of the associated metaphors. While Behemoth and Leviathan embody an otherness which inspires terror, they are both Yahweh's creatures, and Yahweh describes them with fondness and enthusiasm. Likewise the sea is a threat that Yahweh must restrain like a gaoler, but he is also its midwife (38:8–9). 'Indeed, the image of Yam diapered in clouds suggests that this primordial, chaotic force has been integrated into the present world ecology. ... It is a personification of primordial chaos *within* cosmos, intimately related to the divine' (Beal, 2002: 49).

By means of what Perdue calls 'the shock of the absurd' (1991: 226) Job is challenged to restructure his faith and praise the God who allows a place for chaos in his creation.

This reading of the second of Yahweh's speeches is entirely coherent with the message a number of scholars have found in the first speech (e.g., Davis, 2001: 135–40; Fretheim, 2005: 233–45; Schifferdecker, 2008). We have already seen how some of the metaphors used there parallel those in the second speech. In addition we may note how Yahweh turns Job's attention to aspects of creation which are of no direct use or benefit to human beings and therefore, from an anthropocentric perspective, without obvious purpose. God gratuitously sends rain on the wilderness where nobody lives (38:25–27). The questions put to Job in 38:39—39:30 are not intended merely to emphasize Job's ignorance; the animals and birds paraded before Job in this passage are indeed creatures of which he is largely ignorant, but his ignorance is a consequence of their wildness. By means of unanswerable questions 'God takes him ... out to "where the wild things are" ' (Fretheim, 2005: 233). The creatures included here stand in sharp contrast to the domesticated animals mentioned in 1:3 with which Job was familiar. Even the warhorse (39:19–25) is paradoxically useful only because of its untamed will and energy, and is in no way domesticated (Clines, 2011: 1128).

The characteristics of creation depicted in the first speech can be summed up as grandeur, variety, wildness and freedom. There is order in the world too, of course, but of a kind that does not fit with Job's expectations. Summing up the message of both the Yahweh speeches, Davis writes: 'This God's-eye view of the world plays havoc with Job's notion of the way things ought to be—which is to say, sensible, well-adapted to human purposes, and above all, predictable' (2001: 137).

If this is a valid way of understanding the divine speeches, some important consequences follow. Of the many interpretations of the Yahweh speeches that have been offered, most deny that any explanation for the existence of innocent suffering is to be found there. The majority of scholars would agree with Elizabeth Moberly's concise verdict that the book of Job 'questions an answer, rather than answers a question' (1978: 42). But if the above suggestions are correct, the speeches *can* be seen as offering such an explanation (though far from being one that closes down further questions; cf. Fretheim, 2005: 359, n. 146). They say that chaos (experienced on the human level as destructive events and evil acts) is a necessary ingredient in creation and cannot be separated from the rest of God's design. This in turn means that the book of Job is (in its final form, at least) a work of theodicy.

It might be objected that if God's speeches are in fact offering Job an explanation for the existence of innocent suffering, it is strange that they make no reference to the events in the heavenly court with which the book of Job opens. This, I believe, would be to overlook the way in which the argument of the book moves on between the prologue and God's speeches. To begin with, Job's questions and complaints focus on his own suffering, but by the final round of the debate he is demanding answers to more general questions: 'Why do the wicked live on, reach old age, and grow mighty in power?' (21:7); 'Why are times not kept by the Almighty, and why do those who know him never see his days?' (24:1). Reflecting on numerous ways in which the poor are victimized, oppressed and even killed by the powerful, Job wants to know why life for so many is lived without evidence of divine justice. P. C. Craigie describes the shift in the following terms: 'At the beginning of the book, it looks as though Job is on trial . . . But in the development of the book, it is clear that it is God who is on trial; suffering and evil are merely pointers toward the greatest problem of all, namely God!' (1980: 8).

If God (more specifically, God's relationship with and governance of the world) is the ultimate problem, then the divine speeches do indeed address Job's questions at this higher and more general level. Putting it another way, they address Job's questions about global injustice and suffering, but leave aside the question of why Job himself has suffered. That question has been swallowed up in the larger issue of God's relationship with his creation (cf. Fretheim, 2005: 233–40).

The writer of Job in conversation with some modern scientist-theologians

One consequence of this way of reading the divine speeches in the book of Job is that its author becomes a close companion to certain modern theologians.

Scientist–theologians Arthur Peacocke and John Polkinghorne (biochemist and theoretical physicist respectively) have written extensively on God's interaction with the world. Their views do not exactly coincide (for the main differences see Polkinghorne, 1996), but they broadly agree on the importance of chance, randomness or disorder as an ingredient in the process of creation.

> It has become increasingly apparent that it is chance operating within a law-like framework that is the basis of the inherent creativity of the

natural order, its ability to generate new forms, patterns, and organizations of matter and energy. (Peacocke, 2001: 26)

In an evolving world of this kind, death is the necessary cost of life; transience is inevitably built into its physical fabric. New possibilities are realized 'at the edge of chaos,' regimes where there is a balance between order and disorder. (Polkinghorne, 2000: 39)

Elsewhere Polkinghorne has expressed this more theologically:

The Christian God is both loving and faithful. The gift of the God of love to his creation will surely be freedom. ... The gift of the God of faithfulness will surely be reliability. ... We may expect the creation of the God who is both loving and faithful to display characteristics of both openness and regularity, such as are in fact reflected in the physical interplay of chance and necessity in the process of the world. (1991: 83)

He has further developed the concept of 'openness' to serve the interests of theodicy, framing what he calls a 'free-process defence' for the existence of natural evil, analogous to the 'free-will defence' for the existence of moral evil. In this view, the movement of tectonic plates can cause earthquakes, and the multiplication of bacteria can cause disease, 'because they are "free" to act in accordance with their natures, just as we are free to act in accordance with our nature' (1996:49). Indeed Polkinghorne sees a close connection between these two 'freedoms':

The physical universe, with its physical evil, is not just the backdrop against which the human drama, with its moral evil, is being played out, so that the two can be disentangled. We are characters who have emerged from the scenery; its nature is the ground of the possibility of our nature. Perhaps only a world endowed with its own spontaneity and its own reliability could have given rise to beings able to exercise choice. I think it is likely that only a universe in which we could entertain free-process defence, would be one in which there could be people to whom the free-will defence could be applied. (1994: 85)

The philosopher Keith Ward has also used these insights to explain the existence of suffering. Ward suggests that in the kind of universe that God had to create in order to fulfil his purposes, there had to be room for chance and freedom; the many 'necessary interconnections' of our universe 'make the values of that universe inseparable from at least the possibility of suffering, and from a good deal of actual suffering'. In this sense, 'God is the cause of suffering, but does not intend the suffering just out of maliciousness or perverse pleasure. God will ensure that the overwhelming good, of which it is a condition, will at last be realised' (1998: 95, 96; see also 1996: 190ff.; 2001: 159–60.)[9]

These theologians all acknowledge the constraints that such a universe places on God's omnipotence if that word is understood to mean his absolute control through primary agencies (Ward, 1998: 95, 102–3; 2001; Polkinghorne, 2001). Interestingly, Athalya Brenner's reading of the Yahweh speeches in Job involves the conclusion that 'God is not absolutely omnipotent' (Brenner, 1981: 133).[10] For Polkinghorne, however, this restriction of God's power is a voluntary self-limitation, which is an aspect of God's loving gift of freedom to his creation (2001).[11]

Conclusion

It would be a gross anachronism to claim that the author of Job was trying to say exactly the same as the scientist–theologians referred to above, but there are undeniable parallels and he would surely be on warm speaking terms with them. The biblical author was of course no scientist, but he was a close observer of natural processes: he had noted the long-term effects of weather on mountains, as well as the more rapid erosion of rock and soil by water (14:18–19); he also had a fair understanding of the cycle of rain formation, and perhaps even understood how it turned water from the sea into fresh water that human beings could use (36:27–8, on which see Clines, 2006: 870). Combining his observations of nature with deep theological reflection on existing texts and traditions, he arrived at insights into God's relationship with creation which are arguably unique in the biblical canon.

By the use of a rich set of metaphors the biblical writer affirms that 'chaos' exists by God's will as an aspect of his creation. Of course, chaos is not the same as suffering and evil, but it can be viewed as the realm, so to speak, from which they emerge; hence it is associated with them in the writer's imagery. Chaos, as portrayed by the metaphors in the Yahweh speeches, is thus very close to the freedom or disorder which, as Ward puts it, is 'the price of creating a truly emergent universe' (Ward, 1998: 103). The ambivalent metaphors in the divine speeches are totally appropriate for this necessary yet terrifying ingredient in the composition of the cosmos.[12]

It is my hope that this essay will encourage further dialogue between scientist–theologians and the book of Job, and it is offered in warm appreciation of Ernest Lucas's many contributions to the science–faith debate.

Notes

1 Note that in Clines (2011) these levels of meaning have receded somewhat: 'While Yahweh does not state explicitly what meanings these animals have in the divine purposes, the significance of Behemoth and Leviathan is no different from that of the

other animals; these two are just prime examples of the animal creation' (Clines, 2011: 1179). Clines does not now reject symbolic meanings altogether, but he is far less explicit in suggesting what they might be (e.g., Clines, 2011: 1184, 1186, 1201).
2   A student of mine who had been a medical missionary in Africa described a training video used to illustrate the horrendous and often fatal injuries a hippopotamus can inflict.
3   An actual sea-creature may be in view in Ps. 104:26, but Day (1985: 73–4) argues that here 'the mythological chaos monster ... has undergone a process of depotentization'. Similarly Levenson writes that in this verse Leviathan 'has been emasculated into a toy that has always only delighted and never opposed its designer, maker and owner' (1994: 54). M. J. Paul thinks a real creature is referred to in Job 3:8–9 (in VanGemeren, 1996, 2: 779), but a mythological interpretation of these verses is generally preferred.
4   Unless otherwise stated, biblical quotations are from the NRSV.
5   *CTA* 5.I.1–4 = *KTU* 1.5.I.1–4, as translated in Day (1985: 13); see also Driver (1956: 103); Pritchard (1967: 138); Lambert (2003: 148).
6   *CTA* 3.IIID.34–9 = *KTU* 1.3.III.38–42, as translated in Day (1985: 13–14); see also Driver (1956: 87); Pritchard (1967: 137); Lambert (2003: 148).
7   While it is not unknown for the freshwater or Nile crocodile (*Crocodylus niloticus*) to be found around the mouths of estuaries (cf. Driver and Gray, 1921: 359), it is arguable that even such a setting fails to match the language of vv. 31–32. The estuarine or saltwater crocodile (*Crocodylus porosus*, the world's largest reptile, growing up to 5 or 6 metres in length) has been known to cross large stretches of open sea, but it is hardly conceivable that the Job writer knew of this species' existence as its range is limited to the Indo-Pacific coasts and islands between the east coast of India and northern Australia.
8   Fyall (2002), following Gibson (1985), has argued that Behemoth and Leviathan are not merely chaos monsters but images of satanic forces, respectively 'embodiments of the powers of death and evil' (p. 129); indeed, 'Leviathan is the power of evil, the Satan' (p. 137). Like Gibson before him, he has to work hard to make his case, and ultimately (for this reader at least) he fails to convince. In trying to link the divine speeches with the prologue (p. 141), he fails to appreciate how the debate has moved on since those opening scenes (see further below). See also the comment of Bauckham (2010: 187, n. 35).
9   Similar ideas have been explored by Clark Pinnock, champion of so-called 'openness theology' from the evangelical wing (2001: 129–34). However, Pinnock makes additional appeal to the idea of 'rebellious spirits' to explain some forms of natural evil, a move which seems unnecessary in the context, and which depends on the unjustified insertion of an angelic fall into Gen. 1:1–2 (2001: 36, 146).
10 See also Kushner (1981: 43–5) for a popular presentation of a similar reading. In my view Brenner's case is marred by Jungian-sounding references to God's 'dark side' (pp. 134 and 135).
11 It should be emphasized that this is *not* a deist view, in which God, having created the world, is no longer involved with it except in the sense that he somehow holds it in being. Polkinghorne in particular has written extensively on the ways in which God might interact with his creation (e.g., 1997, 2001). For a critique of the earlier paper see Murphy (1997).
12 Although I have used the terms 'chaos' and 'chaos monsters' throughout this chapter,

readers may well have found them increasingly inappropriate as my argument progressed. Indeed, 'chaos' becomes an entirely inadequate word for what I believe the author of the book of Job was trying to evoke if, as I believe, he was aiming to subvert chaos metaphors and chaos-monster imagery and place his own novel stamp on them. (The word may lead to further confusion because of its association with so-called 'chaos theory', which actually involves micro-level determinism.) However, while it may seem like an improvement to replace 'chaos' with terms such as disorder, chance and freedom (all employed by the scientist–theologians I have quoted above), these are also open to misunderstanding if not used with proper care. This is clearly an area in which more thinking on terminology needs to be done!

Bibliography

Ahuis, F. 'Behemot, Leviatan und der Mensch in Hiob 38–42'. *ZAW* 123 no. 1 (2011), pp. 72–91.
Alter, R. 'The Voice from the Whirlwind'. *Commentary* 77 no.1 (1984): pp. 33–41.
Andersen, F. I. *Job*. Tyndale Commentaries (Leicester: Inter-Varsity Press, 1976).
Bauckham, R. *Bible and Ecology: Rediscovering the Community of Creation* (London: Darton, Longman & Todd, 2010).
Beal, T. K. *Religion and Its Monsters* (New York/London: Routledge, 2002).
Ben-Tor, D. *Scarabs, Chronology and Interconnections: Egypt and Palestine in the Second Intermediate Period (Orbis Biblicus et Orientalis 27)* (Göttingen: Vandenhoeck & Ruprecht, 2007).
Brenner, A. 'God's Answer to Job'. *Vetus Testamentum*, 31 no. 2 (1981): pp. 129-37.
Clines, D. J. A. 'Job'. Pages 559-92 in *A Bible Commentary for Today* (ed. G. C. D. Howley; London: Pickering & Inglis, 1979).
———. *Job 1-20*. Word Commentary (Dallas, TX: Word Books, 1989).
———. 'Job'. Pages 459–84 in *New Bible Commentary, 21st Century Edition* (ed. D. A. Carson et al.; Leicester: Inter-Varsity Press, 1994).
———. *Job 21-37*. Word Commentary (Dallas, TX: Thomas Nelson, 2006).
———. *Job 38–42*. Word Biblical Commentary (Nashville: Thomas Nelson, 2011).
Craigie, P. C. 'Biblical Wisdom in the Modern World: III. Job'. *Crux*, 16 (1980): pp. 7–10.
CTA, Corpus des tablettes en cunéiformes alphabétiques découvertes à Ras Shamra-Ugarit de 1929 à 1939 (ed. A. Herdner; Paris: Mission de Ras Shamra 10, 1963).
Davis, E. F. *Getting Involved with God: Rediscovering the Old Testament* (Lanham, MD: Rowman & Littlefield, 2001).
Day, J. *God's Conflict with the Dragon and the Sea* (Cambridge: Cambridge University Press, 1985).
Dell, K. J. *The Book of Job as Sceptical Literature*. BZAW 197 (Berlin: De Gruyter, 1991).
———. *Job*. The People's Bible Commentary (Oxford: Bible Reading Fellowship, 2002).
Dhorme, E. *Commentary on the Book of Job* (London: Thomas Nelson, 1967; English trans. of *Le Livre de Job*, Paris: J. Gabalda & Cie, 1926).
Driver, G. R. *Canaanite Myths and Legends* (Edinburgh: T. & T. Clark, 1956).
Driver, S. R. and G. B. Gray. *The Book of Job*. International Critical Commentary

(Edinburgh: T. & T. Clark, 1921).
Fretheim, T. E. *God and World in the Old Testament: A Relational Theology of Creation* (Nashville, TN: Abingdon Press, 2005).
Fyall, R. S. *Now My Eyes Have Seen You: Images of Creation and Evil in the Book of Job* (Leicester: Apollos, 2002).
Gibson, J. C. L. *Job*. Daily Study Bible (Edinburgh: St Andrew Press, 1985).
———. 'On Evil and the Book of Job'. Pages 399–419 in *Ascribe to the Lord* (ed. L. Eslinger and G. Taylor, JSOTSupp 67, Sheffield: JSOT Press, 1988).
Good, E. M. *In Turns of Tempest: A Reading of Job*. (Stanford, CA: Stanford University Press, 1990).
Gordis, R. *The Book of Job: Commentary, New Translation and Special Studies* (New York: Jewish Theological Seminary of America, 1978).
Gowan, D. E. 'God's Answer to Job: How Is It an Answer?', *Horizons in Biblical Theology* 8 (1986), pp. 85-102.
Habel, N. C. *The Book of Job* (London: SCM, 1985).
Hartley, J. E. *The Book of Job*. New International Commentary on the Old Testament (Grand Rapids: Eerdmans, 1988).
Kahler, B. 'A Four-Legged Creature with Seven Snake-Heads Depicted on a Cylinder Seal of Tell Asmar, Iraq'. Pages 71–5 in *Die Zahl Sieben im Alten Orient* (ed. G.G.G. Reinhold: Frankfurt am Mein: Peter Lang, 2008).
Keel, O. 'Ein weiterer Skarabäus mit einer Nilpferdjagd, die Iconographie der sogenannten Beamtenskarabäen und der ägyptische König auf Skarabäen vor dem Neuen Reich'. *Ägypten und Levante* 6 (1996): pp. 119–36.
———. *Jahwes Entgegnung an Ijob* (Gottingen: Vandenhoeck & Ruprecht, 1978a).
———. *The Symbolism of the Biblical World* (London: SPCK, English trans. 1978b).
KTU, Die keilalphabetischen Texte aus Ugarit (ed. M. Dietrich, O. Loretz and J. Sanmartín; AOAT 24/1, Neukirchen-Vluyn, 1976; 2nd enlarged edn of *KTU: The Cuneiform Alphabetic Texts from Ugarit, Ras Ibn Hani, and Other Places* (ed. M. Dietrich, O. Loretz and J. Sanmartín; Münster: 1995).
Kushner, H. *When Bad Things Happen to Good People* (New York: Avon Books, 1981).
Lambert, W. G. 'Leviathan in Ancient Art'. Pages 147–54 in *Shlomo: Studies in Epigraphy, Iconography, History and Archaeology in Honour of Shlomo Moussaieff* (ed. Robert Deutsch; Tel Aviv: Archaeological Center Publications, 2003).
Lang, B. 'Job XL:18 and the "Bones of Seth"'. *Vetus Testamentum* 30 (1980): pp. 360–61.
Levenson, J. D. *Creation and the Persistence of Evil: The Jewish Drama of Divine Omnipotence* (Princeton, NJ: Princeton University Press, 2nd edn, 1994).
Moberly, E. *Suffering, Innocent and Guilty* (London: SPCK, 1978).
Morrow, J. *Towing Jehovah* (London: Arrow, 1994).
Murphy, N. 'Divine Action in the Natural Order: Buridan's Ass and Schrödinger's Cat'. Pages 325–57 in *Chaos and Complexity: Scientific Perspectives on Divine Action* (ed. R. J. Russell, N. Murphy and A. R. Peacocke; Notre Dame, IN: University of Notre Dame Press, 2nd edn, 1997).
Newsom, C. *The Book of Job: A Contest of Moral Imaginations*. (Oxford: Oxford University Press, 2003).
Peacocke, A. R. 'The Cost of New Life'. Pages 21–42 in *The Work of Love: Creation as Kenosis* (ed. J.C. Polkinghorne; Cambridge: SPCK, 2001).
Perdue, L. G. *Wisdom in Revolt*, JSOTSupp 112 (Sheffield: Almond Press, 1991).
Pinnock, C.H. *Most Moved Mover: A Theology of God's Openness* (Carlisle:

Paternoster, 2001).
Polkinghorne, J. C. *Reason and Reality* (London: SPCK, 1991).
———. *Science and Christian Belief* (London: SPCK, 1994).
———. *Scientists as Theologians* (London: SPCK, 1996).
———. 'The Metaphysics of Divine Action'. Pages 147–56 in *Chaos and Complexity: Scientific Perspectives on Divine Action* (ed. R. J. Russell, N. Murphy and A. R. Peacocke; Notre Dame, IN: University of Notre Dame Press, 2nd edn, 1997).
———. 'Eschatology: Some Questions and Some Insights from Science'. Pages 29–41 in *The End of the World and the Ends of God: Science and Theology on Eschatology* (ed. J. C. Polkinghorne and M. Welker; Harrisburg, PA: Trinity Press, 2000).
———. 'Kenotic Creation and Divine Action'. Pages 90–106 in *The Work of Love: Creation as Kenosis* (ed. J.C. Polkinghorne; Cambridge: SPCK, 2001)
Pope, M. H. *Job*, Anchor Bible (New York: Doubleday, 3rd edn, 1973).
Pritchard, J. B. ed. *The Ancient Near East in Pictures Relating to the Old Testament* (Princeton: Princeton University Press, 1954).
———. ed. *Ancient Near Eastern Texts Relating to the Old Testament* (Princeton: Princeton University Press, 3rd edn, 1969).
Schifferdecker, K. *Out of the Whirlwind: Creation Theology in the Book of Job* (Cambridge, MA: Harvard University Press, 2008).
Tsevat, M. *The Meaning of the Book of Job and Other Biblical Studies* (New York: Ktav, 1980): pp. 1–37.
VanGemeren, W. A. ed. *New International Dictionary of Old Testament Theology and Exegesis*, 5 vols (Carlisle: Paternoster, 1996).
Wakeman, M. K. *God's Battle with the Monster: A Study in Biblical Imagery* (Leiden: E. J. Brill, 1973).
Ward, K. 'Cosmos and Kenosis'. Pages 152–66 in *The Work of Love: Creation as Kenosis* (ed. J.C. Polkinghorne; Cambridge: SPCK, 2001).
———. *God, Chance and Necessity* (Oxford: One World, 1996).
———. *God, Faith and the New Millennium* (Oxford: One World, 1998).
Williams, C. *War in Heaven.* (London: Victor Gollancz, 1930).

God
>   For the gift of minds we give you thanks:
>   minds that tussle with myths, monsters and
metaphors
>   seeking insight, chiselling understanding
>   from primordial rock and ancient analogies
>   in pursuit of you.
>
>   For the gift of sight we give you thanks:
>   eyes that observe the workings of the world
>   of clashing freedoms and forms of harmony
>   vision that delights in new discovery
>   and recognizes chaos in creation
>   as it resonates with the deep places and anxieties
>   of the human heart.
>
>   For the gift of mystery we give you thanks:
>   hiddenness of the unknown and unknowable,
>   and that in all things, in all seeking,
>   in all struggling, in all seeing,

3

The Traditional Israelite Legal Settings: Social Contexts in Proverbs?

Hillary Nyika

Introduction

Over the years studies in Old Testament have focused on the royal court as an educational setting. But one wonders why other legal settings[1] such as the gates and royal court, which are also important social contexts where proverbs were used in Israelite society, have not received due attention in Old Testament wisdom studies. So the chapter mainly investigates the possible usage of proverbs in these judicial institutions as a treasure of wisdom, ethics, morals and teachings accumulated over many generations. Their usage may have included reinforcing societal values and criticizing the corrupt practices associated with the judiciary, for example, bribing the elders or judges, false witnessing and the use of the judiciary to oppress the poor by denying them justice. In order to clarify the possible usage of proverbs in Israelite legal settings, the paper will, first, explore the gate as a legal social setting; second, investigate the royal court as a legal institution, not as an educational institution; and finally, illustrate the possible usage of proverbial sayings in these two Israelite legal settings.

The gate

The gate is an important legal setting talked about in the book of Proverbs and other Old Testament literature. It was used for different activities in Israelite society. For instance, a social setting reserved for settling legal matters (Josh. 20:4; Deut. 21:19–20; 22:15; 25:7; Job 5:12; 31:21; Isa. 29:21; Amos 5:10,12,15; Ruth 4:1,11; Prov. 22:22; 24:7). Also, it was used as a market place where community inhabitants could congregate (Prov. 1:21; 2 Kgs 7:1) and transact business (Ps. 121:8; Ruth 4:1; Prov. 8:3–4). Quintessentially, it was a leisure area of the Palestinian town and a place where people met and socialized, travellers were received, news of the outside world learnt, and legal matters were settled (Boecker, 1980: 31).

In order to clarify the gate as a legal social setting, let us look at what Proverbs and other Old Testament literature say. Proverbs 22:22-3, for example, underpins that the gate was a legal social setting in Israelite society. We concur with Fox (2009: 714), Whybray (1994c: 329) and Longman (2006: 416), who suggest that reference to 'the gate' at least points towards a public setting, in particular a legal setting where justice was administered. The gate is 'the centre of communal justice and power' (Yoder, 2009: 232) (Prov. 1:21; 8:1-3; 24:7; Deut. 21:19). As Proverbs 22:22 underscores, to rob and oppress the poor who are already in difficult straits is a heinous crime. Proverbs 22:22 is reminiscent of Isaiah 10:1-2, which pronounces judgment in the form of defeat and captivity on those who oppress the poor by manipulating the judicial system. Also, Amos 5:10-15 condemns a corrupt legal system at the very site of legal proceedings: the city gate where truth is rejected, the poor are plundered, and witnesses bribed. Consequently, the needy, the poor, widows and orphans are turned aside from justice in the gate (Amos 5:12).

Proverbs 22:23 underlines that 'Yahweh will plead their cause'. This term is also a forensic term connected with or used in a court of law, 'but is used here metaphorically of Yahweh's protection of the poor' (Whybray, 1994c: 329). Yahweh vindicates the poor and executes judgment to their oppressors (Exod. 22:21-4; Deut. 24:14-15; Lev. 19:13). Yahweh as the 'redeemer' pleads the case of the poor in the legal setting and ensures that justice prevails. Indeed, what is being underlined here is that these texts warn individuals against using the legal setting of 'the gate' as an instrument for exploiting and oppressing the poor.

Moreover, other literature emphasizes that 'the gate' was a legal setting. So, for example, Job 5:4 talks about the children of fools who are far from safety, they are crushed in the gate and there is no one to deliver them. The children of the fools are the focus of attention, since their foolish fathers left them in a miserable position. As Clines (1998) notes, if this is not precisely a case of the sin of the father being visited on the children (Job 21:19-20), then it is at least an illustration of the crippling effect of sin on all that belongs to the fool, his 'habitation'. His children are, as orphans, without a strong protector to ensure them justice in the legal and business transactions that take place in the city gate. Additionally, Job 5:4 echoes Proverbs 22:22, particularly the words יִדַּכְּאוּ 'crush' and בַשָּׁעַר 'in the gate'. The phase וְאֵין מַצִּיל 'with no one to deliver' is also found in Isaiah 5:29; Psalms 7:3 [2]; 50:22. Following this line of argument, we can underline that elders met at the gate to adjudicate disputes (Josh. 20:4; Deut. 21:19-20; 22:15; 25:7; Job 29:7-17; 31:21; Ruth 4:1-12; Amos 5:10,12; Isa. 29:21). In fact, these elders were leading and influential men of the community (Deut. 19:12; 22:15; 25:7; 1 Sam. 16:4; Exod. 3:16; Josh. 24:1).

In order to further clarify the importance of the gate as a legal setting, let us examine some of the legal cases brought before the elders at the gate. For instance, in Deuteronomy 21:18–21, flagrant and sustained disobedience is a capital offence. Parents brought their stubborn and rebellious son before the elders at the gate, and gave parental testimony about their son's stubborn, rebellious, gluttonous and drunken behavior. All the men of the town would stone him to death. Also, in Deuteronomy 22:13–20, a young woman was stoned for committing a disgraceful act in Israel by prostituting herself in her father's house. Additionally, if a young woman, a virgin already engaged to be married, committed adultery with a man in her town, she was brought before the town gate and stoned to death (Deut. 22:23–24).

There are also other cases and penalties mentioned in the Old Testament. For example, suppose two disputing individuals enter into litigation and brought their case before the judges or elders to judge between them. If the guilty party deserved to be flogged, he was beaten forty lashes in the presence of the judge(s) (Deut. 25:1–3). Cases of levirate marriage were also before the judges (Deut. 25:5–10). In summary, we have been trying to show that the gate was an important legal setting where elders played a pivotal role in the administration of justice. As shown by the examples of cases brought before the gate, justice was close to the people. By contrast, it was not centralized, like the royal court during the monarchy.

The royal court: a legal social setting?

The royal court was a legal setting associated with the king's orderly administration of justice and the functioning of the kingdom (Prov. 25–9; 31:1–9). In order to clarify this issue, let us examine the Israelite king's legal role and then show examples of legal disputes brought before the king at the royal court.

The king as supreme judge

Indeed, the king became the 'supreme judge' during the time of the monarchy. In clarifying this issue, we will explore what the biblical literature says about the king's juridical role. Proverbs 16:10–11 emphasizes the king's legal acumen. Heim observed a link between Proverbs 16:10 and verse 11 in saying verse 10 introduces the king as a divine agent. He further notes that the verse legitimizes the king's recourse to divination in the form of casting lots to settle legal disputes when all other methods have failed due to insufficient evidence. In verse 11, Yahweh is identified as the 'source' of accurate means of measurement. Heim argues that the inverted arrangement between verses 10 and 11 not only serves to link the two verses, 'but also forms a casual link between the king's legal activity and his divine source of guidance' (2001:

211). What Heim says about the king's legal role is plausible.

However, McKane (1970: 499), Longman (2006: 331) and Whybray (1994a) note that the reference to קֶסֶם 'inspired decisions' is strictly condemned elsewhere in the Old Testament as it is associated with heathen divination (Deut. 18:10; 1 Sam. 6:2; 28:8; 2 Kgs 17:17; Isa. 44:24–5). But here alone it is used in a positive sense as it is paralleled by the king's pronouncement of judgment; of a judicial decision made with respect to cases brought before the king as judge. While no acceptable interpretation has been found on the use of קֶסֶם here, it probably reflects an unusual view of the royal judicial pronouncements akin to the woman of Tekoa. In asking for a legal decision, she presented her fictitious story and claimed to believe that David was 'like the angel of God to discern good and evil' (2 Sam. 14:17, ESV).

Essentially, the woman of Tekoa attributed legal acumen to David. If that is the case, Proverbs 16:10 may not be concerned with a decision produced by oracular machinery as noted by Gemser (1960: 102–28) who refers to the king's use of Urim and Thummim. Rather, the verse may refer to an 'ability to sift evidence, to get the truth and arrive at a fair verdict' (McKane, 1970: 500). Nevertheless, this does not mean that the king was believed to be God's mouthpiece, but Yahweh bestowed upon him the aptitude to make the right judgments Whybray, 1994c: 243–4). Thus, in the context of administering justice, this may denote the king's ability to discern between good and evil, distinguishing right from wrong (see Anderson's 1998 comment on 2 Sam. 19:28). Quintessentially, 2 Samuel 14:17 supports the sayings in Proverbs 16:10 and 20:8 that the king has absolute competence to deal with all legal cases since he is Yahweh's earthly representative (Whitelam, 1979: 135). As McKane notes, Proverbs 16:10 underscores that a legal judgment given out by a king has the quality of inerrancy which attaches to an oracular decision (קֶסֶם), just as the woman of Tekoa asserts that 'the king is like the angel of God discerning good and evil' (2 Sam. 14:17,20) (McKane, 1970: 500). What the woman of Tekoa says about David is similar to Mephibosheth's courtly flattery in 2 Samuel 19:28 (see Anderson's 1998 comment on 2 Sam. 19:28).

Also, Proverbs 20:8 says: 'A king who sits on the throne of judgment winnows all evil with his eyes.' This verse is similar to Proverbs 20:26 where 'A wise king winnows the wicked and drives the wheel over them'. These texts both express confidence in royal justice as 'winnowing' refers to the king's function as judge (Prov. 16:10) (Murphy, 1998, on Prov. 20:8). It is the king's legal responsibility to ensure that the wicked are punished (Dell, 1998: 176). This portrayal of an ideal king is also found in other literature, for instance, Isaiah 16:5 where the king 'seeks justice and is swift to do what is right'.[2]

In addition, Proverbs 20:28 says, 'Loyalty and faithfulness preserve the king, and his throne is upheld by righteousness.' Golka (1993) suggests a popular origin for Proverbs 20:26 and 20:28 as he sees overtones of the people warning the king. But we concur with Dell's observation that this overtone is not clear here (1998: 176). However, what is apparent and central in these texts is the issue of justice. There is also a close link between the divine and the king, thus, the king and his God-given authority. The king as God's representative on earth is expected to uphold justice because the royal throne is established by righteousness. This echoes Proverbs 21:1 that refers to the king's dependence on divine control. As Dell notes, the text shows a 'closeness of the two rather than the distance' (Dell, 1998: 177). Also, Proverbs 29:14 talks about the ideal of justice as the king has a moral responsibility supported by divine blessing.

Furthermore, Proverbs 29:4 says, 'By justice a king gives stability to the land, but one who makes heavy exactions ruins it.' As Murphy rightly suggests, this text refers to 'the ideal of the just king and the corresponding security of the throne' (1998, on Prov. 29:4). Golka comments, 'A deeply felt sigh of ordinary people, perhaps against Solomon's taxation?' (1993: 33). Although the meaning of this text is not clear-cut, as Whybray remarks, 'it is probably an attack on ruinous taxation, or, possibly; on the acceptance of bribes by the king' (1990: 53). Nonetheless, we concur with Dell's suggestion that this text could 'be a wider comment on the centrality of justice and of the possibility of the possible abuse of power' (1998: 180).

Moreover, Proverbs 31:1–9 contains the only example of a royal instruction given by a mother rather than a father. Nonetheless, 'the queen mother occupied a position of power in Judah, and apparently also in some other kingdoms of the ancient Semitic world' (Whybray, 1994c: 422). Additionally, this 'royal instruction' has been compared with the Egyptian *Instruction for King Merikare* and the *Instruction of King Amenemhet*, and its contents closely resemble the Akkadian *Advice to a Prince* (see Whybray, 1994a: 153; 1994c: 422). The instruction presents a picture of a model ruler as it primarily contains a series of admonitions to the young king about his juridical duties (Whybray, 1994c). The instruction is of non-Israelite origin as a reference to Proverbs 30:1 הַמַּשָּׂא with an article referring to the 'words of Agur' also מַשָּׂא occurs in Proverbs 31:1. Commentaries and translations are divided as to its meaning[3] and the translation of מַה־בְּרִי at the beginning of Proverbs 31: 2 is also problematic.[4]

Nevertheless, the queen mother gives precepts to her son about the proper comportment of kings and rulers. She uses the masculine plural מְלָכִים 'kings' and רוֹזְנִים 'rulers or dignitaries reliable in judgment' (Prov. 8:15; Ps. 2:2; Hab. 1:10) with the preposition לְ 'for' being used as an indirect object of the teaching of the queen mother. She instructs her son Lemuel[5] against women and strong intoxicating wine or beer, seen here as weakening distractions, lest he neglect his duty to care for the powerless. Excessive drinking was regarded as disgraceful conduct because it made kings and rulers forget their status and pervert the right of the afflicted, which is a reflection of one's turning away from the basic rules in the social and religious spheres (Prov. 31:4–5).

Against this background, the queen mother's instructions to her son have both educational and legal significance. Thus, the king is instructed to be the voice of the voiceless, the defender of the defenceless and to judge righteously.

The king had to deliver legal judgments as he had the ultimate responsibility for the administration of justice (Prov. 31:8–9).[6] Notably, שְׁפָט־צֶדֶק 'judge righteously' (v. 9) here brings out the connection between jurisprudence and righteousness. צֶדֶק 'righteousness' permeates and sustains the life and rights of individuals in the community, and the queen mother tries to reinforce the need for social justice and the virtues of moral life which needed to be implemented by the kings and rulers in order to safeguard communal existence.[7] Thus, Proverbs 31:1–9 emphasizes the king's fundamental legal duty, delivering and executing justice and protecting the rights of the weak and vulnerable (also see Dell, 1998: 181–82). Furthermore, the king had a duty to safeguard the well-being of society in legal matters (Pss. 45:7; 72:2,4,12–14; 101). Indeed, as the human representative of Yahweh, the king's authority was meant to reflect Yahweh's attributes of righteousness and fairness (Pss. 9:16; 11:7; 1 Kgs 3:28).

The king's legal role

We are now going to further clarify the king's legal role by examining some examples of legal cases brought at the royal court. The king's legal acumen and royal super intelligence is noted in 1 Kings 3:28, which makes reference to and acknowledges that Solomon's wisdom proceeds from God. For Solomon executed מִשְׁפָּט 'justice', which is a judicial decree, a case to be judged, the act of judging, or a case that has received judicial attention (see DeVries, 1998 on 1 Kgs 3:38). While the story in 1 Kings 3:16–28 serves to demonstrate the practical aspects of the wisdom promised to Solomon in 1 Kings 4:12, it has been suggested that the story has folkloristic rather than a historical character as similar stories came from India and China (see Mulder, 1998: 154). Nevertheless, the historicity of this story cannot be dismissed because the story is folkloristic in character. Certainly, this does not prove that the story is historically untrustworthy.

In 1 Kings 3:16–28, we read the story of the two harlots who came before the king in pursuit of justice. Harlots were social outcasts who were despised, poor, powerless and defenceless (see DeVries, 1998 on 1 Kgs 3:38). In this story, the women lived by themselves in the same house since there was no witness when the incident occurred. Nonetheless, the story underlines the king's absolute competence in dealing with all legal cases. It also reflects the simple faith ordinary people had in the impartiality and effectiveness of the royal administration of justice (Prov. 16:10,13; 20:8,28).

In 2 Samuel 8:15, David reigned as the sole judge in Israel above the local courts—'gates'—as he did not delegate legal authority (2 Sam. 15:3). Consequently, his cunning son Absalom criticized and accused him of negligence (see Anderson, 1998 on 2 Sam. 15:2–6). Indeed, petitions came from outlying areas of Jerusalem, the residential capital of the monarchy, for the king to judge in concrete cases. Evidently, this shows that the royal court embodied a judicial status and function. Israelite kings were also known for their sagacity and knowledge of judicial affairs (2 Sam. 8:15; 14:17,20; 1 Kgs 3:27–28; 10:9).

The story of the Shunammite woman also shows a widow who seeks justice at the royal court as she appeals for her house and land (2 Kgs 8:1–6). This woman was wealthy (1 Kgs 4:8) and had been self-sufficient (1 Kgs 4:13) but is forced to flee her homeland in time of famine (1 Kgs 8:1–2). While the woman was away, the story implies, someone took her house and land. When she returned, she set out to appeal at the royal court. Suggestions have been made to the effect that the crown may have taken possession of her abandoned property (Alt, 1955: 364). However, there is insufficient biblical evidence in support of this view; therefore, this case cannot be taken as general principle for the crown's administration of state property. The fact remains that the woman appealed to the king for the restoration of her property.

Probably, the lodging of a legal appeal before the king and seeking his justice shows her faith in the king, the supreme judge responsible for the welfare of his subjects (2 Sam. 8:15). Consequently, the king took the woman's plight seriously enough to appoint one of his own officials to be in charge of the restoration of her property (2 Kgs 8:6). Indeed, the king's judgment is in sharp contrast to the land-grabbing activities of Ahab who had no respect for the law and justice. That is, in 1 Kings 21:1–17, Ahab committed heinous crimes—the murder of Naboth and then taking possession of his ancestral land. Ahab particularly disregarded the Israelite law that was designed to inhibit the alienation of family property (Lev. 25:8–34; Num. 27:9–11). Indeed, the wealthy's unjust and inhuman practice of expropriating the ancestral land of the socially vulnerable through the manipulation of the courts is frequently condemned (Isa. 5:8–12; 32:7 and Mic. 2:1–2 recall Prov. 15:25).

Furthermore, the story of the Queen of Sheba (1 Kgs 10:1–10) demonstrates Solomon's international fame, which attracted foreigners to his court (1 Kgs 4:34). The Queen of Sheba's visit confirms King Solomon's status as the wise king par excellence who executes justice and righteousness (1 Kgs 10:9) and whose throne is established in righteousness (Prov. 25:5). Solomon is hailed as one whose justice is honored and revered by Israel's lowest of the low by bringing their case before him (1 Kgs 3:16–28) and by the rich and powerful or the highest of the foreign high (1 Kgs 10:1–10). In summary, these notable stories underline the king's national and international reputation, his duty and responsibility to protect the vulnerable and the importance of the royal court as a legal setting.

The use of proverbs in Israelite legal settings

We are now going to examine the possible usage of proverbs in Israelite legal settings in:

1 Condemning the taking of bribes, partiality, and penal practices
2 Warning against perjury
3 The need to protect the socially vulnerable and advising those profiteering from the misfortunes of the poor
4 Overhasty legal accusation
5 The use of proverbs by advisers, judges, defendants and plaintiffs.

In clarifying this issue, we will explore what Proverbs says in relation to other Old Testament texts. So, proverbs with legal links will be divided into two groups: the strongest, and the weakest.

The strongest legal links

Proverbs that condemn

The taking of bribes

The word מַתָּן 'gift' is used neutrally in Proverbs 19:6. However, another word שֹׁחַד 'bribe' is used in Proverbs 17:23; 21:14. In addition, Proverbs 21:15 refers to the practice of מִשְׁפָּט 'justice'. Indeed, the placement of Proverbs 21:15 immediately after Proverbs 21:14 that talks about bribery is probably significant. The content of these proverbs echoes seventh- and eighth-century prophets who were critical of the corrupt judicial process, its officials and the rich who manipulated the legal system and deprived the poor of their legal rights as they perverted the legal system by accepting bribes (Isa. 1:23; 5:23; 10:1–2; Amos 2:6; 5:10,12; Mic. 3:9,11). Additionally, Isaiah 3:13–15 underlines the indictment of state leadership. The language is forensic, which presupposes a legal setting where Yahweh rises to deliver the indictment.

Also, Amos 2:5–16 shows that Israel (Northern Kingdom, not the nation as a whole) stands under divine judgment for the oppression of the poor and for immorality. Amos 5:10–13 explicitly condemns the corrupt legal system, particularly at the gate, where the truth is rejected, the poor are plundered, and witnesses are bribed. Furthermore, Amos 5:12 strongly condemns corruption in the Israelite legal system because of bribes from influential citizens; the judiciary intimidated the poor plaintiffs to drop their exaction or compensation. Consequently, the judiciary became a partisan instrument of oppression of the poor by the ruling class.

Thus, Amos' lament attacks the criminals (עֲצוּמִים) and sinners (חַטֹּאתֵיכֶם). That is, the corrupt elders, jurists at the court trials. Israelite leading citizens were purposely persecuting the righteous (or 'innocent' צַדִּיק) by taking bribes either for declaring poor peoples' cases against the rich to be without merit, or by ruling in favor of rich plaintiffs or defendants against poor plaintiffs or defendants (cf. Exod. 23:6–8; 1 Sam. 12:3; Isa. 10:2; 29:21; Mal. 3:5). Indeed, such a direct covenant violation (Exod. 23:1–8; Deut. 16:18–20) is heinous. But Yahweh, who is surely the speaker here, knows it (יְדַעְתִּי). So, those who paid the bribes were also guilty. However, the focus is on the jurists, trusted to be impartial, yet they do the opposite (see Stuart, 1998 on Amos 5:12). Besides, Micah 3:3a talks about eating 'the flesh of my people' which does not mean cannibalism, but is a metaphorical word used elsewhere in the Old Testament to denote wicked actions against defenceless individuals (Prov. 30:14; Hab. 3:14).

The practice of bribing witnesses and judges was evidently a common practice severely condemned in the laws (Exod. 23:8; Deut. 16:19; 27:25) and other Old Testament literature (Isa. 1:23; 5:23; Ezek. 22:12; Ps. 15:5b; Eccl. 7:7). Proverbs 15:27 also condemns the greedy for unjust gain—those who take bribes. It is not clear whether this practice refers to bribing witnesses and/or judges. But Proverbs 17:23 condemns this practice particularly when its purpose was to pervert the course of justice and secure the condemnation of an innocent person. Whybray notes that the emphases in Proverbs 15:27 seems to be on 'the heinousness of the crime rather than on the means by which it is committed. Its precise nature is not stated here, but the parallel in the second line suggests that it is some kind of extortion' (1994c: 236). Similarly, Murphy notes that 'the parallelism indicates that the "gifts" are not innocent; they are bribes' (see Murphy, 1998 on Prov. 15:27).

Proverbs 17:23 also refers to מִשְׁפָּט 'justice' which may explicitly suggest a legal context (Longman, 2006: 350). If so, it is highly probable that proverbs were used in Israelite legal settings to condemn the crime of taking bribes in order to pervert justice. Perhaps their usage and criticism specifically focused on the corrupt judiciary officials, false witnesses, and the rich who manipulated the legal system.

Partiality and injustice

In Proverbs 18:5, there is an injustice because the judge is partial to one of the parties without regard to the merits of the case. Thus, a righteous or innocent person is denied justice. To show favor or partiality is literally 'to lift up the face' of the one who is favored. This phrase is used of judicial bias in Leviticus 19:15, Psalm 82:2 and in Deuteronomy 10:17 where it is associated with the taking of bribes. It reflects a situation in which a superior instructs an inferior, who has bowed down, to stand up, and thus he lifts up the face. Here it describes the action of a judge who blatantly issues an unjust decision (cf. Prov. 17:23) (see Murphy, 1998 on Prov. 18:5).

Proverbs 18:5 condemns the corrupt judges (Whybray, 1994c: 266). The wicked man 'רָשָׁע', and the innocent or righteous man 'צַדִּיק' are technical terms used for 'guilty' and 'innocent' (Whybray, 1994c: 266). So Proverbs 18:5 is concerned with judicial procedures. Let us clarify how the words רָשָׁע and צַדִּיק are used in the judicial pronouncement of guilt/wickedness. The verb רשׁע occurs thirty-four times in the Old Testament; nine times in the qal and twenty-five times in the hiphil. In the qal, it refers to wicked conduct, while in the hiphil, it can connote either wicked conduct or the pronouncement of guilt. Several instances of the hiphil denote the pronouncement of guilt against a judicial background. A forensic nuance is, for example, prominent in Deuteronomy 25:1, where a tribal court adjudicates an interpersonal dispute, acquitting the innocent צַדִּיק and condemning the guilty רָשָׁע, and in Exodus 22:9 [8], where judges pronounce guilt in cases of misappropriated property. Any reversal of true justice, for instance, acquitting the guilty and condemning the innocent as is the case in Proverbs 17:15, constitutes an abomination before Yahweh (Isa. 50:9).[8] Also, the hiphil of נטה 'deprive or subvert . . . of מִשְׁפָּט justice', is literally 'thrust aside' and is frequently used in other Old Testament literature, for instance Exodus 23:6; 1 Samuel 8:3, in connection with the condemnation of taking bribe(s) (Van Gemeren, 2004).

Similarly, Proverbs 24:23b–24 condemns partiality in the administration. Proverbs 24:23b is almost identical with Proverbs 28:21a and is a variant of Proverbs 18:5a. The phrase 'partiality in judging' is indicative of Deuteronomy 1:17 in its address to the judges, and Deuteronomy 16:19, which is addressed to the whole people. Actually, the administration of justice in Israel was not confined to 'professional' judges. Ordinary Israelites were also responsible, 'not only as witnesses but also as judges' (Whybray, 1994c: 353). We concur with Whybray's observation that the similarity of Proverbs 24:23b to these 'laws in Deuteronomy suggests that it was generally familiar as a legal maxim' (1994c: 353). If so, this underpins what we are trying to illustrate about the usage of proverbs within Israelite legal settings.

Proverbs 24:24 condemns a judge who shows favoritism to one of the litigants in giving a verdict. Whybray notes that צַדִּיק אָתָּה 'You are innocent' was probably the legal phrase used as a declaration of acquittal by the judge. For instance, this verse recalls Ezekiel 18:9 where a second-person formulation 'You are righteous', as is the case here in Proverbs 24:24, 'seems to reflect civil law' (see Allen, 1998 on Ezek. 18:9). The Proverbs reference mentions the communal curse of nations while the Ezekiel text is about individual retribution, which represents a bizarre turnaround of the normal individual importance in Proverbs and a new emphasis on the individual in Ezekiel. Nonetheless, the need to judge justly is underlined in both cases (Dell, 2006: 177).

In addition, McKane notes that the phrase הכרפנם conjures up a situation where personal factors influence the verdict, whether the defendant is a crony of the judge or the judge takes a liking to one and is antipathetic to the other (1970: 573). The Hebrew idiom for showing partiality is either 'lifting the face of' (Prov. 18:5; 28:21b) or, as is the case here, 'recognizing the face' (see Murphy, 1998 on Prov. 24:24). If so, whoever obstructs the course of justice is cursed in the community.

By contrast, those who judge with equity will be rewarded as society blesses those who bless it and curses those who curse it (Prov. 24:25). In essence, what we are trying to emphasize here is that the primary focus and possible usages of Proverbs 24:24–25 is the legal setting. Probably, the proverbs were used to comment on the administration of justice outside the legal settings. Also, other literature, for instance, Leviticus 19:15, warns against partiality in judging. The text prohibits judges and councils from being partial to the poor or honoring the great. Thus, no favoritism is to be shown to anyone, regardless of status. The command not to favor the poor is surprising given concern for them in the Old Testament (Exod. 22:20–26 [21–27]; 23:6; Deut. 24:17–18; 27:19). Nonetheless, this prohibition seeks to prevent that concern from causing the elders to lean a judgment in favor of the unfortunate solely because that person is poor (Exod. 23:3) (see Hartley, 1998 on Lev. 19:15). So, we are trying to emphasize that these texts underscore that not only judges but all Israelites must establish justice in their legal settings as the foundation of their community and covenant relationship with Yahweh.

Penal practices in the legal settings

Longman notes that the likely primary setting for Proverbs 17:26 is legal because it condemns those who would render an improper verdict in a court case (2006: 351). Similarly, Whybray supports this view in saying Proverbs 17:26, like Proverbs 17:23, refers to corruption in the law courts. The word צַדִּיק 'righteous' here has its proper legal sense of 'innocent'. Also, the verb עָנוֹשׁ 'to impose fine' may have rather a broader sense of 'punish' here (Whybray, 1994c: 262). Additionally, עָנוֹשׁ in this broader sense is used in Proverbs 17:26; 19:19; 21:11; 22:3; 27:12, similar to the restrictions in Exodus 21:22; 22:25 and Deuteronomy 22:19 where the verb is used in its narrower sense.

Commenting on Proverbs 17:26, Waltke asserts, 'the tyrant in view is a magistrate because he is in a position to flog subordinate nobles in the government's hierarchical structure' (Eccl. 5:8 [7]). Further, its synonymous parallel pairs two forms of legal punishment, 'to fine' and 'to flog' for two kinds of virtuous citizens, 'an innocent person' and 'nobles', and two negative evaluations 'is not good' and 'is against what is upright' (Waltke, 2005: 63).

Also, McKane supports what we are trying to demonstrate, saying that the verse 'contains two random examples of bad penal practice. It is bad to fine an innocent man and it is improper to degrade noblemen by punishing them with scourging' (1970: 506–7). What these scholars say is plausible and indicates that the verse has a forensic sense. While the evidence to show the usage of proverbs in a legal setting is scanty, the balance of evidence presented here is critical of the judiciary; therefore, it is likely that proverbs may have been used in Israelite legal settings and society in condemning legal personnel known for bad penal practices or legal abuses.

Proverbs and legal warning against perjury

Proverbs 24:28 matches Proverbs 24:23–25 in warning against false witnessing in a court of law, which recalls the ninth commandment in Exodus 20:16 and Deuteronomy 5:20. The language of witness in Proverbs 24:28 suggests a legal setting because false accusations made in court are perjury (Longman, 2006:442; Whybray, 1994c: 355). The phrase 'without cause' implies that the person concerned has no reason to give witness. This proverb is likely to have been used to warn individuals against committing perjury and abusing the legal processes by becoming involved with other people's litigation as false witnesses bent on incriminating their neighbour.

We concur with Longman's suggestion that Proverbs 25:18 has a primary legal setting (2006: 455). Perjury is also condemned in Proverbs 14:5,25, which show that it might have lethal consequences. Similarly, McKane underscores that one who gives a false testimony against a neighbour makes a savage assault on his reputation and inflicts grievous bruises and wounds. So, committing perjury is likened to the use of lethal weapons (a war club, sword, sharp arrow). Though the perjurer does not take part in crude physical violence, he or she is a character assassin whose work of defamation is fundamental as false witness could result in fatal penalties (McKane, 1970: 506–7). A clear instance is the falsified case against Naboth in 1 Kings 21. Also, Proverbs 6:19 underlines that perjury is 'an abomination to the LORD' (Whybray, 1994c: 366).

In addition, Whybray notes that the situation envisaged in Proverbs 12:17 is that of legal testimony (see also McKane, 1970: 445). Indeed, the vocabulary indicates a judicial setting as shown by the words עֵד 'witness', which is predominantly used in a forensic context (Heim, 2001: 155) and יָפִחַ 'speaks', literally, 'breathing out'. This verb יָפִחַ 'speaks' is used on numerous occasions in Proverbs (Prov. 6:19; 14:5,25; 19:5,9) with reference to giving legal testimony (Whybray, 1994c: 196; Longman, 2006: 276). Lying witnesses seem to have been a major problem in the Israelite community (Prov. 6:19; 12:17; 14:5,25; 19:9; 21:28). As McKane notes, the contrast is between the truthful witness and the perjurer. The truthful witness honestly testifies, advances the course of justice, and facilitates a right verdict. By contrast, the perjurer through his falsification defeats the course of justice (McKane, 1970: 445). What McKane says is parallel to Proverbs 19:28, which condemns 'the false witness, particularly in a court of law' (Longman, 2006: 373) as the person is guilty of contempt of court and deliberately perverts the course of justice. This verse recalls the false witness mentioned in Proverbs 19:5,9 (Heim, 2001: 269).

Furthermore, Heim makes a connection between Proverbs 12:17,18 and 19. The false witness mentioned in v. 17b is also referred to in v. 18. Thus, he gossips trying to harm like a sword-thrust. By contrast, the astute converses wisely so that his words bring healing and justice. Proverbs 12:19 underlines the outcome of such behavior. 'Thus truthful testimony prevails, while false evidence will be exposed and punished' (Heim, 2001: 156). This also echoes Proverbs 19:5,9; 21:28.

Protection of the vulnerable

Proverbs 23:10–11 underscores the need to protect the rights of the poor and prohibits the greedy that remove an ancient landmark—the boundary markers set by the ancients—or encroach on the fields of orphans. The maintenance of the ancient landmark is also mentioned in Proverbs 22:28. The prohibition is probably against the powerful elites who grabbed land from vulnerable members of society (1 Kgs 21:1–24). Also, this prohibition evokes Deuteronomy 19:14; 27:17; Job 24:22; Isaiah 5:8–10 and Hosea 5:10. In Deuteronomy 19:14, this admonition appears as a law of Moses. Those guilty of the crime of moving a neighbor's boundary marker are cursed (Deut. 27:17). The inclusion of the curse here sheds light on the difficulty in producing sufficient evidence in a court of law to obtain a conviction of an offender. Family land was the economic basis for households in Israel and Judah. It was handed through generations or inherited at the father's death; therefore, land was not an economic asset to be bartered. For, instance, Naboth in 1 Kings 21:3 refers to 'the inheritance of my fathers', inheritance—inalienable property—was a sacred right that must not be tampered with, even by the present holder.

In addition, Leviticus 25:33 speaks about the prohibition against selling land rights because when these ordinances gave way to the greedy, it created a class of landless, homeless and unemployed Israelites without livelihood or civil rights. So, given this background, traditions and laws were developed pertaining to land distribution (Lev. 25:10–12, 24–5; Josh. 13–22; Ruth 4:10). As Longman notes, the prohibition against raiding the property of those socially powerless was supported by a strong sanction (Lev. 25:25–30, 47–55; Ruth 3; Jer. 32:1–15) (2006: 426).

Similar to Proverbs 23:10–11, Proverbs 30:13–14 talks about the oppression of the poor by the greedy. These two texts are reflective of the greedy in Israelite society, those who devour the poor of their community. The content and tone in these texts recollects Isaiah 5:8–10; Amos 2:6–7; 4:6; 5:11; Micah 2:1–2; 1 Kings 21. These issues become clearer when we interpret them in the context of monarchical Israel, especially its political, economic, social and cultural changes that had serious implications (positive and negative) on Israelite society. Indeed, the control of economic routes in the Near East and the tribute from subjugated states gave rise to Israel's economic and social growth at the expense of the old egalitarian structures of society (1 Kgs 10:14–29). Thus, the royal court (as a political institution) and its administration levied taxes on its citizens and vassal states (1 Kgs 4:7–20).

Additionally, deserving state officials were rewarded with gifts of land (1 Sam. 8:14; 22:7). The crown accrued land (1 Kgs 21:15–16) and redistributed it (2 Kgs 9:7–10; 16:4; 19:29–30). Those who had sufficient economic, political and judicial power deprived a man and his household of their inheritance which was a part of covenant right. The covenant stipulated that every man in Israel was equal before God and the law; the subject of Israelite land-tenure has been discussed above.

So the violent acquisition of land by the crown threatened Israelite families with their inherited smallholdings. This disregard for justice and violent seizure of other people's inherited property is demonstrated by the prophetic outcry (Mic. 2:1–2). In addition, the new regulation that barred state officials and members of the royal family from accumulating land was announced (Ezek. 46:16–18). Furthermore, the prophets criticized the upper class for forcibly removing small farmers and their families from their ancestral properties (Amos 8:4; Isa. 5:8; Mic. 2:9). Quintessentially, since it was the king and his officials' responsibility to protect the rights of the poor, probably the proverbs that prohibit the powerful from seizing the property of the vulnerable were used in Israelite legal settings to protect the poor's civil rights and to enforce social justice in Israelite community.

Profiteering from the misfortunes of the poor

Proverbs 28:8 warns against lending at interest to fellow Israelites. This is redolent of the law in Exodus 22:25; Leviticus 25:35–38; Deuteronomy 23:19–20 and the two passages in Ezekiel 18:8,13 that are based on the Pentateuch. The unspoken motivation in Proverbs 28:8 is that Yahweh will act, by preventing the ruthless wealthy person from enjoying his ill-gotten profits. Rather, a generous person will enjoy the profits (Prov. 14:31; 19:17). Proverbs 28:8b repeats the idea of 13:22b (see Murphy, 1998 on Prov. 28:8). So, Proverbs 28:8 underlines that no interest is to be charged since charging interest would be tantamount to profiteering from the misfortunes of the poor. In fact, this practice defeats the primary purpose of lending, which was meant to provide a means of social support for the poor (Exod. 22:25; Deut. 23:19–20). Further, Exodus 22:25 and Deuteronomy 24:10–14,17 reinforce the notion that if a garment is held as collateral, it must be returned before its absence causes hardship (see Durham, 1997 on Exod. 22:25).

The interpretation of Proverbs 13:23 is disputed. Some scholars argue that the poor in Proverbs were very destitute with no land, not even rough, previously cultivated land, and it was unlikely that such land could produce a bumper harvest (see Whybray, 1994c: 209). However, we concur with scholars who argue that in Proverbs 13:23 poverty is a result of some injustice perpetrated toward the poor by the wealthy and powerful. The chapter has previously discussed the condemnation of moving the landmarks and the abuse of the ancient law of credit. This suggests that the poor had land (see Nyika, 2008: 193). If so, 'lack of food for the hard working poor is due to tyranny, rather than the environment' (Longman, 2006: 291; Waltke, 2004, 573). So the proverb condemns the powerful who, by flouting the sanction of the corrupt legal process, took away the poor's hard-earned livelihood. Accordingly, this recalls Amos 5:10–12 that has been previously discussed (see Nyike, 2008: 178). So, probably, proverbs that echo laws that condemn the abuse of the ancient law of credit and the charging of interest had a forensic usage.

Overhasty legal accusation

Proverbs 25:7c–8 warns against an overhasty legal accusation or acting as witness against someone observed committing a criminal act. Longman notes that *rîb* 'legal accusation or case' may have legal connotation although the proverb may have a wider application (2006: 291). Whybray notes that the MT has 'do not go'; but the RSV, like the majority of commentators, re-points the verb as causative. If the MT is correct, then *rîb* refers to a legal process, as the verse appears to be a caution against hurrying to go to law or act as witness against someone observed committing a crime. But it is not clear why something which has merely been witnessed should be the occasion of precipitate litigation, unless the thought is that of Proverbs 24:28 which cautions one from becoming a 'professional' witness who has a habit of intervening in other people's law suits by giving evidence without any legal obligation to testify (McKane, 1970: 580).

Furthermore, Whybray notes that some scholars like Symmachus, Toy, Gemser and McKane interpret לָרִב 'into the court' as לָרֹב 'to the crowd'. If this interpretation is correct, the caution is not concerned with legal proceedings but scandal-mongering (Waltke, 2005: 295–6; Whybray, 1994c: 362). Similarly, McKane is in favor of seeing a reference here to reckless gossip and broken confidence rather than making a hasty, ill-considered, legal action (1970: 581). However, Murphy notes that the interpretation depends on the nature of the conflict whether it is private or public in a judicial setting. He emphasizes that either situation is possible. The prohibition argues against making hasty legal accusations or judgments based on visual evidence and readiness to enter into a dispute with a neighbour. He concludes that some commentators interpret the verse as an admonition against making the affair public by judicial litigation (see Murphy, 1998 on Prov. 25:7c–8). What Murphy asserts is plausible especially if one interprets vv. 7b–10 as a unit, a quatrain. These proverbs seem to be referring to judicial proceedings, 'The "one who hears" in v. 10a can have the technical sense of "judging" (in a legal dispute)' (see Murphy, 1998 on Prov. 25:9–10). If the topic in these verses is the same, namely, a judicial contention with a neighbour, then this interpretation is laudable.

Use of proverbs

By advisers

Possibly, the Israelite king had advisers who were consulted in matters relating to the administration and execution of justice. The following proverbs might support this. While Proverbs 11:10–11 are concerned with the well-being of urban life, they also refer to the effects of evil speech and the fact that the community's well-being depends on the respective fates of the righteous and the wicked (Heim, 2001: 138; Whybray, 1994c: 180). Perhaps, as Longman suggests, the flourishing of the righteous entails that they are in positions of influence. Thus, they occupy royal positions where their behavior leads 'to social justice and the alleviation of oppression' (Longman, 2006: 254). This is significant for Proverbs 16:13, which possibly has a royal court background. By contrast, the wicked are defined by their practice of injustice, oppression and offer of bad advice, which causes the collapse of the community. This thought expressed in Proverbs 11:10 and is also echoed in Proverbs 14:34; 28:12,28 and 29:2 where 'the contrast between the just community and the single unjust ruler should be noted' (Murphy, 1998 on Prov. 29:2).

Whybray further notes that Proverbs 25:4–5 reflects an awareness of injustice done by wicked people standing near the throne. They offer fatal advice which may endanger the king's throne (cf. 1 Kgs 12:6–15) (Whybray, 1994c: 359–61). These dangerous people are likely to have been the king's advisers working within both the judiciary and administrative setting. Indeed, Proverbs 11:14 highlights that good advice promotes success. In addition, the advisers' guidance may refer to military strategy as in Proverbs 20:18 and 24:6. Nevertheless, Whybray notes that the term 'royal counsellor' also has the general sense of one who gives private advice (Prov. 12:20) (Whybray, 1994c: 181). While these verses have a general application, they may well have a royal court usage. Essentially, we are trying to underline that the royal advisers or counsellors played an influential role in the king's administration of the kingdom and execution of justice among his subjects (cf. 1 Kgs 12).

By judges, defendants and plaintiffs

In Proverbs 18:5,17 the term צַדִּיק 'innocent or righteous' has a forensic sense, suggesting a legal setting (Waltke, 2005: 82; Whybray, 1994c: 271). In Proverbs 18:17, the one who first states a case (the defendant) seems right, until the other (the plaintiff or accuser) comes and cross-examines. Indeed, the verse shows that the plaintiff argues his case and the defendant is given the opportunity to defend himself. The fact that both parties are given opportunities to argue their case enables the judge to cross-examine and sift the evidence in order to arrive at a fair verdict; thereby doing justice. The proverb underscores the equality of disputants. As Whybray rightly notes, 'The verse is addressed to judges, warning them against making premature judgments before all the evidence and arguments have been heard' (Whybray, 1994c: 271; Longman, 2006: 358). In addition, 'a firsthand witness to a crime had a legal obligation to testify in court' (Lev. 5:1–6; Prov. 29:24) (Waltke, 2005: 296; Whybray, 1994c: 405). If so, this supports our argument that Israelite judges, defendants and plaintiffs, probably used proverbs in their legal procedures. This is similar to the Shona people and their use of proverbs in traditional legal courts (discussed in Nyika, 2008: 159–73).

The weakest legal links

The admonitions of Proverbs 1:24–31 are indicative of condemnation of pre-exilic and exilic prophets with accusation followed by declaration of unavoidable judgment (Isa. 6:9–13; Ezek. 3:7) (Dell, 2006: 165). Proverbs 1:24 and 28 both echo Isaiah 65:1–2, the commencement of Yahweh's judgment (Dell, 2006: 165). However, the similarities between Proverbs 1:24,28 and Isaiah 65:1–2 are not adequately close to assert a direct link between the two passages (Whybray, 1994c: 48). Yet, the pronouncement of the sentence (Prov. 1:26–7), which follows with the accusation (vv. 24–25) (Waltke, 2004: 206), suggests forensic links. Nevertheless, it is not clear here whether 'the gate' (v. 21) refers to a legal or commercial setting. As Waltke rightly notes, 'the gate designates both the monumental edifices shading the narrow passageway through it and the side chambers where the elders sat on stone benches to adjudicate and discuss local affairs' (2004: 202).

The mention of false weights in Proverbs 11:1; 16:11; 20:10; 20:23 as 'an abomination to the LORD' recalls both law and prophecy (Lev. 19:35–37; Deut. 25:13–16; Ezek. 45:10; Hos. 12:7; Amos 8:5b–6; Mic. 6:10–11). In fact, Proverbs 11:1 talks about God's abomination of fraud (Heim, 2001: 137) and dishonest trade. Heim further notes that this verse establishes God's 'concern for fair trade, which can be generally applied in human affairs' (2001: 138). Fraudulent business practice is forbidden in the Old Testament as an 'abomination to Yahweh'. As Van Leeuwen notes, the language of the phrase is evocative of Israel's legal codes (Lev. 19:35–37; Deut. 25:13–16), and prophetic condemnation of commercial greed and deception (Ezek. 45:10; Hos. 12:7; Amos 8:5; Mic. 6:11) (1997: 117). In addition, Proverbs 11:1 echoes Proverbs 16:11; 20:10,23. Whybray notes 'in view of the wide spread usage of the texts which condemn "false balances or scales" and similarity of terms employed, it is hardly possible to determine whether it was legal, wisdom (or prophetic) tradition that the topic first appeared in Israel' (1994c: 176).

Furthermore, Whybray says 'abomination' is frequently used in Proverbs. For instance, it occurs in Proverbs 10:32 and 11:1 though the topics dealt with in these verses are not the same; they set out criteria of acceptable behavior to distinguish the righteous from the wicked. He concludes that Proverbs 11:1 may be a comment on Proverbs 10:32 since it explicitly clarifies that moral and immoral conduct are matters not only for the approval of society but also for the judgment of Yahweh himself (1994c: 176). Similarly, Murphy notes that deceitful practice in business is prohibited in the Hebrew Bible, both in the Torah (Lev. 19:35; Deut. 25:13–16, with 'abomination') and often in the prophets (e.g., Amos 8:5), and it is echoed in Proverbs 16:11; 20:10,23. This probably suggests that the practice was widespread, and never stamped out (see Murphy, 1998 on Prov. 11:1). However, it is difficult to suggest a forensic context for Proverbs 11:1 because people pass moral judgment in all kinds of non-legal settings. If so, the usage of this verse probably lies in a broader-than-legal setting, as reference to fairness and integrity permeates all dealings in daily life.

In Proverbs 20:22, the statement that Yahweh avenges crime is closely related to legal terms and implies giving assistance to those in trouble rather than rescuing them from it, an 'interpretation that gives a better parallel with to "to repay" than "to save, to deliver" ' (Waltke, 2005: 153). Whybray suggests, 'This verse must be presumed to refer to offenders that could not for some reason be dealt with by the judges, or cases where the offender had been wrongfully acquitted' (1994c: 300–301). While this text refers to judicial procedures for justice, it is difficult to link it to Israelite legal settings since it explicitly refers to divine justice.

Proverbs 25:6–7b warns against self-aggrandisement in the presence of the king. Whybray rules out the possibility that these verses are addressed specifically to the courtier (1994c: 362). But, Longman suggests, 'the most natural primary audience for this warning is the sage who serves in the court, though the principle may have wide application' (2006: 452). McKane advocates a formal court occasion as a possible social setting for these verses (1970: 580). Though the balance of evidence seems to be in favor of the royal court, it is difficult to pinpoint whether these verses have a legal setting.

Conclusion

Although we cannot conclusively prove the usage of proverbs in Israelite legal settings due to lack of Israelite legal documents, what proverbs say and the balance of evidence presented is in favor of that possibility. It is probable that biblical proverbs, most of which can be read simply as comments on legal matters, were used in legal proceedings. The chapter strongly suggests that the Israelite royal court also had a juridical role. This is supported by the examples of legal cases brought before the royal court which have been discussed in this chapter. Besides, the fact that King Solomon was renowned for his oratory, wisdom and knowledge of the people's customary law suggests that the king and his advisers may have used proverbs in the royal court (1 Kgs 3:27–8; 10:9).

The chapter has also shown that proverbs are critical of the Israelite judiciary; therefore, it is likely that they have a judicial interest. They were probably used in the judicial process. Besides, this shows that the sages were deeply concerned about the legal process in Israel in particular, that it should not be corrupted or abused. It is therefore reasonable to suppose that they may have been involved in presenting and arguing cases in which individuals would have used proverbial wisdom. Additionally, it is logical to presume that proverbs may have been involved in Israelite legal settings to condemn the taking of bribes, partiality and injustice, and regarding penal practices in Israelite legal settings.

Moreover, the Israelite kings, advisers, litigants and witnesses possibly drew analogies from proverbial images and skilfully introduced proverbs into speech at crucial moments during legal proceedings. So it seems reasonable to suggest that Israelite kings, elders, advisers, judges, defendants, plaintiffs, prophets and, perhaps, ordinary people may have used proverbs to comment, advise or rebuke, smoothing disagreements and bringing cases to a close. Further, it is possible that proverbs were used to criticize and condemn the abuses associated with the Israelite legal settings, to warn against perjury, to promote the need to protect the socially vulnerable, and to censure those profiteering from the misfortunes of the poor and making overhasty legal accusations.

Notes

1 Due to the word limit of this paper, we will not discuss the role of the family as a legal domestic court.
2 Biblical quotations are from the NRSV, unless otherwise indicated.
3 Massa, as in Prov. 30:1, is understood here as an area in North Arabia, over which Lemuel is king; this interpretation disregards the *athnach* under מלך in the MT. Some follow a literal interpretation of the MT: 'the burden (or, instruction) with which his mother instructed him'. Also see Whybray (1995: 99–100).
4 There are varying interpretations of מה, e.g., 'hear,' based on Arabic; so Plöger following Ben Yehuda. It has also been interpreted as a negative particle 'no'; so Barucq, citing Joüon §144h. But the MT can be rendered literally as 'what?' with a verb of some kind such as 'say' being understood. The word for 'son' is the Aramaic form בר (Murphy, 1998: 239).
5 Lemuel is otherwise unknown, and efforts to associate him with Edom are guesswork. In v. 2, it seems that the mother of the king is speaking, although it is not clear if she is the real queen mother, or the mother of one of the palace heirs who rose to the kingship. The nuance of her statements is not clear; see Dell (1998: 177). But she is certainly calling attention to the advice she is about to give. Moreover, she emphasizes her authority by referring to her maternal privilege; she has not only borne him, but apparently dedicated him as well ('son of my vows'; like Hannah in 1 Sam 1:11, 28).
6 Although King Lemuel is unknown and non-Israelite, what is important is the motif as the king is instructed not to neglect duty, to judge righteously and to defend, care and speak for the powerless which are similar characteristics to those of Israelite kings. Also, the meaning of חלוץ, 'one passed on or over or away', is difficult to determine (ὑγιῶ, 'soundly'; 'judge all things soundly' in LXX). The root of this word means 'change disappear', etc. Various translations have been proposed, but

ultimately it is the context that suggests something like 'weak, abandoned, unfortunate', etc. The dittography of ץ suggested in *BHS* yields חלי, 'sickness' or 'suffering', etc. See Murphy's (1998) comment on Prov. 31:8–9.
7 The notion of justice and righteousness is also an issue, which dominates the prophetic indictments.
8 For further reading on the use of רשע in the Old Testament, see Van Gemeren (2004).

Bibliography

Allen, L. C. *Ezekiel 1–19*, Word Biblical Commentary, vol. 28 (electronic edn), Logos Library System (Dallas, TX: Word, 1998).

Alt, A. 'Der Antel des Königtums an den sozialen Entwicklung in der Reichen Israel und Juda'. Pages 348–72 in *Kleine Schriften*, vol. 3 (Munich: Beck, 1955).

Anderson, A. A. *2 Samuel*, Word Biblical Commentary (electronic edn), Logos Library System (Dallas, TX: Word, 1998).

BHS, Biblia Hebraica Stuttgartensia (ed. K. Elliger and W. Rudolph; Stuttgart: 1983).

Boecker, H. J. *Law and the Administration of Justice in the Old Testament and Ancient East* (London: SCM Press, 1980).

Clines, D. J. A. *Job 21–42*, Word Biblical Commentary, vol. 18a (electronic edn), Logos Library System (Dallas, TX: Word, 1998).

Dell, K. J. *The Book of Proverbs in Social and Theological Context* (Cambridge: Cambridge University Press, 2006.)

———. 'The King in the Wisdom Literature'. Pages 163–8 in *King and Messiah in Israel and the Ancient Near East* (ed. J. Day; JSOTS 270; Sheffield: Sheffield Academic Press, 1998).

DeVries, S. J. *1 Kings*, Word Biblical Commentary (electronic edn), Logos Library System (Dallas, TX: Word, 1998).

Durham, J. I. *Exodus,* Word Biblical Commentary (electronic edn), Logos Library System (Dallas, TX: Word, 1997).

Fox, M. V. *Proverbs 10–31: A New Translation with Introduction and Commentary*, Anchor Bible, 18B (New Haven: Yale University Press, 2009).

Gemser, B. 'The Instructions of Onchsheshonqy and Biblical Wisdom Literature', VTS vii, pp. 102–128.

Golka, F. W. *The Leopard's Spots: Biblical and African Wisdom in Proverbs* (Edinburgh: T. & T. Clark, 1993.).

Hartley, J. E. *Leviticus*, Word Biblical Commentary, vol. 4 (electronic edn), Logos Library System (Dallas, TX: Word, 1998).

Heim, K. M. *Like Grapes of Gold Set in Silver.* Beihefte zur Zeitschrift für die alttestamentliche Wissenschaft, 273 (Berlin: Walter de Gruyter, 2001).

Longman, T. III. *Proverbs* (Grand Rapids: Baker Academic, 2006).

McKane, W. *Proverbs: A New Approach* (London: SCM Press, 1970).

Mulder, M. J. *1 Kings*, vol. 1, Historical Commentary on the Old Testament (Leuven: Peeters, 1998).

Murphy, R. E. 'Kerygma of the Book of Proverbs', *Interpretation* 20 (1966): pp. 3–14.

———. 'Wisdom-Theses and Hypotheses'. Pages 35–42 in *Israelite Wisdom:*

Theological and Literary Essays in Honour of Samuel Terrien (ed. J. G. Gammie, W.A. Brueggmann, W. L. Humphreys and J. M. Ward (New York: Scholars Press, 1978).

———. *Proverbs*, Word Biblical Commentary, vol. 22 (electronic edn), Logos Library System (Dallas, TX: Word, 1998).

Nyika, H. *The Use of Proverbs to Inculcate and Reinforce Shona and Israelite Values* (Unpublished PhD thesis, Bristol University, 2008).

Stuart, D. *Hosea-Jonah*, Word Biblical Commentary (electronic edn), Logos Library System (Dallas, TX: Word, 1998).

Van Gemeren, W. A. ed. *New Dictionary of Old Testament Theology and Exegesis* (5.1, CD ROM edn) (Grand Rapids: Zondervan, 2004).

Van Leewen, R. C. 'Proverbs'. In *The New Interpreter's Bible* (ed. L. E Keck; (Nashville, TN: Abingdon, 1997).

Waltke, B. K. *The Book of Proverbs: Chapters 1–15* (Cambridge: Eerdmans, 2004).

———. *The Book of Proverbs: Chapters 15–31* (Cambridge: Eerdmans, 2005).

Whitelam, K. W. *The Just King: Monarchical Judicial Authority in Ancient Israel* (Sheffield: JSOT Press, 1979).

Whybray, R. N. *The Book of Proverbs: A Survey of Modern Study* (Leiden: Brill, 1995).

———. *Composition of the Book of Proverbs* (Sheffield: JSOT Press, 1994b).

———. *The Intellectual Tradition in the Old Testament*, Beihefte zur Zeitschrift für die alttestamentliche Wissenschaft,135 (Berlin: Walter de Gruyter, 1974).

———. *Proverbs*, The New Century Bible Commentary (Grand Rapids: Eerdmans, 1994c.)

———. 'The Structure and Composition of Proverbs 22:17–24–22'. Pages 83–96 in *Crossing the Boundaries: Essays in Biblical Interpretation in Honour of Michael D. Goulder* (ed. S. E Porter, P. Joyce and D. E. Orton; Leiden: Brill, 1994a).

———. *Wealth and Poverty in the Book of Proverbs* (Sheffield: JSOT Press, 1990.).

———. *Wisdom in Proverbs: The Concept of Wisdom in Proverbs 1–9*, Studies in Biblical Theology 45 (London: SCM Press, 1965).

Yoder, C. R. *Proverbs* (Nashville, TN: Abingdon Press, 2009).

God of justice
> we give you thanks for Scripture's steady pulse,
> > revealing your heart for justice expressed in the gift of
law.

We thank you for the sayings and stories surrounding legal codes,
> the gate, the royal court and the role of the king as judge.

We thank you for the setting down of boundaries of behavior
> that lead to the prospering of all people.

We thank you for the unmasking power of due process
> exposing wrong, exploitation and violence.

We thank you for all who diligently seek to exercise justice
> in a world still riddled with corruption, greed and
> > partiality.

We pray for all who administer justice, who seek justice,
> and who find in you their strength, their advocate and

4

Personified Wisdom in Early Judaism

Knut M. Heim

In his influential textbook on the Psalms and Wisdom Literature, Ernest Lucas asked: 'is Wisdom depicted as simply *present* or as *active* during the process of creation? (2003: 107). Since the meaning of the word *'amon* in Proverbs 8:30 (a key text for understanding wisdom's role in creation) is uncertain, he concluded that 'it seems best to see Wisdom in Proverbs 8:22–31 as a vividly portrayed personification of an attribute of Yahweh rather than as a hypostasis' (2003: 107–8). The word 'hypostasis' is a complex term that is frequently misunderstood. Lucas' minimalist definition, in the glossary, explains it as 'a distinct individual entity' (2003: 204). The personification of wisdom in Proverbs 1–9 had a vivid afterlife, and in the following study I will sketch some of the highlights of her career in early Judaism in order to explore how active her role in creation was. As a by-product, this will shed some light on how early Christians drew on their Jewish heritage in their understanding of Jesus of Nazareth.

A history of the reception of personified wisdom in Early Judaism

Early Judaism's portrayal of wisdom took its cue from the personification in Proverbs 8 and related texts, including Job 28, but with significant and peculiar nuances that broadly fall into two categories. One category developed personified wisdom into a metaphoric concept that appears to picture her as a superhuman being with quasi-Godlike features. This may be illustrated with passages from the Wisdom of Solomon. The other category developed in a different direction. The personification was maintained on a literary level, but was ultimately turned on its head by the reification of wisdom: Personified wisdom was identified with the Torah. This interpretative move is exemplified by Ben Sira and Baruch.

Significantly, however, the portrayal of humanity's approach to wisdom in both categories involved romantic or 'erotic' overtones. The following paragraphs will illustrate this with key texts from Ben Sira, Wisdom of Solomon and Baruch.

Personification, reification and erotic language in Ben Sira

The most celebrated passage regarding the personification of wisdom in Ben Sira is chapter 24, but the following quote illustrates how the personification shaped the way in which the acquisition of wisdom was envisaged:

> Happy is the *man* who meditates on wisdom and reasons intelligently, who reflects in his heart on her ways and ponders her secrets, pursuing her like a hunter, and lying in wait on her paths; who peers through her windows and listens at her doors; who camps near her house and fastens his tent-peg to her walls; who pitches his tent near her, and so occupies an excellent lodging-place; who places his children under her shelter, and lodges under her boughs; who is sheltered by her from the heat, and dwells in the midst of her glory. (14:20–27)[1]

Surprisingly, this striking presentation of a rather intrusive kind of male pursuit of a female figure has rarely caused offence. As recently as 1970 German Old Testament scholar Gerhard von Rad could comment innocently: 'Nowhere else has the image of the erotic appeal which the cognitive process has on man been described in a more beautiful and chaste manner' (1970: 219).[2] Yet if wisdom were thought of as a real-to-life woman, the only way to label the recommended behavior towards her is 'stalking'. Why, then, has this imagery not been perceived as offensive in the past? In my view, this is not so much because male readers in the past were insensitive to obtrusive behavior of fellow males towards females (although they often were and often still are); rather, the personification of wisdom was appropriately recognized as what it was: a literary figure of speech.

'Stalking' wisdom was not perceived as problematic because in early Jewish circles the *literary personification* of wisdom remained transparent, and the book's readers readily recognized it for what is really was—a *conceptual reification:* personified wisdom *was* the Torah, a book, a body of teaching rather than of flesh and blood. The model for reading such texts about personified wisdom were personifications of wisdom like the one in Ben Sira 24:1–22, closely fashioned on Proverbs 8, which culminates in the identification of wisdom with the Torah in verse 23: 'All this is the book of the covenant of the Most High God, the law that Moses commanded us.'

In conclusion, our analysis of the acquisition of wisdom in Ben Sira has demonstrated that in one tradition of early Judaism, wisdom was stripped of any potentially supernatural vestments and insignia. Literarily personified, she was expressly reified, stripped of her human clothes, conceptually tamed and theologically sanitized into an instrument or medium of Yahweh's self-revelation.

The personification as such continued to have an impact on the acquisition of wisdom. Wisdom was perceived as a highly desirable but exalted prey worthy of the most rapacious and strenuous pursuit, for it gives access to God's self-revelation and to divine guidance in all matters of conduct. Yet this heightened desirability came at a price. In this tradition, wisdom is no longer a living being reaching out to humans and inviting them to share pleasant company and enjoy good food for life (cf. Prov. 1–9). Rather, she has become a prey that needs to be caught, something that needs to be taken by force. The cognitive process is now portrayed as a forceful and passionate pursuit of an attractive but passive and unresponsive entity. Humans no longer respond to an invitation to learn; they are on the prowl for knowledge.

In the next section, we will look at further developments in this tradition's interpretation of the wisdom personification.

Personification, preexistence, incarnation and reification in Baruch 3–4

A large part of chapter 3 in the book of Baruch is taken up with wisdom terminology. Fear of the Lord, one of the key terms in Proverbs 1–9, is used to paraphrase the faith of Israel: 'you have put the fear of you in our hearts so that we would call upon your name' (Bar. 3:7). The promise of 'life' for those who 'possess' wisdom is echoed in the following words: 'Hear the commandments of life, O Israel; give ear, and learn wisdom!' (3:9). The evocative metaphor 'fountain of wisdom', well known from the book of Proverbs, also appears: 'You have forsaken the fountain of wisdom' (3:12).

A significant paragraph takes up and alludes to various key promises and benefits associated with the possession of wisdom in Proverbs 1–9 and Job 28.

> Learn where there is wisdom, where there is strength, where there is understanding, so that you may at the same time discern where there is length of days, and life, where there is light for the eyes, and peace. Who has found her place? And who has entered her storehouses? Where are the rulers of the nations, and those who lorded it over the animals on earth; those who made sport of the birds of the air, and who hoarded up silver and gold in which people trust, and there is no end to their getting . . . ? (Bar. 3:14–17)

The following verses allude to Job 28:

> Later generations have seen the light of day, and have lived upon the earth; but they have not learned the way to knowledge, nor understood her paths, nor laid hold of her. Their descendants have strayed far from her way. She has not been heard of in Canaan, or seen in Teman; the descendants of Hagar, who seek for understanding on the earth, the merchants of Merran and Teman, the story-tellers and the seekers for understanding, have not learned the way to wisdom, or given thought to her paths. (Bar. 3:20–3)

Personified Wisdom in Early Judaism 59

We can see that the personification metaphor as developed in Baruch 3 focuses on wisdom's dwelling-place, which, in line with the imagery of Job 28 but in contrast with personified wisdom's portrayal in Proverbs 1–9 (e.g., Prov. 9:1–6), is pictured as a remote and inaccessible location far removed from ordinary human dwellings. The 'path to wisdom' is thus pictured as a strenuous journey. Whereas in Ben Sira wisdom is 'hard to get,' in Baruch she is 'hard to get to'.

The most sustained discussion of wisdom is found in the following longer passage, the end of Baruch 3 and the beginning of Baruch 4. Throughout, wisdom is personified as a woman.

> O Israel, how great is the house of God, how vast the territory that he possesses! It is great and has no bounds; it is high and immeasurable. The giants were born there, who were famous of old, great in stature, expert in war. God did not choose them, or give them the way to knowledge; so they perished because they had no wisdom, they perished through their folly. Who has gone up into heaven, and taken her, and brought her down from the clouds? Who has gone over the sea, and found her, and will buy her for pure gold? No one knows the way to her, or is concerned about the path to her. But the one who knows all things knows her, he found her by his understanding. The one who prepared the earth for all time filled it with four-footed creatures; the one who sends forth the light, and it goes; he called it, and it obeyed him, trembling; the stars shone in their watches, and were glad; he called them, and they said, 'Here we are!' They shone with gladness for him who made them. This is our God; no other can be compared to him. He found the whole way to knowledge, and gave her to his servant Jacob and to Israel, whom he loved. Afterwards she appeared on earth and lived with humankind. (Bar. 3:24–37)

In modern Bible translations, such as NRSV, the following statements belong to a new chapter, Baruch 4:1–2, but in the original they continue the same paragraph: 'She is the book of the commandments of God, the law that endures for ever. All who hold her fast will live, and those who forsake her will die. Turn, O Jacob, and take her; walk toward the shining of her light' (Bar. 4:1–2).

A number of important motifs familiar from earlier wisdom personifications are taken up: the 'house' (Bar. 3:24; cf. Prov. 9:1), the 'way to knowledge/wisdom' (Bar. 3:27; cf. Job 28). There is also the assumption that wisdom is located in 'heaven' (Bar. 3:29), inaccessible and extremely valuable. No one knows the way to her (Bar. 3:30–31; cf. Job 28). Only God knows her and found her in the context of creation (Bar. 3:32: cf. Prov. 8), implying, at least on the level of the metaphor, that she is a being/an entity separate from and to a degree independent of God. God gave wisdom only to Israel (Bar. 3:36). Most intriguingly, 'afterward she appeared on earth and *lived* with humankind' (Bar. 3:37), which comes close to the idea of the 'incarnation' of a heavenly, pre-existent being (cf. Bar. 3:37 with vv. 32 and 29, above). It is precisely at this point, however, that the personification metaphor is diffused into a reification of wisdom. This interpretative step occurs in Baruch 4:1: 'She is the book of the commandments of God, the law that endures for ever.' As in Ben Sira, then, wisdom is initially personified *as a woman* only to be reified in turn—turned into the 'the book of the commandments of God', his 'law'. In Ben Sira and Baruch, then, we see one and the same interpretative move that appears to do justice to the female personification (βίβλος, 'book' is a feminine noun), only to turn the female figure into an object for study, albeit a supremely valuable one (νόμος, 'law' is a masculine noun). Baruch 3 differs from Ben Sira and Wisdom of Solomon (on which see below) inasmuch as erotic language and romantic sentiments are entirely absent.

Personification, apotheosis, and romantic language in Wisdom of Solomon

The personification of wisdom pervades the book. In Wisdom 6:17–18a the erotic language of love and desire for wisdom is deconstructed, and the literary function of the personification comes to the fore: 'The beginning of wisdom is the most sincere desire for instruction, and concern for instruction is love of her, and love of her is the keeping of her laws.' Quite literally, the 'beginning' of wisdom, the first step to the acquisition of wisdom, is a desire to learn. And to 'love' wisdom is to keep a set of instructions contained in wisdom teaching.

In 6:13–16 the apparent dichotomy between the lectures (the acquisition of wisdom requires strenuous effort) and the wisdom interludes (personified wisdom herself takes the initiative) of Proverbs 1–9 is resolved by combining human effort and wisdom's self-giving:

> She hastens to make herself known to those who desire her. One who rises early to seek her will have no difficulty, for she will be found sitting at the gate. To fix one's thought on her is perfect understanding, and one who is vigilant on her account will soon be free from care, for she goes about seeking those worthy of her, and she graciously appears to them in their paths, and meets them in every thought.

A number of statements have usually been described as containing erotic language (cf. also 6:13–16, quoted above):

> I loved her and sought her from my youth; I desired to take her for my bride, and became enamoured of her beauty. (Wisdom 8:2)

> Therefore I determined to take her to live with me, knowing that she would give me good counsel and encouragement in cares and grief. (Wisdom 8:9)

When I enter my house, I shall find rest with her; for companionship with her has no bitterness, and life with her has no pain, but gladness and joy. (Wisdom 8:16)

The language in these statements, however, is *romantic* rather than erotic. Commensurate with the consistently developed personification of wisdom as a noble woman with a highly exalted status (see immediately below), the mutual attraction between humans and wisdom is described in terms of the attraction between a woman and a man. In contrast to Ben Sira, however, this is the stuff of romance, of courtship, love and marriage, where a proper distance and respectful propriety (chastity in Von Rad's terms) is maintained, picturing a dynamic two-way relationship. This is not surprising in view of high, almost Godlike qualities ascribed to wisdom. I am listing some of these qualities in the following:

- Wisdom as Creatrix: 7:12,22; 8:5–6; 9:9 and especially 8:3–4: 'She glorifies her noble birth by living with God, and the Lord of all loves her. For she is an initiate in the knowledge of God, and an associate in his works.'
- Wisdom's noble birth (of God?): 8:3 (quoted above).
- Wisdom 'one' with God: 7:25–26: Wisdom is a 'breath of the power of God, and a pure emanation of the glory of the Almighty', a 'reflection of eternal light, a spotless mirror of the working of God, and an image of his goodness'.
- Wisdom brings immortality: 6:18; 8:17.
- Λόγος and σοφία are treated as parallel: 9:1–2.
- Wisdom sits 'by' God's throne: 9:4,10.
- Σοφία and God's 'holy spirit' are treated as parallel: 9:17.
- Wisdom and God are used interchangeably: 10:1—12:2.

At first sight, at least, these statements come close to assigning divine status to personified wisdom. Nonetheless, even in the monotheistic milieu of contemporary Judaism, this apparent 'apotheosis' of wisdom was generally not considered heretical. How could personified wisdom acquire quasi-divine features in Second Temple Judaism? The answer lies in a fuller appreciation of the wisdom personification as a particularly potent literary metaphor. In the context of Wisdom of Solomon in particular and within the wider cultural milieu of contemporary Judaism, the identity of personified wisdom as a *literary* creation that ultimately was to be identified with the 'law' of God always remained transparent.

Consequently, statements about wisdom's exalted status go hand in hand with expressions about the subordination of wisdom to God (see Wisdom 7:15 and esp. 8:21—9:4). The wisdom figure, however exalted, did not pose a threat to Israel's belief that the Lord was one (cf. the Shema, Deut. 6:4–5).

Furthermore, several statements in Wisdom of Solomon suggest an equation between personified wisdom and the 'word' (= 'logos') of God: 'O God . . .

who has made all things by your word (λόγος), and by your wisdom (σοφία) has formed humankind' (Wisdom 9:1-2). On the one hand, personified wisdom in Wisdom of Solomon emerged as a particularly effervescent and animated persona. On the other hand, she remained reified as the Torah, the written word of God, or conceptualized as God's own wisdom.

This oscillation between figurative and various non-figurative interpretations of personified wisdom has remained a viable and acceptable option for interpreters from various backgrounds through different historical periods precisely because of the literary nature and the creative power of the personification metaphor, which by its very nature prompted imaginative engagement and permitted different—and sometimes conflicting—interpretations all at the same time.

Summary

An examination of two specific developments in the personification of wisdom in Ben Sira, Baruch and Wisdom of Solomon has demonstrated that the personification metaphor has a significant impact on how the acquisition of wisdom was perceived and portrayed. In Ben Sira, where the personification is turned on its head by means of its reification into the Torah, the language is intrusive and overtly erotic. In Baruch, the wisdom personification is overtly and consistently reified, and her identification as the 'law' and 'book' of God remains transparent throughout. Erotic or romantic language is absent. Instead, relational aspects are expressed in terms of a journey towards wisdom's dwelling-place. In Wisdom of Solomon, where the personification is developed further and where wisdom acquires quasi-divine traits, the language is romantic.

To sum up, the statements about pre-existent wisdom proceeding from God and being a 'mediator' in creation in Proverbs 8 were developed in two distinct ways in Second Temple Judaism. Its application to the Torah, as exemplified in Ben Sira, is probably the more pervasive. The verdict of Klaiber and Marquardt (1993: 155 n. 236), however, that statements about pre-existent wisdom were applied to the Torah in early Judaism, while early Christian teaching applied them to Christ, is too simplistic: The 'apotheosis' of wisdom in Wisdom of Solomon remained influential in Hellenistic Judaism. In Hellenistic Jewish philosophy, most notably in the thought of Philo (cf. e.g., *Leg. All.* 1.65), exalted wisdom became identified with the (male) *logos*, the divine word or spirit. Thus the 'apotheosis' of personified wisdom in the style of Wisdom of Solomon furnished a genuinely orthodox Jewish model which 'paved the way' (cf. Bar.) for the identification of personified wisdom with the Son of God.

Greek philosophy and Philo

Philo's speculative thinking about wisdom and its acquisition is deeply embedded not only in his own Jewish cultural milieu, but also in the wider philosophical thought of his day. His approach is eclectic, as he draws upon a wide range of philosophical thought and combines his influences into a new philosophical concept that also influenced early Christian thought.

Logos and nous in Greek philosophy

Greek philosophy is concerned with wisdom, as the name suggests. The term philosophy is a compound noun made up of the verb φιλῶ (*philo* = to love) and the noun σοφία (*sophia* = wisdom). Greek philosophy, quite literally then, is the *love* of wisdom, a metaphoric expression suggestive of wisdom's personification. The very name for philosophy thus highlights the relational aspects of the acquisition of wisdom.

From the second half of the sixth century BC, two related ideas emerged in Greek philosophy that later were to have a profound impact on the understanding of personified wisdom in Judaism and Christianity: the 'logos' and the 'nous'. The understanding of the logos and the nous in the various philosophical systems went through many transformations.

The first philosopher to speak of 'the logos' was Heraclitus of Ephesus (*c*.540–475 BC). Behind the eternally changing realities lies a kind of 'world order'. There is unity in diversity and diversity in unity, held together by the 'logos', the all-pervading harmony of universal reason. Trying to explain the aesthetic order of the visible world, Heraclitus therefore postulated the 'logos' as the power behind the cosmic process, in analogy with human reasoning, which imposed order on things in ordinary human affairs (Salmond and Grieve, 1911: 919). Analogical conclusions like this, often arrived at through metaphorical extension from observation of physical phenomena to metaphysical ideas, form a typical pattern for human thinking about the complex issues that are the themes of philosophy. Things metaphysical are explained in analogy with the visible world that is open to human perception and interpretation. The unknown is explained with the help of a metaphorical extension of what is known and perceived to be in some way analogous or similar.

Heraclitus himself did not furnish a clear definition of the term 'logos', and this vagueness was probably deliberate. For Heraclitus fire is the principle of empirical experience, and this 'primordial fire' is the divine process which constitutes the law of the universe, the logos, who rules the world and whom humans should obey (Störig, 1985: 136–37; Mitchell, 1910: 309–10; Salmond and Grieve, 1911: 919–21). 'The law of things is a law of Reason Universal (λόγος), but most men live as though they had a wisdom of their own' (Mitchell, 1910: 310).

Anaxagoras (*c*.500–428 BC) spoke of a supreme, intellectual principle, not identified with the world but independent of it, which he called nous (νοῦς) rather than logos. From here there is a direct line to the nous or wisdom (rather than logos) in Plato. (The *Epinomis*, in which the logos appears as synonym for nous, is pseudo-Platonic.)

Similarly, Aristotle (384–322 BC) later identified the principle which sets all nature under the rule of thought and directs it to a rational end as nous or the divine spirit itself. Plato and his immediate followers, then, used the term nous rather than logos.

Plato's (427–348/7 BC) thinking about the nous would later be conflated with various aspects of philosophical thinking about the logos. Therefore we will treat his contribution here slightly out of sequence, and afterwards return to our discussion of the logos in our treatment of the term's use in Stoicism and Philo. Some key features of Plato's cosmology are presented in the *Timaeus*, the account of an extended philosophical conversation between Socrates, Timaeus, Hermocrates and Critias as told by Plato.[3] The first part *(Timaeus*, 29D–47E) deals with the works of reason, those elements of the world which clearly manifest an intelligent and intelligible design, focusing especially on the *demiurge*, 'the benevolent maker and the Forms which provide his model', to use Cornford's memorable summary (1948: 32). The term is a transliteration of the Greek word δημιουργὸς, 'craftsman'. This deity, one among many other gods in Plato's pantheon, is fashioned upon the *human* image of a master craftsman who builds artefacts with his hands.

Hence the human analogy provides our philosophers with the conceptual framework to envisage what may have happened when the universe was created. Plato's cosmology is founded on a complex metaphor, for this is how human thinking probes into new realms of knowledge (see Lakoff and Johnson, 1981; Lakoff and Turner, 1989). Since the reality of creation that the metaphor aims to describe is complex and beyond direct human observation, the metaphoric image of the demiurge constitutes a particularly rich conceptual metaphor with a range of associated metaphorical entailments and extensions.

The image of the human craftsman becomes the guiding metaphor for envisaging various details of the creative process. Since a craftsman by definition does not create his artefacts from nothing (*ex nihilo*), the demiurge is envisaged as forming the universe out of pre-existing matter, his main achievement being the imposition of *form* on the raw materials of the universe. He creates *order*.

Since the universe is not a simple artefact like a tool or other utensils that can be held in the hand, but a huge, complex space, the craftsman does not create from his own imagination, but he needs to use *a blueprint, a plan, an image or model*.

Behind this idea, of course, lies the metaphor of the *creator as architect*. This is not yet explicit in Plato's cosmology, but his metaphor of the demiurge–craftsman creator will become *the* guiding metaphor for future thought about creation, including the idea of the creator as architect. The idea of the architect is more fully explored in the second part of the *Timaeus*, with the help of space and mathematics, the basic 'toolbox' of the architect.

Several key features of Plato's cosmology are relevant for our study. As far as we know, Plato was the first Greek philosopher to introduce the image of a creator god (Cornford, 1948: 34). This creator god was introduced in the form of an 'image', for the pioneering way in which Plato had Socrates and his companions talk about creation was in the form of mostly human analogies, that is, personifications. We now turn to the nous and the logos in Greek philosophy after Plato, for the logos made a forceful comeback in the philosophical system of the Stoics (on Stoicism, see Hicks, 1911: 942–51).

Stoicism, which flourished for several centuries, is a branch of Greek philosophy founded by Zeno of Citium (340–260 BC) on the Mediterranean island of Cyprus. Its teachings are a development of the Socratic school of the so-called Cynics,[4] combined with other earlier systems, such as that of Heraclitus. Relevant for our purposes is the doctrine of a strict law or order that is immanent to and permeates the whole world. This power the Stoics called 'logos', 'nous', 'soul', 'necessity', 'providence', and sometimes 'god' (with reference to Zeus).

Crucially, the understanding of the logos proceeded from a perceived parallel between macrocosm and microcosm. The logos, the 'soul' of the world which fills and permeates it, is postulated in analogy with the human soul, which according to the scientific knowledge of the times was thought to pervade and to breathe through the whole human body.[5] In Stoicism, logos and nous are conflated. Again we find that various parts of a philosophical system are formulated by way of analogy and metaphorical extension. Metaphysical problems were solved by explaining the unknown with the help of what was thought to be known. Also important for our purposes is Stoicism's pantheism: god is in everything and everything is god. The divine is ultimately identical with the whole living world.[6]

The importance of the Stoic philosophy continued through the fourth to second centuries BC, but eventually came to be superseded by what has sometimes been called 'eclecticism' (Störig, 1985: 200–202). The great philosophical schools of the Greek era were no longer seen as mutually exclusive systems but as a rich treasury of human thought from which the most suitable philosophical aspects could be chosen and reformulated into new, composite philosophical systems.

The most important representative of eclecticism for our purposes was the Jewish philosopher Philo of Alexandria, who epitomizes what has been called 'Alexandrian eclecticism'.

Personified wisdom, logos and demiurge
(= craftsman–creator) in Philo of Alexandria

Philo (*c*.25 BC—AD 50) lived and worked in Alexandria, at the time the cultural centre of the Eastern Mediterranean. Philo's God is quite different from the God portrayed in the Hebrew Bible. Philo's God is utterly transcendent and above human comprehension. In the creation of the world, his transcendent nature precluded his direct contact with matter. In order to impose his will on matter, Philo's God used corporeal forces 'whose true name is [*sic*] *ideas*'—in direct dependence on Plato. The eclectic nature of Philo's cosmogony is shown in the name that he gave to the essence of these ideas. He called them 'the logos'—and this choice of terminology demonstrates Stoic and other Greek influences on Philo. The logos is not identical with God, but takes second position. Philo also calls him 'Son of God'. He is mediator between God and humanity and intercessor for humans before Philo's God (Störig, 1985: 202). At issue in Philo is an elaborate attempt to reconcile the idea of a transcendent god becoming manifest to humans, which in the intellectual climate of Greek philosophical circles in Philo's time seemed contradictory (Hurtado, 2003: 575–6).

Heavily influenced by Platonic thought, Philo made the logos (λόγος) together with wisdom (σοφία) the central theme of his thought.[7] Frequently Philo simply replaced personified wisdom with the term logos when he spoke of 'her' or rather 'his' active role as God's 'tool' (ὄργανον) in the creation of the world (see Schimanowski, 1985: 85–94). A key passage from Philo illustrates this well:

> To speak of or conceive that world which consists of ideas as being in some place is illegitimate; how it consists (of them) we shall know if we carefully attend to some image supplied by the things of our world. When a city is being founded to satisfy the soaring ambition of some king or governor, who lays claim to despotic power and being magnificent in his ideas would fain add a fresh lustre to his good fortune, there comes forward now and again some trained architect (ἀνηρ ἀρχιτεκτονικὸς) who, observing the favorable climate and convenient position of the site, first sketches in his own mind well-nigh all the parts of the city that is to be wrought out, temples, gymnasia, town-halls, market-places, harbours, docks, streets, walls to be built, dwelling-houses as well as public buildings to be set up. Thus having received in his own soul, as it were in wax, the figures of these objects severally, he carries about the image of a city which is the creation of his mind. Then by his innate power of memory, he recalls the images of the various parts of this city, and imprints their types yet more distinctly in it: and like a good craftsman (οἷα δημιουργὸς ἀγαθὸς) he begins to build the city of stones and timber, keeping his eye upon his pattern and making the visible and tangible objects correspond in each case to the incorporeal ideas.

> Just such must be our thoughts about God. We must suppose that, when He was minded to found the one great city, He conceived beforehand the models of its part, and that out of these He constituted and brought to completion a world discernible only by the mind, and then, with that for a pattern, the world which our senses can perceive. As, then, the city which was fashioned beforehand within the mind of the architect held no place in the outer world, but had been engraved in the soul of the artificer as by a seal; even so the universe that consisted of ideas would have no other location than the Divine Reason (θεῖον λόγον), which was the Author of this ordered frame. (Philo, 17–20; 1929a: 15–17)

Numerous features in this passage take up previous thought or inaugurate future patterns of thinking. In the phrases 'how it consists (of them) we shall know if we carefully attend to some image supplied by the things of our world' and '[j]ust such must be our thoughts about God' Philo highlighted that he envisaged the creation of the world by means of human analogy.

The expressions 'some trained architect' and 'like a good craftsman' signal Philo's dependence on Plato's image of the demiurge and his development of the idea via the specific image of the demiurge as *architect*.

The designation of 'Divine Reason' (lit. 'divine logos') as the 'author' of the universe shows Philo's conflation of Platonic, Stoic and other Greek ideas. His eclectic absorption of various Greek concepts, most notably Stoic pantheism, also comes through in the following statement, a few lines later: 'Should a man desire to use words in a more simple and direct way, he would say that *the world discerned only by the intellect is nothing else but the Word of God* (θεοῦ λόγον) when he was already engaged in the act of creation' (Philo, 24; 1929a: 21). He expressly based these statements on Genesis 1:

> It is Moses who lays this down, not I ... when setting on record the creation of man, that he was moulded after the image of God (Gen. 1. 27). Now if the part is an image of an image, it is manifest that the whole is so too, and if the whole creation, this entire world perceived by our senses (seeing that it is greater than any human image) is a copy of the Divine Image, it is manifest that the archetypal seal also, which we aver to be the world descried by the mind, would be *the very Word of God* (θεοῦ λόγος). (Philo, 25; 1929a: 21; emphasis added)

The 'archetypal seal', which Philo identified with the pattern of the world that can only be seen by the mind, is the logos of God. Thus the logos (= personified wisdom) is the blueprint according to which Philo's God creates the physical world. Essentially, Philo offers a creative midrash, summarized well by Skarsaune: 'Like a master architect, God first made a mental plan of the world in his mind, i.e., in his Logos, and then proceeded to create the visible world after its pattern' (2007: 402).[8]

Similar to Hebrews 1:1–3 and Wisdom of Solomon 7:26 is Philo's statement concerning the creation of light mentioned in Genesis 1:3–4: 'Now that invisible light perceptible only by mind has come into being as an image of the Divine Word (θείου λόγου) Who brought it within our ken: it is a supercelestial constellation, fount of the constellations obvious to sense' (Philo, 31; 1929a: 25). For Philo the light which was created on the first day—before the rest of creation (cf. Prov. 8:22–30)—is personified wisdom.

In Philo's writings, personified wisdom also appears as mediator in creation, as the following discussion shows. Often this mediatorial role is expressed through the image of personified wisdom as 'mother' of the universe, as in the following extract:

> Now 'father and mother' is a phrase which can bear different meanings. For instance we should rightly say and without further question that the Architect who made this universe was at the same time the father of what was thus born, whilst its mother was the knowledge possessed by its Maker. With his knowledge God had union, not as men have it, and begat created being. And knowledge, having received the divine seed, when her travail was consummated, bore the only beloved son who is apprehended by the senses, the world which we see. Thus in the pages of one of the inspired company, wisdom is represented as speaking of herself after this manner: 'God obtained me first of all his works and founded me before the ages' (Prov. viii. 22). True, for it was necessary that all that came to the birth of creation should be younger than the mother and the nurse of the All. (Philo, 30–31; 1929b: 333–35)

Later in the same text Philo speaks of the matriarch Sarah as a *type* of personified wisdom: 'She [sc. Sarah as a type of personified wisdom] is not born of that material substance perceptible to our senses, ever in a state of formation and dissolution, the material which is called mother or foster-mother or nurse of created things by those in whom first the young plant of wisdom grew; *she is born of the Father and Cause of all things*' (Philo, 61; 1929b: 349).

The first part of the quote denies that Sarah = personified wisdom is to be equated with Plato's *hulae*, who is described as 'the mother of all that has come into being' (*Timaeus* 51 A). The second part (in italics) is an allusion to Proverbs 8:22.

The next quotation demonstrates the complex and bewildering ways in which Philo appropriated and creatively reused the personification of wisdom as a female authority figure in close relationship with God: 'Moses says that he cannot defile himself either for the father, the mind, nor for the mother, sense-perception (Lev. xxi. 11), because, methinks, he is the child of parents incorruptible, and wholly free from stain, his father being God, who is likewise Father of all, and his mother Wisdom, through whom the universe came into existence' (Philo, 109; 1929c: 68–69).

It is not really clear how the father = mind and the mother = sense-perception of the first part of this quotation relate to the F/father = Philo's God and the mother = wisdom of the second part. Nor is it clear how some aspects of this statement can be reconciled with Philo's other statements about wisdom. The complexity of the metaphorical conflagrations in Philo's statements about personified wisdom in his various works are evidence of the extraordinary capacity of the wisdom metaphor to evoke a multiplicity of associations that are mutually enriching and cumulatively influential for later thinking about the subject. In conclusion, Philo's ideas and related Jewish interpretations of wisdom's role in creation furnish further milestones on the interpretative road that lead to the earliest writings of the Christian church.

Summary and conclusions

Our survey has demonstrated that when the writers of the New Testament predicate Jesus the Christ with the designation 'logos', as most prominently in the Prologue to John's Gospel (John 1:1–18), then they have combined Israelite/Jewish, Greek and Christian concepts.

In one commentator's view, 'OT, Platonic and Stoic concepts come together in a *bewildering* unity' (Haenchen, 1984: 126). However, our survey has shown the rich facets of personified wisdom's role in the imagination of various Jewish writers. And it has demonstrated the categorical similarities between Jewish thinking about wisdom and Greek philosophical thinking about the logos. When these aspects are taken into consideration together, then this fusion of concepts in the poetic and theological imagination that fuelled the faith of the New Testament writers is perhaps not quite as 'bewildering' as some have assumed.

The rich diversity of Jewish thinking about personified wisdom's role in creation, her combination with Greek thinking about creation and her propensity for adaptation and application to Jesus in Christian thinking lie in the metaphorical nature of wisdom's personification as a *literary* figure and in the ingeniously evocative use of the *female* persona. Personified wisdom became a central figure for understanding God's ways with his world. In her various guises, wisdom came to be understood as his collaborator in the creation, redemption and sustenance of the world, combining Israelite/Jewish, Greek and Christian thinking into an extraordinarily evocative and rich concept of God's engagement with the world. We cannot but be impressed with the creativity and theological productivity of the authors and interpreters of the past.

Notes

1 Note the frequency of statements that carry overtones related to gender-sensitive issues. The translation (like others in this chapter) is taken from NRSV, but I have replaced NRSV's 'person' in v. 20 with the literal 'man', as NRSV's inclusive rendering obscures the very issue at stake.
2 I have translated Von Rad's generic term 'Menschen' with the term 'man' rather than 'humanity' because 'Mensch' is a male noun in German. Similar statements by Von Rad include: 'an almost mystical deliverance of man into the glory of being itself (*Herrlichkeit des Seins*)'; 'sublime love covenant between man and the divine mystery of creation'; 'here man throws himself lustfully at a meaning which penetrates him; he discovers a mystery that has already been on the way to him in order to give itself to him' (*Herrlichkeit des Seins*: 220).
3 The Greek text side-by-side with a (slightly dated) English translation can be found in Bury (1929: 1–253). It is, of course, Plato's cosmology that is presented, who puts his words into the mouths of Socrates, Timaeus and the others.
4 Cynicism was a 'materialist' school of philosophy. The logos played an important role in their ethical system.
5 The soul was thought to permeate the body through the arteries. Around 330 BC Praxagoras had discovered that, in contrast to the veins, the arteries in corpses were empty. This led to the conclusion that the arteries were the vessels through which the soul breathed and through which it reached the different parts of the body (Hicks, 1911: 944–5).
6 The beginning of a hymn to Zeus by the stoic philosopher Cleanthes demonstrates the central role that the all-ruling divine reason played in stoic thought, and shows some similarities with the personification of wisdom. Cf. Störig (1985: 194–5).
7 'Philon, P. von Alexandria, Philo Judaeus'. *Brockhaus Enzyklopädie*, vol. 17 (Mannheim: Brockhaus Verlag, 19th edn, 1992, p. 103. On Platonic thought about creation, see Cornford (1948: esp. 34–9).
8 Ref. to Philo, 17–20 (1929) and the comments on this passage in Urbach (1975: vol 1, 199–200).

Bibliography

Bury, R. G. *Plato: With an English Translation*, vol. 7, Loeb Classical Library; London; New York: Heinemann, Putnam's, 1929).

Cornford, Francis M. *Plato's Cosmology: The Timaeus of Plato Translated with a Running Commentary*. International Library of Psychology Philosophy and Scientific Method (London: Routledge & Kegan Paul, 1948).

Ford, David. *Christian Wisdom: Desiring God and Learning in Love*. Cambridge Studies in Christian Doctrine 16 (Cambridge: Cambridge University Press, 2007).

Haenchen, Ernst. *John 1: A Commentary on the Gospel of John Chapters 1–6* (Philadelphia: Fortress Press, 1984).

Hicks, Robert Drew. 'Stoics', *Encyclopedia Britannica*, vol. 25 (Cambridge: Cambridge University Press, 11th edn, 1911), pp. 942-51.

Hurtado, Larry W. *Lord Jesus Christ: Devotion to Jesus in Earliest Christianity* (Grand

Rapids: Eerdmans, 2003).
Lakoff, G. and Mark Turner. *More than Cool Reason: A Field Guide to Poetic Metaphor* (Chicago: University of Chicago Press, 1989).
Lakoff, George and Mark Johnson. *Metaphors We Live By* (Chicago: University of Chicago Press, 1981).
Lucas, Ernest. *The Psalms and Wisdom Literature.* Exploring the Old Testament 3 (London: SPCK, 2003).
Klaiber, Walter and Marquardt, Manfred. *Gelebte Gnade: Grundriss einer Theologie der Evangelisch-methodistischen Kirche* (Stuttgart: Christliches Verlagshaus, 1993).
Mitchell, John Malcolm. 'Heraclitus', *Encyclopedia Britannica*, vol. 13 (Cambridge: Cambridge University Press, 11th edn, 1910), pp. 309–10.
Philo. *On the Creation of the World.* Loeb Classical Library 1 (trans. F. H. Colson and G. H. Whitaker, 1929a).
———. *On Drunkenness.* Loeb Classical Library 3 (trans. F. H. Colson and G. H. Whitaker, 1929b).
———. *On Flight and Finding.* Loeb Classical Library 5 (trans. F. H. Colson and G. H. Whitaker, 1934).
Salmond, Stewart Dingwall Fordyce and Alexander James Grieve. 'Logos'. *Encyclopedia Britannica*, vol. 16 (Cambridge: Cambridge University Press, 11th edn, 1911), pp. 919–21.
Schimanowski, Gottfried. *Weisheit und Messias: Die jüdischen Voraussetzungen der urchristlichen Präexistenzchristologie.* Wissenschaftliche Untersuchungen zum Neuen Testament 2.17 (Tübingen: Mohr, 1985), pp. 85–94.
Skarsaune, Oskar. 'Jewish Christian Sources Used by Justin Martyr and Some Other Greek and Latin Fathers'. Pages 379–416 in *Jewish Believers in Jesus: The Early Centuries* (ed. Oskar Skarsaune and Reidar Hvalvik; Peabody: Hendrickson: 2007).
Störig, Hans Joachim. *Kleine Weltgeschichte der Philosophie* (Stuttgart: Kohlhammer, 13th edn, 1985).
Urbach, Ephraim E. *The Sages: Their Concepts and Beliefs* (trans. Israel Abrahams; 2 vols.; Jerusalem: Magnes, 1975).
Von Rad, Gerhard. *Weisheit in Israel* (Neukirchen-Vluyn: Neulirchener Verlag, 1970).

God beyond our imagining
> we are grateful for the yearning for wisdom
> that you have planted deep within us;
> we are grateful for the stretched sinews
> seeking knowledge and understanding
> of all those who have gone before us
> and have entrusted to us their soul's journey.

    And as wisdom dances her dance of invitation
> or speaks truth from law
> or helps us to engage in creativity
> beyond our wildest dreams,
> she sings of you,
> you, Creator, Maker, Sustainer,
> and finds her home in Jesus Christ,

PART TWO

Science and Christian Faith

5

Ancient and Modern Wisdom: The Intersection of Clinical and Theological Understanding of Health

Paul S. Fiddes

In the last two decades there has been an increasing volume of voices in healthcare circles about the need for 'wisdom' in medicine. Usually, what is meant by 'wisdom' here is the clinical judgment of the practitioner, shaped by his or her experience over the years, and this is often contrasted with 'evidence-based medicine' or EBM.

EBM approaches rely on guidelines supplied by databases of evidence culled from tests and from observed outcomes over a wide range of the population (EBM Working Group, 1992:2420–25; Sackett et al., 1996: 71–2; 1997: 2–5), and the guidelines for good practice may well be formulated and disseminated by a government agency, notably in the UK by NICE (National Institute for Health and Clinical Excellence). So there has been a vigorous debate in which 'wisdom' has been asserted over against mere 'evidence' (see e.g., Edmondson and Pearce, 2007: 233–44; Smith, 1991: 798–9; Szawarski, 2004: 185–93) Pellegrino, 2002: 378–84; Litchfield, 1999: 62–73; Howie, 1984: 1770–72). All discussion in the medical literature acknowledges that an element of EBM is essential for successful and responsible practice. But there has been an anxiety that a purely scientific approach has begun to *dominate* medical decision-making at the expense of more human and social factors, and so to threaten the 'art' or wisdom of medicine. There has been a demand either to 'balance' or 'limit' EBM by the wisdom of the doctor, and the exact relation of the two continues to be a matter of contention.

I want to bring this present-day appeal to wisdom into interaction with a more ancient tradition—that of wisdom in the literature of ancient Israel—to see what illumination might come. In the medical literature the notion of 'wisdom' is often related to Aristotle's concept of *phronesis*, or practical wisdom, a judgment to be exercised where the complexity of a situation means that it cannot be resolved simply by the application of either moral or scientific principles.[1] Virtually no reference is made in the current debate to the ancient Hebrew concept of wisdom or *hokmah*, and this is what I propose to do in this paper. *Hokmah*, rather than *phronesis*, also brings theology into play, and enables us to do what is understandably absent from the medical literature on the subject: that is, to dare to talk about the relevance of the presence and activity of God in the world, a world in which medicine is seeking to promote the everyday phenomenon of health. For Aristotle, health was a 'flourishing' of human life; in modern existentialism or phenomenology the term often used is an 'authentic' life. Where then does God fit into a world in which medicine aims to bring about such flourishing and authenticity?

I hope that the project in this essay may honor the outstanding work in the academy and the church of my friend and colleague Ernest Lucas, since he has himself written on issues of both biblical wisdom and the nature of healing. On the former area he has written a well-received and highly accessible introduction (Lucas, 2003), and his interest in the latter area stems from his long-standing concern for the relation between theology and science, having research doctoral degrees in both fields. He was clearly the most appropriate person to edit, and contribute to, a collection of essays on Christian healing which issued from a research consultation on this theme sponsored by the Margaret Houghton Trust, extending from 1991 to 1994 (Lucas, 1997), and he returned to the theme of the 'healing' of creation in an article on the New Testament teaching on the environment in 1999. However, I do not think that he has himself explicitly combined his interests in wisdom and in healing, at least in print. I am delighted to celebrate his high achievements as a Christian theologian by attempting this task myself, and I look forward to a typically acute response in due time.

But first, to illustrate what the exercise of wisdom in medicine might look like in a concrete situation, I want to offer a case-study given by Trisha Greenhalgh in an article in the *British Medical Journal* entitled 'Narrative Based Medicine in an Evidence Based World', in which she aims to explore 'the dissonance between the "science" of objective measurement [EBM] and the "art" of clinical proficiency and judgment'. She cites an actual report from a GP in Cardiff, whom she names Dr Jenkins, who records that 'I got a call from a mother who said her little girl had had diarrhoea and was behaving strangely. I knew the family well, and was sufficiently concerned to break off my Monday morning surgery and visit immediately' (Greenhalgh, 1999: 324). Greenhalgh now constructs a 'hypothetical case' based on this comment which apparently indicates the following of a 'hunch' by the physician: 'Dr Jenkins contemplates the brief history hastily obtained by the receptionist over the telephone and, using his intimate knowledge of the family, begins to put together the story of this illness.' In Greenhalgh's version, Dr Jenkins suspects meningoccocal meningitis, on the basis of two symptoms which are not specific to meningitis (diarrhoea, strange behavior) and, by what seems on the face of it to be a lucky intuition, his diagnosis turns out to be correct. The doctor has only seen one case of meningoccocal meningitis in his 96,000 consultations, but he still gets it right.

However, if we reflect a little on this example with the help of Greenhalgh, we may see that 'luck' is hardly the apt word; we can demystify a little the wisdom which the doctor shows. On the one hand, the doctor's diagnosis seems to run *counter* to the available evidence-based guidelines. Specific symptoms for meningoccocal meningitis are neck stiffness and a rash, neither of which are reported. Diarrhoea in previously well children, which *is* mentioned, is generally viral and self-limiting. There is also the practice guideline to be considered, that doctors cannot commit themselves completely and immediately to all patients who seek their help. Dr Jenkins has a surgery full of people needing attention. On the other hand, the evidence base also produces the guideline that early meningoccocal meningitis often presents itself with non-specific symptoms in a primary care situation, and there is the practice guideline that if meningoccocal meningitis *is* suspected the doctor must make the patient a priority, and penicillin must be administered urgently. EBM therefore plays a part in this diagnosis, but it is clearly not sufficient. To this the doctor adds first his personal knowledge of the family: here (with Greenhalgh) we speculate a little, but from his alarm we may suppose that they have an uncomplaining track record, that the mother has good sense and that the child's behavior when well has been nothing out of the ordinary. Second, the doctor reflects on his own experience of many thousand stories of illness, where the phrase 'behaving strangely' has been very rarely used to describe symptoms of non-specific illness, and therefore the odd expression rings warning bells. All this merges to produce a strong suspicion, which is later confirmed.

The example is not *typical* of instances where the clinical judgment of the doctor is critical, since an initial diagnosis is made here on the basis of a second-hand report. As we shall see, the place for wisdom to be exercised is usually the clinical encounter, a dialogue betweeen doctor and patient in which two life-worlds and stories are opened to each other and interpretation happens. But the example does still illustrate a threefold model of wisdom-reasoning urged by the researchers Ricca Edmondson and Jane Pearce in an article on 'Wisdom as a Model' in healthcare. They argue that an interpretation emerges from interaction between three elements: attention to the problem itself, awareness of the capacities and experience of the self in dealing with the presenting problem, and empathy with the feelings, capacities and situation of the other: so—problem, self, other (Edmondson and Pearce, 2007: 238–39). They summarize these three aspects with the classical terms 'logos', 'ethos' and 'pathos' (drawn from Aristotle's *Rhetoric*, 1356a.2–3). The first (the problem) must include reference to an evidence base and the guidelines drawn from it. But conflict between different maxims abstracted from the evidence makes necessary the further elements of self-awareness and sensitivity to the other. The three aspects can in fact, I suggest, be reduced to two overall. The first is the wisdom of careful observation, and the second two—I propose—are both a wisdom of attunement to what the philosopher Hans-Georg Gadamer, when reflecting on the nature of health, calls 'the rhythm of life' (1993: 145). This is an expression to which I wish to return.

Now, however, I want to turn to the wisdom of ancient Israel, which envisaged precisely these two aspects of wisdom within its concept of *hokmah*. The first is about observing the world around, the second about living in tune with the world. We might call these Wisdom A and B.

Wisdom A: confidence and caution in observation

This is not the place to debate the origins of the wisdom enterprise in ancient Israel. Suffice it to say that this movement gave to us the books of Proverbs, Job and Ecclesiastes in the Hebrew Bible; later products of this school of thought can be seen in the the Wisdom of Jesus Ben Sira (translated from Hebrew into Greek) and the (so-called) Wisdom of Solomon in the Greek Septuagint.

Reading this literature, we catch a glimpse of a class of people called 'the wise', a diverse group of literate people who probably included scribes, teachers, public administrators and royal advisors (see Scott, 1970: 20–45; Crenshaw, 1998: 20–24; Fontaine, 1993: 100–108). As they show themselves to us in their writings, the wise are fairly confident that they can cope with experience through careful observation of how things are. From their own experiments in living, and from the reports of others back through the generations, they can deduce the reasonable thing to do in any particular circumstances. Their technique is to collect and pass on deductions from experience, on the assumption that the natural and human world is amenable to being understood by patient investigation, built up over many years.[2] From this observation of the world, the wise find patterns of meaning and detect regularities that can offer guidance to those who are willing to listen to their teaching. Their observations are fixed in proverbs, riddles, and lists of natural phenomena, by which they begin to bring some order to a vast and complex area of investigation. So, for example, they note *analogies* between events in the natural and human world, pointing out that 'this is like that'. Here is an example:

Three things are stately in their tread;

four are stately in their stride:
the lion, which is mightiest among beasts
and does not turn back before any;
the strutting cock, the he-goat,
and a king striding before his people. (Prov. 30:29–31[3])

The lion, the cock and the goat are all like a king leading his people: we cannot miss the tone of social satire in this saying. Most frequently the wise observe the link between cause and effect, warning that 'if you do this, then that will happen'. For instance:

Pride goes before destruction
and a haughty spirit before a fall. (Prov. 16:18)

It is these cause–effect patterns from experience that have the largest place in the sentence literature of the book of Proverbs, which now occupies most of chapters 10–29 of the collection, and which is a kind of text book of wisdom in different editions, gathered together over hundreds of years.

Sayings can combine both the elements of analogy and consequence, as does this one:

The beginning of strife is like letting out of water [analogy];
so quit before the quarrel breaks out [consequence]. (Prov. 17:14)

The consequences of allowing a quarrel to get under way are, it is implied, as disastrous as the small trickle of water from a dam which, if not mended, will become a flood.

Thus, when the wise have to cope with a situation, to 'steer' their way through the maze of events, they appeal to the guidelines gleaned from experience; these represent order won from the chaos of life. As the opening to the book of Proverbs urges us:

For gaining instruction in wise dealing,
righteousness, justice, and equity . . .
let the wise also hear and gain in learning,
and the discerning acquire skill,
to understand a proverb and a figure,
the words of the wise and their riddles. (Prov .1:3–6)

But there is a dual mood in this wisdom literature. Alongside confidence there is a strong note of caution. For all the hard discipline, the teacher of wisdom was prepared to recognize an element of the unpredictable in all calculations; there are unknown factors which the wise person must reckon with (see Von Rad, 1972: 97–112; Crenshaw, 1998: 189–90). The multiplicity and variety of the world order with which the wise are dealing can never be completely mastered, and always have the capacity to surprise. Here is a witness to this from another wise man writing in the book of Proverbs.

Three things are too wonderful for me;
four I do not understand:
the way of an eagle in the sky,
the way of a snake on a rock,
the way of a ship on the high seas,
and the way of a man with a girl. (Prov. 30:18–19)

This beautiful little piece is an attempt to catalogue similar phenomena, namely the movement of something through some element: the eagle through the air, the snake over rock, the ship through water, and the human being in and through the body. Despite his confidence in cataloguing, the wise person here admits a limit in understanding: 'Three things are too wonderful for me; four I do not understand.'

So the wise are aware of the uncertainties that arise out of the very material they are dealing with. There is a hiddenness about wisdom, but not because it is concealed somewhere—say in heaven. It is hidden because of the complexity of the world, its vast scope, on which the wise can never get a complete grip. Now it is in this situation that talk about God gets started. There are unknown factors with which the wise must reckon, and it is in this context that it becomes appropriate to talk about God. In a significant group of sayings there is a recognition of something which cannot be calculated in experience, and in this connection the name of Yahweh, God the Lord, is invoked—referring to Yahweh's presence or purpose or activity (Prov. 16:1,2,3,9,20,33; 19:14,21; 20:12,24; 21:30,31). This cluster of sayings connects Yahweh explicitly with the *limits* of human wisdom. Here is an example from Proverbs 16:

> The plans of the mind belong to mortals,
> but the answer of the tongue is from [Yahweh].
> All one's ways may be pure in one's own eyes,
> but [Yahweh] weighs the spirit. (Prov. 16:1–2)

So people can plan to say something in their mind, but there is something they cannot control about the way that their words actually come out, and God has a part to play there. There is a sense of limitation upon human wisdom, and a cautiousness in using the guidelines of experience. There is something uncertain too about the achievement of happiness (16:20), or victory in battle (21:31) or the choice of a right wife (19:14). In the last case we read:

> House and wealth are inherited from parents:
> but a prudent wife is from the Lord.

These proverbs urge that in all these areas there needs to be a humility before *God*. This humble approach to life can take the form of admonitions about 'the fear of the Lord', a phrase that appears some nine times in the sentence literature of Proverbs.[4] The primary meaning of this phrase 'the fear of the Lord' is a humility in the midst of calculations. Some scholars have suggested that this is a development in Israelite wisdom, not typical of the early period in which wisdom was (supposedly) an essentially secular venture (e.g., McKane, 1970: 279–81);[5] it is wisdom getting religious as time goes on. However, we note that there is a *continuity* between sayings in the wisdom collections of Proverbs which do not mention God, and those which do. The constant feature here is a sense of limitation upon human wisdom which is a cautiousness in using the guidelines of experience. For example, with the text, 'The human mind plans the way, but the LORD directs the steps' (Prov. 16:9), we may compare a similar saying that does not invoke God: 'There is a way that seems to be right, but in the end it is the way to death' (Prov. 16:25). There is a kind of humble 'fearing' that can be both secular and religious, with a shifting borderline between. One saying (Prov. 14:16), for instance, simply commends 'fearing', in a kind of secular version of the 'fear of the Lord':

> The wise are cautious [fearers] and turn away from evil,
> but the fool throws off restraint and is careless.

The point in the sayings that *do* combine a sense of limit with a reference to Yahweh is not that God suddenly intervenes to trip the wise man up, or that God *only* acts where there are 'gaps' in human knowledge. Rather, the sayings affirm that God has the perfect wisdom to operate successfully in *all* areas, *including* those where human wisdom falters through lack of grasp on the situation. Where the human capacity to see is limited, God has total vision of everything that is there to be seen. God is always on the scene, always involved in the world, and the moments when a sense of the limits of wisdom is sharpest are only reminders of what is always the case, points of focus. We find that the limitation of the wisdom method arises out of the very material which wisdom concerns itself with; so we picture this limit not as a boundary *beyond* which God is, but as a continual extension of the known into the unknown. It is a question of complexity and multiplicity, of limitation consisting in the 'limitless'scope of things that cannot be grasped. What defeats wisdom is not a boundary, but boundlessness. In this boundless expanse, God is at home as we are not.

Here is a little piece from Proverbs 30:3-4 which expresses this thought:

> I have not learned wisdom,
> Nor have I the knowledge of the Holy One.
> Who has ascended to heaven and come down? . . .
> Who has wrapped up the waters in a garment?
> Who has established all the ends of the earth?

Here the extent of wisdom is described in terms of the height, breadth and depth of the world—heaven, earth and sea. The writer complains that he is exhausted with trying to grasp it, and here he speaks for all students:

> Thus says the man: I am weary, O God,
> I am weary, O God. How can I prevail? (Prov. 30:1)

Wisdom B: Lady Wisdom—the way of attunement

Alongside the wisdom of observation, combining both confidence and humility, we find a second portrayal of wisdom in this early literature. What we might call Wisdom B is the appearance of a personified figure of wisdom, usually depicted as an attractive and enticing woman, who walks along the paths of the world. Lady Wisdom is out on the road of life, issuing an invitation to those who are foolish to come and live and learn with her. She cries out her invitation in the streets and in the marketplace, like a wisdom teacher setting out a prospectus, inviting pupils into her school; 'you who are ignorant' she cries, 'turn in here' (see Prov. 9:4, cf. Prov. 8:1–5; see Whybray, 1965: 76–104; Perdue, 1994: 77–100; Joyce, 2003: 89–101). This wisdom danced on the earth at the beginning of creation when God made the mountains and the seas; she played on the earth and delighted in the company of newly created human beings (Prov. 8:30–1). This wisdom walks through the world here and now, following the path of the sun from its rising to its setting on the far horizon (Ben Sira 24–26); she seeks for somewhere to dwell, longing for those who will make their home with her. She looks for those who will walk with her, for 'her ways are ways of pleasantness, and all her paths are peace' (Prov. 3:17).

While Wisdom A is a hard and disciplined skill, resulting in a great deal of uncertainty as well as knowledge, Wisdom B is available, offering herself to human beings, out on the road of life: 'For she ranges in search of those who are worthy of her; on their daily path she appears to them with kindly intent, and in all their purposes meets them half-way . . . a concern for learning means love towards her' (Wisdom of Solomon 6:16–17, NEB).

The point of the image is to hold out a promise of having a *relationship* with wisdom, to be in tune with the wisdom that shapes the world, to walk with her and dwell with her. Alongside the wisdom of observation, there is a wisdom of participation. Using a later image, there is a spirit of wisdom with which the wise can be filled (Wisdom of Solomon 7:23—8:1). God comes into this aspect of wisdom, because Lady Wisdom is presented as keeping company with God, knowing God intimately; indeed, she can be seen as an extension of God's own personality—significantly female. This has led some scholars of this literature to propose that there are two totally different kinds of wisdom in view, a human wisdom and a divine wisdom. There is, they suppose, a practical wisdom, collecting guidelines from experience (my Wisdom A), and there is theological wisdom that only God bestows (my Wisdom B) (see Ringgren, 1947: 93–94; (Von Rad, 1972: 144–57). Lady Wisdom would then be a kind of mediator of transcendent reality, a bridge between divine and human life.[6]

But this, I believe, is a total misreading of the pictures of wisdom. Lady Wisdom is a thoroughly practical woman; she is depicted as a wisdom teacher, looking for pupils to instruct in the art of seeing the world properly. Above all, God is represented in the wisdom texts as exercising a highly *practical* kind of wisdom in creating and sustaining the world. In the poem of Job 28, a riddling question is posed:

Where shall wisdom be found?
And where is the place of understanding? (v. 12)

Wisdom is said to be at least partly hidden to human beings, but not because it is a divine quality which God can conceal in heaven. I suggest that wisdom is hidden, as in the book of Proverbs, because of the extent and complexity of the world under observation.[7] God knows wisdom because God knows the *world* perfectly; wisdom is presented as an *object* which God surveys, counts, establishes and searches out:

God understands the way to it,
and he knows its place . . .
When he gave to the wind its weight,
and apportioned out the waters by measure:
when he made a decree for the rain,
and a way for the thunderbolt;
then he surveyed it and counted it;
He established it and searched it out. (Job 28:23-27)

Like the practical wisdom of the wise, God's wisdom as Creator is a matter of observing and handling the world. Wisdom is depicted as an object of God's activity because his surveying of wisdom is synonymous with his operation upon the world in creation. It was when God gave 'weight', 'measure', 'decree' and 'way' to the elements (vv. 25-26) that he did corresponding things to wisdom: he 'surveyed' it, 'counted' it, 'established' it and 'searched it out' (v. 27). The two sets of activities are not even cause and effect; they are identical. When God gave proportion to the world, that *was* his searching out of wisdom. To know wisdom is to handle the world successfully. Wisdom is thus presented as an object that God knows well because it is *the world itself* as an object of study and activity. The riddle of Job 28 asks: 'where is the place of wisdom'? The answer is: 'wisdom is not found in any particular place, but lies in knowing every place'. Human wisdom is then bound to be limited, but it is not of a different kind from divine wisdom. God is supremely wise, the supreme interpreter of the world.

Wisdom A and B are thus not two wisdoms but one, displaying two different *aspects* of wisdom. On the one hand, wisdom comes from observation, from the careful collecting of evidence; it is a technical skill requiring discipline and humility, or the 'fear of the Lord'. On the other hand, wisdom has a personal, relational quality, symbolized by the figure of Lady Wisdom; wisdom is learning to be attuned to creation and to its Creator, vibrating with its rhythms of life, living in sympathy with others. In this theological dimension, the wise live in a world where they are always receiving the offer to participate in God's own wisdom, seeing the world as God sees it. Technical and relational wisdom thus belong together, each assisting the other. Now, there is an intriguing parallel here with the modern dispute about the relation between appeal to evidence and clinical judgment in medicine. Wisdom A is gleaned from observation, and might be called 'evidence-based' in so far as it is communicated and passed down in the public arena of teaching as the results of experience which are collected, documented and made available to all who want to learn. Wisdom B also depends on experience and observation, but issues in a wisdom that forms the character of the investigator and enables him or her to respond in sensitive ways to a situation. How *illuminating* the parallel between ancient wisdom and modern medical wisdom might be, and whether the theological framework still has meaning in the medical arena, are matters I now want to go on to consider.

Only one kind of wisdom

We begin with the insight from ancient wisdom that there is only one wisdom, whether technical or personal. This might well lead us to agree with Malcolm Parker, in his article entitled 'Whither Our Art? Clinical Wisdom and Evidence-Based Medicine'. Parker argues that it is quite misleading to set EBM over *against* wisdom, and so to speak of 'balancing' or 'limiting' EBM by the wisdom of the practitioner. EBM, he suggests, is not in a separate category from the wisdom of medical judgment—both involve observation, learning from experience, and the forming of patterns of interpretation. The difference lies between the experience of the individual doctor, and experience drawn from a much wider area of public life (Parker, 2002: 274–76). We should recognize then, he says, that EBM is *part* of the very practice of wisdom itself, and the public and individual areas of experiential wisdom are both essential.

Jane Macnaughton, in a significant article on the nature of evidence (1998: 89–92), also argues for an integration of EBM with clinical judgment, pointing out the very collection of information and its transformation into 'evidence' in the first place requires a process of judgment. Evidence is not a matter of cold facts, merely hard-nosed data. Human judgment is needed in seeing the significance of certain observations and turning them into a hypothesis to be tested, and evidence is the result (Macnaughton, 1998: 90–91).[8] We notice that all this is quite reminiscent of the relation we have seen between Wisdom A and Wisdom B in ancient Israelite literature.

Advocates of EBM such as Malcolm Parker therefore insist that there is no question of the individual being bypassed. There has to be a sensitive application of evidence to particular cases. Skill and judgment are needed in matching a particular patient to a population database. Once the databases have told us what the probability factors in certain procedures might be, he urges that the practitioner must then take full account of the factors in individual cases, such as the characteristics of particular patients, their preferences, personal values, social circumstances and beliefs. EBM cannot simply dictate either a diagnosis or a treatment, while it remains an essential element in both. We have seen that the practice of wisdom in ancient Israel recognized a hiddenness and ambiguity in all observation of the world. Talk of 'wisdom' in medicine arises because there is a level of complexity here which cannot be dealt with simply by scientific deduction.

The large question, of course, is *how* the matching of the individual to the available base of evidence takes place. It is here that sensitive practitioners can feel an element of dissonance. On the one hand, the element that we have called Wisdom A demands that the factors of probability and risk are presented to the patient. Deriving from the testing of whole population groups, there are probable outcomes and quantifiable risks: there is, for instance, about a one in a thousand risk of a complication following the stenting of a coronary artery, such as a stroke, a puncture or tearing of the artery (perhaps I might add that I personally turned out to be that one in a thousand in my own experience of angioplasty). On the other hand, beyond statistical probabilities there is the element that we have called Wisdom B, involving factors of empathy and attunement, both to the doctor's own attitudes and capacities and to the patient's fears, hopes and expectations.

The three-way relation between the problem, the self and the other to which I have already referred might be seen as an interaction of three *stories* which overlap: there is the corporate, social story which is told by the database of evidence; there is the story which the patient tells, and there is the story of the doctor's own experience. Diagnosis and treatment can only emerge by a careful listening to all three kinds of story. The interpretation which emerges is not then just a matter of truth, but of what is 'good' for the particular patient here and now.

In her article about the nature of evidence, Jane Macnaughton gives what seems at first sight to be a trivial example about choice of treatment, but which highlights the need to find what is 'good', and what belongs to the 'good life'. Evidence-based medicine proposes that in mild to moderate acne the applying of an antibiotic cream is just as effective as a whole course of oral antibiotic pills. There are also good reasons for being cautious about prescribing antibiotics, since frequent use builds up immunity. But Macnaughton asks us to 'consider the case of Susie, a 17-year-old who has recently started on the combined oral contraceptive pill and attends her doctor with acne, compared with that of Liz, a 21-year-old presenting with the same problem, who is about to get married and is on a 3-monthly depot progesterone injection for contraception'. Both have mild to moderate acne, and so EBM would indicate that for both of them the cream is really what is needed. But in the case of Liz there are social and personal factors to be taken into account; she may wish to keep her face clear of medications on her forthcoming honeymoon (some sympathetic imagination is needed by the doctor here), and so the doctor prescribes the pills. Susie, on the other hand, needs to avoid oral antibiotics which might interfere with her contraceptive pill, and she doesn't have a honeymoon coming up. The cream definitely seems to be indicated. However, Macnaughton suggests that 'if Susie declares that a friend of hers got antibiotic tablets and his acne disappeared "like magic", the wise doctor would comply with the patient's desire and so make use of the additional benefits that the patient's belief in the treatment might convey' (Macnaughton, 1998: 91).

Even in this non-critical example, we can see that a consultation is an event of dialogue, in which the life-worlds of the doctor, the patient and the wider population are opened to each other. From this dialogue a shared interpretation of the issue should emerge, in which the doctor must always be open to the horizon of the patient. Evidence should not be set against wisdom, but take its place within it. But can the theological perspective of wisdom contribute anything to an understanding of what is going on in this dialogue? To answer this, we need to think more about the relation of subject to object in the way that we experience the world and other people.

Overcoming the gap between subject and object

Those who are suspicious of EBM accuse it of being a last fling of modernism, an arrogant confidence that the world can be treated as a mere object of investigation, something to be controlled and mastered. They accuse EBM of losing the subject in attention to mere objectivity, and suggest that the cultivation of wisdom can restore the subject, with all its experience and motivations, to its rightful place. In the 'postmodernist paradigm', urge J.J. and J.E. Chan, 'the validity of intuition and experience is considered equal to that of traditional methods of observation, induction and experimentation' (2000: 332). Actually, the problem we face in our time is more complex than the loss of a subject. Modernism has not in fact neglected the subject, but rather opened up a *gap* between subject and object, driving a wedge between the human person and the world of nature. The general danger is that of the *domination* of the object by the subject, and in medicine the specific danger would be an imposing of solutions on the patient. This could certainly be the result of an inflexible appeal to EBM, but—as Parker rightly points out—it could also be the result of ignoring the wider experience that EBM provides (2002: 278–79). Practitioners who rely simply on their own experience can become equally dominating, indeed Godlike in their paternalism, confident that they know best.

Wisdom in ancient Israel is both subject and object at the same time, crossing the boundaries between the human consciousness and the world. In its 'A' type of wisdom, the word *hokmah* (wisdom) stands on the one hand for a *faculty of mind*, a skill of approach gained through experience, an ability to 'steer' through life. It is a capacity of the subject. On the other hand it stands for the *area of knowledge* itself, a 'body' of instruction. It is subject *and* object. Wisdom can be something not yet known to a person, knowledge which waits exploration within the world order itself, an *area of knowledge corresponding to the world*, the world as an object of study. Here the concept of *hokmah* has an advantage over the Aristotelian term *phronesis*, which is simply subjective, an intellectual virtue. Appealing to *hokmah*, the mind of the wise can never stand above and beyond the objective world whose signs they are interpreting. Wisdom requires empathy with the other, whether other persons or the natural realm, and this is the point of the figure of wisdom who offers a relationship with herself ('Wisdom B'). Lady Wisdom is a symbol of participation, and she stands as a sign that in any situation where one subject is assymetrical in relation to another, or has an advantage over the other, such as a doctor to a patient, empathy is needed to enter the world of another.

In this context talk about God becomes appropriate. God who 'sees all' is supremely wise (Prov. 5:21; 15:11), and to use this descriptor means that—like human wise people—God is always committed to the signs of the material world; indeed, God is deeply immersed in them and in the time and history in which they exist. Now, let us take what may seem to be a large doctrinal leap, and say that this perception about God has been best expressed in Christian thought within the concept of Trinity. To be sure, the figure of Lady Wisdom in the Hebrew Bible does not yet imply a doctrine of the Trinity, although she points to a certain complexity within God, together with ideas of the Word and the Spirit of God. However, the witness she makes to a participatory form of life and being comes to fullness in the later church doctrine of the Trinity.

The doctrine of the Trinity has sometimes been presented as a kind of numerical puzzle in which God is supposedly one individual being and three individuals at the same time. This is less a complexity than a contradiction. The language of the early theologians was not about self-contained individuals, but about personal realities (*hypostases*) whose very being is in relationship.[9] Trinity is a vision of God as relational being, and this communion is open to embrace created beings within it. Talk of God as Trinity is about three interweaving relationships of giving and receiving in love. Taking a clue from Karl Barth's insistence that 'with regard to the being of God, the word "event" or "act" is final' (1936–77, II/1: 263), we may speak of God as an 'event of relationships'. Of course, it is not possible to visualize, paint, or etch in stone or glass three interweaving relationships, or three movements of being characterized by their relations. But then this ought to be a positive advantage in thinking about God, who cannot be objectified like other objects in the world.

Talk about God as 'an event of relationships' is not therefore the language of a spectator, but the language of a *participant* (see, extensively, Fiddes, 2000: 28–55). It only makes sense in terms of our involvement in the complex network of relationships in which God happens. Let me spell out a typical experience of this participation, in the practice of prayer. The New Testament portrays prayer as being 'to' the Father, 'through' the Son and 'in' the Spirit (see, e.g., Matt.6:6; John 14:16; Heb. 7:25; Eph. 6:18). This means that when we pray to God as Father, we find our address fitting into a movement like that of speech between a son and father, our response of 'yes' ('Amen') leaning upon a child-like 'yes' of humble obedience that is already there, glorifying a father (2 Cor. 1:20; cf. Rom. 8:34; Heb. 7:25). At the same time, we find ourselves involved in a movement of self-giving like that of a father sending forth a son, a movement which the early theologians called 'eternal generation' and which we experience in the mission of God in history. These movements of *response* and *mission* are interwoven by a third, as we find that they are continually being opened up to new depths of relationship and to new possibilities of the future by a movement that we can only call 'Spirit'; for this third movement the Scriptures give us a whole series of impressionistic images—a wind blowing, breath stirring, oil trickling, wings beating, water flowing and fire burning—evoking an activity which disturbs, opens, deepens and provokes. The traditional formulation that the Spirit 'proceeds from the Father through the Son' points to movement which renews all relations 'from' and 'to' the Other.

Thus, through our participation, we can identify three distinct movements of ecstatic, outward-going love. While I have used the traditional male terms 'father and son', the movements I have described cannot be gender-specific, and we can also express the experience of participation as being like a relationship from a mother to a daughter, or any combination of these metaphors.

Such participation is a form of knowing which bridges the gap between subject and object. If God is related to the world, then the world must be participating in God, immersed into the movement, the interweaving dance of these relations. From a Trinitarian perspective we may say that God limits God's self in 'making room' for creation to indwell the divine life, and in redemption God draws created beings ever more deeply into the communion of relationships in which God's being consists. The triune God might then be conceived as the total environment within which complex systems develop; everything that exists is embraced within relational movements of self-giving and self-realizing love.

Participation, dialogue and interaction

In his work on the nature of health and medicine I have already cited, the philosopher Hans-Georg Gadamer describes medicine as a dialogue in which the doctor and patient together try to reach an understanding of why the patient is ill. Such a dialogue requires empathy and participation on the part of the doctor, opening his or her own horizon of understanding to that of the patient's, and entering the patient's world.[10] Leaning on Heidegger's phenomenological portrayal of 'being in the world', Gadamer sees the aim of this dialogue as the re-establishing of a healthy balance or equilibrium which has been lost. The point of the dialogue is to produce health, which he says:

> manifests itself in a kind of feeling of well-being ... we are open to new things, ready to embark on new enterprises and, forgetful of ourselves, scarcely notice the demands and strains which are put upon us. ... Health is not a condition that one introspectively feels in oneself. Rather it is a condition of being there (*Da-Sein*), of being in the world (*In-der-Welt-Sein*), of being together with other people (*Mit-den-Menschen-Sein*), of being taken in by an active and rewarding engagement with the things that matter in life. ... It is the rhythm of life, a permanent process in which equilibrium re-establishes itself. (Gadamer, 1993: 143–45; trans. Svenaeus, 2003: 422)

The dialogue between doctor and patient is an opportunity for wise choices to be made which will re-establish connection with the rhythms of life. The good life consists in 'being there with others' and, referrring back to Aristotle's concept of *phronesis* or wise judgment, Gadamer sees the doctor–patient dialogue as an opportunity for making wise choices that open up a situation to that good end. Now, from the perspective of Christian theology, I suggest that this is possible because 'being in the world with others' is a participation in a deeper and more primal rhythm of life, the movements of giving and receiving that are symbolized in the life of the Trinity. Sensitivity to others awakens us to that rhythm which is already there before us; correspondingly, to live in the faith and expectation that the rhythm is there should help us to find the wise decision in interaction with others.

In their article about wisdom as a model for healthcare, Edmonson and Pearce do not open up this transcendent dimension, but they do stress the need to open up a sensitive interaction between the three elements of self-consciousness, empathy with the other and attention to the presenting problem. The practitioner, they stress, needs to know how to engage the patients' own efforts in recovery, knowing how they will react, and incorporating an awareness of what their predicament means to them. Treating mainly the issue of mental health, they give a vivid example of a failure to engage in this kind of interaction. As they tell the story,

The case involves a woman patient admitted to an acute hospital after a stroke, who was subsequently transferred to a rehabilitation ward. The patient, because of the effects of the stroke, had great difficulty making her needs known and called for the nurses' attention repeatedly. The skills of the physiotherapist and occupational therapist could not be applied because of her agitated state. The team set up a care plan giving her highly personal attention, situating her next to the nursing station, using reassurance, offering distraction, and trying to identify her needs through regular enquiry. They tolerated her level of need until their concern for other patients' well-being became compromised through the noise she made, and a nurse was injured when the lady pushed a table onto her foot. It seems that the members of the team too were becoming agitated by this stage, and when the doctor was called to see the patient he seemed to share their distress. He supported the team consensus that she should be managed on a psychiatric ward because of her disturbed behavior. (Edmondson and Pearce, 2007: 240)

However, Edmonson and Pearce now add that during this entire period it had been overlooked that the lady was not just recovering from a stroke; she was suffering painfully from breast cancer which had already been detected to be spreading. Only in a much later case review was attention given to this probable cause for her disruptive attempts to communicate.

Reflecting on this story of what Pearce and Edmonson call a 'disastrous' decision, despite the staff's best intentions, they ask 'in what way could wisdom have guided the team's plans, above and beyond just taking more time or gaining more staff (possibilities which are not inexhaustibly available)'? Following their own suggestions, we can detect the way that procedures and established guidelines were allowed to dominate more rounded processes of reasoning. Taking the three elements they identify, we find first a distinct lack of self-awareness; missing was a self-critical approach to the management of the team's interpersonal emotions; frustration and even anger outweighed attention to moral issues about the patient's human status. Team members might have checked their responses to the situation, and asked themselves what use might be made of past experiences colleagues had had in comparable situations. Second, there was lack of imaginative engagement with the world of the patient. They could have drawn on ordinary, everyday wisdom concerning what is important to people and *why* they do things. This might have underlined the possibility that the patient was trying to communicate something they had not guessed. Third, the pressures of the situation led to a neglect of the evidence base itself. The lady's removal from her original ward to a rehabilitation ward, perhaps driven by externally imposed targets, led to a loss of knowledge of her situation. The decision to transfer her to yet another situation, a psychiatric ward, only compounded the problem. A wisdom-based approach, urge Edmondson and Pearce, 'can help keep in mind a range of questions which recognises *the breadth of the considerations* required in health care' (2007: 242).

Finding the rhythm of life

Health is a way of being in the world, an engagement with the rhythm of life; in the words of Gadamer, it is 'a permanent process in which equilibrium re-establishes itself'. In terms of medical practice, finding health entails treating evidence in a flexible way within the context of exercising wisdom. In the more dramatic portrayal of Old Testament wisdom literature, it is a walking with Lady Wisdom through the world in the company of others. In the Christian context of the doctrine of the Trinity, it is also expecting to find rhythms of giving and receiving in love, relations which are wider and deeper than ourselves in which we can participate. This last perspective does not mean expecting a supernatural intervention, but seeking to cooperate with a gentle but effective flow of life which does not overwhelm or replace human action but which has a gift-like quality ('grace' is the theological word) which continually sustains natural processes and promotes human flourishing.

Here we might reflect theologically on a medical case-study which is recorded in a chapter co-authored by Ernest Lucas and a medical doctor, Peter May, in the book on Christian healing to which I referred earlier, a case which was earlier written up in the *British Journal of Cancer* as 'the first reported case of spontaneous regression of a fibrosarcoma' (Madden et al., 1992: S72–75) and which even formed the subject of a television programme.[11] The story goes that a newborn baby had a tumour of the arm, and an NHS consultant had caused a stir by announcing to the press that the tumour had been malignant and had been 'miraculously' healed. Our authors take up the account:

> It turned out that the doctor who presented the case [to the media] had not actually been involved in the care of this child nor in the medical decisions that were made. ... The surgeon was reluctant to perform mutilating surgery if it could possibly be avoided, as he could see no surgical alternative to amputating the arm. The cancer specialist thought the tumour would respond to chemotherapy, but such high doses of drugs would be needed that they would have very serious effects on such a small baby. As it was a rare tumour, they took advice from other specialists. They were given good reason to believe that this type of tumour could well resolve spontaneously if left alone. Soft tissue tumours in the newborn commonly do. As it was unlikely to spread to other parts of the body, the doctors in charge of the case decided to keep the child under review, holding their therapeutic options in reserve. As they hoped, over the next six months the tumour gradually disappeared. The surgeon and cancer specialist were both indignant that the recovery had been presented as being miraculous. There was certainly nothing instantaneous about it. (Lucas, 1997: 104–5)

One thing to notice here is an ambiguity over whether the tumour should have been described as 'malignant' at all: some unusual tumours may be technically classified as 'malignant' without the implication that they will *necessarily* spread through the body. But more significantly, the story shows the same blend of reliance on an evidence base and a willingness to take decisions based on 'wisdom' that we have seen already in other situations. Evidence from similar cases showed a high probability that the tumour could resolve itself, but a risk still had to be taken based on the 'wisdom' of those involved, drawing on personal experience and a sympathetic and imaginative engagement with the child and, probably, the parents. They decided not to 'play safe' with either a radical surgical or chemical intervention. The case was, at any rate, sufficiently unusual to be written up in a medical journal.

If one reflects on the reaction of the consultant who was only remotely involved, it may be that he meant by 'miraculous' that it was an event 'arousing wonder', which John Macquarrie names as the 'minimal meaning' of the word (1977: 247). But he also clearly wanted to find some kind of activity of God within this medical procedure. For those who do not have a religious worldview this is merely an outrageous claim. But Christian theologians will want—like the ancient Israelite wise—to find some way of articulating the activity of God in the world, and more precisely relating human 'wisdom' (including wisdom in medicine) to the presence of God in creation. If we were to take the perspective already outlined in this essay, then we must say that God never acts in a coercive way. We could not speak of this particular event as a unilateral intervention of God. But we do want to say that the doctors were 'walking with Lady Wisdom', which is theologically more than 'working with Mother Nature'. While those without a religious understanding of life will understand their wisdom as an attunement to the rhythms of nature, I do not believe that it impugns their integrity for a theologian to interpret all life-enhancing actions as being attuned to the rhythms of divine wisdom, engaging in the flow of Trinitarian life. As in ancient *hokmah*, a secular caution in the face of a complex world can modulate into a 'fear of God', or a humble approach to the world can become humility before the Creator. Doctors who do have a religious faith might then find in prayer a means of becoming *more* sensitive to these rhythms of life and love, which are to be understood theologically as movements of relationship.

Moreover, we might conceive of a God who takes creation and its freedom so seriously as to need this responsive attunement of what is created in order to carry through divine purposes. Traditionally, the 'aseity' of God, or God's existing only from God's self (*a se*) has been understood to entail a complete freedom from any need of the world, in a 'simple' state of being totally unconditioned by anything outside God's self. But self-existence should not be confused with self-sufficiency (so Ward, 1982: 10, 81–86, 121). In God's own freedom, God can choose to be in need, to work in creation only through cooperation with beings who are also creative. As the theologian Karl Barth puts it, '[God] ordains that He should not be *entirely* self-sufficient as He might be' (1936–77, II/2: 10).

We can then conceive of God's influencing and persuading created beings, or luring them with love, to cooperate with divine aims. There is no mechanical causality here, no inevitable link between cause and effect. As H. H. Farmer put it, God as supremely personal does not seek to manipulate our wills, but persuades by 'haunting the soul with the pressure of an unconditional value' (1935: 24, cf. 70). To return to the vision of Trinity I proposed earlier, this divine persuasion is based in attraction, in the attractiveness of *movements* of love, rhythms of a dance into which we are swept up, so that our actions follow the same divine purpose. We are offered, or presented with, aims through being engaged in the purposeful flow of the divine love. Human beings, exercising wisdom, walk with Lady Wisdom through the world or—to change the metaphor—engage in the movement within God that the early theologians called 'eternal Sonship' or logos.

Now, some Christian thinkers are happy enough to speak of God's loving persuasion in the human consciousness, and especially in what we have been calling the exercise of wisdom, but can conceive of God's action within physical matter only as purely unilateral. In this case, a God who is active in health and healing would be acting differently in the mind of the doctor and the body of the patient. But we can surely have no such mind–body dualism. If human beings are psychosomatic unities and are truly involved in their environment, it makes no sense to speak of persuasive action in human consciousness and coercive action everywhere else, whether in the human body or the many bodies of the world. If the mind is not separable from the physical substratum of the brain (though this is not the same thing as saying that mind is simply reducible to brain; see Swinburne, 1986: 29–31, 298–300), and the physical brain is embedded in the materiality of the world, then we cannot have any duality in the activity of God. If we are to conceive God's action in and through human wisdom as persuasive, then we must also conceive God as working in this way within the whole of nature, guiding it patiently, offering innovation through the influence of the Holy Spirit and calling out response from it. If the world is an organic community, then all its members work together, affecting each other. If the human mind can respond to God, then it is not unreasonable to think that there must be something at least akin to response to God at all levels of creation, some 'family-likeness' within the cosmos. Even if we cannot describe exactly how this relationship between God and the physical world works, we do have various kinds of language to point to the mystery.

One kind of language is offered by 'process theology', which envisages all entities in the world as having the capacity for feeling enjoyment, and reaching after satisfaction. In the process vision, 'actual entities' are the smallest building-blocks of the universe, sub-atomic particles in the process of becoming; they aggregate together to form larger scale objects or 'societies', whether persons or inanimate objects such as rocks. All entities are 'dipolar', with a mental as well as a physical dimension, though at this lowest level of reality 'mind' has not yet reached consciousness as it has in persons. Individual entities and 'societies' work together in the organic community of the world, influencing and being influenced by others, moving towards the achievement of value and beauty (Whitehead, 1967: 27–39, 163–66, 373–75). God offers an aim—or at least parameters for development—to every entity in creation to enable it to grow into fullness of life, and because there is a mental element (or a 'feeling' aspect) in everything, all can accept, reject or modify the divine purpose (Ford, 1978: 82–85; Hartshorne, 1976: 134–38).

While thorough-going adherents of process philosophy take this picture of the world as a scientific description, I suggest that it may be better to regard it as metaphor, pointing to an underlying reality which is finally inexpressible. As we have seen, the wise of ancient Israel were reaching towards this in their own way, by speaking of Yahweh as active and present in every part of the world, even where human vision is limited. Another pathway of thought, based on more recent physics than process philosophy, observes that causality in the world is of two types: there is 'energetic' causality (where one thing makes a physical impact on another), and there is 'informational' causality, where the input of information into a system forms its patterns of behavior. Some theologians, and notably the former quantum physicist John Polkinghorne, have suggested that while creaturely acts involve a mixture of energetic and informational causalities, God acts through making a pure entry of information into nature. This is a holistic kind of causation, affecting the patterns of whole, large-scale systems, which then have an influence on their smaller component parts (Polkinghorne, 1998: 62–64; Peacocke, 1995: 263–64, 272–75, 285–87).

I suggest that we can place this 'pattern-inducing' activity in the context of the triune life of God. As I have been proposing, the triune God acts in the world through being in movement within God's self, and by drawing created realities into the momentum of divine relationships. We can thus take up the insight of 'pattern making', though without having to restrict it to the particular scientific language of an 'input of information'. We can envisage the influence of the patterns of the divine 'dance' of relationships on the patterns of behavior of natural systems, human persons (mind and body) and human societies. We are confident that God's persuasive lure towards life will reach into the whole pattern of the human being, crossing all boundaries between spirit and body. Correspondingly, we are hoping for a response to God's purpose which cannot be isolated in the mind alone but which somehow, at the same time, arises from the body which the mind transcends.

The result of such holistic response to the divine initiative may be an enriching of a pattern of nature that is already there, such as the receiving of a sense of peace despite the presence of disease and disability, or an easing of symptoms and pain though the cause of them is still there. But a theologian may well think that there is room in the partnership between God and nature for something new to happen which is not already part of the regular flow of events; there might, for example, be some inexplicable remission in the onward march of a disease, or the unusual disappearance of damaged cells, or some hastening of a process that usually takes longer, or some recovery of function to an area of the brain that seemed previously to have been defunct. We might call these events 'miracles' in the sense of both 'arousing wonder' and 'disclosing' continuous divine activity, yet we should agree with both Thomas Aquinas and Karl Barth[12] that these are not 'breaches' in nature, but grace finding new paths through nature. They have a sufficient natural explanation, but one that from a perspective of faith is not exhaustive.

Wisdom in ancient Israel was characterized both by observation ('Wisdom A') and participation ('Wisdom B'). Wisdom in modern medicine is both evidence-based and dialogical. Allowing ancient texts to speak into situations of healthcare today provides, for Christian theologians, a concrete instance where talk of God as Trinity can come alive, and where ideas of divine action in the world can be explored. For medical practitioners, the comparison between biblical wisdom and clinical practice may prompt the use of judgment in drawing on wisdom-based approaches to care. Whether practitioners have a religious faith or not, it may also encourage them to cultivate an 'attunement' in imaginative ways to the rhythms of life in body, nature and society.

Notes

1 Aristotle, *Nichomachean Ethics* 1139b.16; 1140a.25–29; 1140b.6–8. For appeal to *phronesis* in the medical literature, see for example Fugelli (1998: 184–88); Macnaughton (1998: 89–92); Svenaeus (2003: 407–31).
2 For the experiental method of wisdom, see Von Rad (1972: 24–50, 74–82, 113–20); Schmid (1966: 155–60); Zimmerli (1964: 146–58); Murphy (1969: 293–7); McKane (1965: 46–51). A challenge to the idea of a distinctive educational technique has, however, been mounted by Whybray (1974: 69–70).
3 All biblical quoteations are from the NRSV, unless otherwise indicated.
4 Seven examples of the formula with the noun (10:27; 14:27; 15:16,33; 16:6; 19:23; 22:4) and two with the verb (14:2,26).
5 This thesis has been contested by Weeks (1994: 57–73).
6 Rudolph Bultmann even postulates an ancient 'wisdom myth' in which Wisdom descends from heaven, searches for a home on earth, is rejected by all and returns to heaven where she now dwells hidden from mortal beings; see Bultmann (1923); similarly, Wilckens (1959: 181).
7 For the following, see my argument in Fiddes (1996: 171–90).
8 Similarly Svenaeus (2003: 408–9), argues that the physician does not aim only at treatment but 'the good life'.
9 e.g., Athanasius, *Contra Arianos* 3.4–6, cf. 1.9, 39, 58; Gregory Nazianzen, *Orationes* 29.16; Augustine, *De Trinitate* 5.6–13.
10 This is worked out extensively throughout Svenaeus (2001).
11 *The Heart of the Matter*, Roger Bolton Productions, BBC 1 (1 August 1992).
12 Aquinas, *De Malo* 6, cf. Aquinas, *Summa Theologiae* 1a.22.3; Barth (1936–77, III/2, pp. 125–28).

Bibliography

Barth, Karl. *Church Dogmatics* (trans. and ed. G. W. Bromiley and T. F. Torrance: 14 vols; Edinburgh: T. & T. Clark, 1936–77).
Bultmann, Rudolph. 'Der Religionsgeschichtliche Hintergrund des Prologs zum Johannes-Evangelium' (1923), repr. in *Exegetica* (Tübingen: Mohr, 1967).
Chan, Jonathan J. and Julienne E. Chan. 'Medicine for the Millennium: The Challenge of Postmodernism'. *Medical Journal of Australia* 172 (2000), pp. 332–34.
Crenshaw, James L. *Old Testament Wisdom. An Introduction* (Louisville, KY: Westminster/John Knox Press, 1998).
Edmondson, Ricca and Jane Pearce. 'The Practice of Health Care: Wisdom as a Model'. *Medicine, Health Care and Philosophy* 10 (2007).
Evidence-Based Medicine Working Group. 'Evidence-Based Medicine: A New Approach to Teaching the Practice of Medicine'. *Journal of the American Medical Association* 268 (1992).
Farmer, H. H. *The World and God* (London: Nisbet, 1935).
Fiddes, Paul S. *Participating in God: A Pastoral Doctrine of the Trinity* (London: Darton, Longman & Todd, 2000).
———. ' "Where Shall Wisdom be Found?" Job 28 as a Riddle for Ancient and Modern Readers'. Pages 171–90 in *After the Exile. Essays in Honour of Rex Mason* (ed. John Barton and David Reimer; Macon, GA: Mercer University Press, 1996).
Fontaine, Carole R. 'Wisdom in Proverbs'. Pages 100–108 in *In Search of Wisdom* (ed. Leo G. Perdue et al.; Louisville, KY: Westminster/John Knox Press, 1993).
Ford, Lewis S. *The Lure of God. A Biblical Background for Process Theism* (Philadelphia: Fortress Press, 1978).
Fugelli, P. 'Clinical Practice: Between Aristotle and Cochrane'. *Schweizerische Medizinische Wochenschrift* 128 (1998).
Gadamer, Hans-Georg. *Über die Verborgenheit der Gesundheit* (Frankfurt: Suhrkamp Verlag, 1993).
Greenhalgh, Trisha. 'Narrative Based Medicine in an Evidence Based World'. *British Medical Journal* 318 (1999).
Hartshorne, Charles. *The Divine Relativity. A Social Conception of God* (New Haven: Yale University Press, 1976).
Howie, J. G. R. 'Research in General Practice: Pursuit of Knowledge or Defence of Wisdom?' *British Medical Journal* 289 (1984).
Joyce, Paul. 'Proverbs 8 in Interpretation'. Pages 89–101 in *Reading Texts, Seeking Wisdom* (ed. David Ford and Graham Stanton: London: SCM, 2003).
Litchfield, Merian. 'Practice Wisdom'. *Advances in Nursing Science* 2/2 (1999).
Lucas, Ernest, ed. *Christian Healing. What Can We Believe?* (London: Lynx, 1997).
———. *Exploring the Old Testament: A Guide to the Psalms and Wisdom Literature* (Downers Grove, IL: InterVarsity, 2003).
———. 'The New Testament Teaching on the Environment'. *Transformation* 16/3 (1999).
Macnaughton, Jane. 'Evidence and Clinical Judgment'. *Journal of Evaluation in Clinical Practice* 4/2 (1998).
Macquarrie, John. *Principles of Christian Theology* (London: SCM Press, rev. edn, 1977).
Madden, N. P., R. D. Spicer, E. B. Allibone and I. J. Lewis. 'Spontaneous Regression of

Neonatal Fibrosarcoma'. *British Journal of Cancer* 66 (1992), supp. vol. 8, S72–75.
McKane, W. *Prophets and Wise Men* (London: SCM Press, 1965).
———. *Proverbs—A New Approach* (London: SCM Press, 1970).
Murphy, R. E. 'The Interpretation of Old Testament Wisdom Literature'. *Interpretation* 23 (1969).
Parker, Malcolm. 'Whither Our Art? Clinical Wisdom and Evidence-Based Medicine'. *Medicine, Health Care and Philosophy* 5 (2002), pp. 273–80.
Peacocke, Arthur. 'God's Interaction with the World'. In *Chaos and Complexity. Scientific Perspectives on Divine Action* (ed. R. J. Russell, N. Murphy and A. R. Peacocke; Vatican City State: Vatican Observatory/ Berkeley: Center for Theology and Natural Sciences, 1995).
Pellegrino, Edmund. 'Professionalism, Profession and the Virtues of the Good Physician'. *Mount Sinai Journal of Medicine* 69/6 (2002).
Perdue, Leo G. *Wisdom and Creation. The Theology of Wisdom Literature* (Eugene, OR: Wipf & Stock, 1994).
Polkinghorne, John. *Belief in God in an Age of Science* (New Haven: Yale University Press, 1998).
Ringgren, H. *Word and Wisdom* (Lund: Haken Ohlssons, 1947).
Sackett, D. L., W. M. C. Rosenberg, J. A. M. Gray, et al. 'Evidence Based Medicine: What It Is and What It Isn't'. *British Medical Journal* 312 (1996).
Sackett, D. L. et al. *Evidence-Based Medicine: How to Practise and Teach EBM* (New York: Churchill-Livingstone, 1997).
Schmid, H. H. *Wesen und Geschichte der Weisheit* (Berlin: W. de Gruyter, 1966).
Scott, R. B. Y. 'The Study of the Wisdom Literature', *Interpretation* 24 (1970), pp. 20–45.
Smith, Richard. 'Where Is the Wisdom? The Poverty of Medical Evidence'. *British Medical Journal* 303 (1991).
Svenaeus, F. *The Hermeneutics of Medicine and the Phenomenology of Health: Steps Towards a Philosophy of Medical Practice* (Dordrecht: Kluwer, rev. edn, 2001).
———. 'Hermeneutics of Medicine in the Wake of Gadamer: The Issue of Phronesis'. *Theoretical Medicine* 24 (2003).
Swinburne, Richard. *The Evolution of the Soul* (Oxford, Clarendon Press, 1986).
Szawarski, Zbigniew. 'Wisdom and the Art of Healing'. *Medicine, Health Care and Philosophy* 7 (2004).
Von Rad, Gerhard. *Wisdom in Israel* (trans. J. Martin; London: SCM Press, 1972).
Ward, Keith. *Rational Theology and the Creativity of God* (Oxford: Blackwell, 1982).
Weeks, Stuart. *Early Israelite Wisdom* (Oxford: Clarendon Press, 1994).
Whitehead, A. N. *Process and Reality: An Essay in Cosmology* (New York: Macmillan, 1967).
Whybray, R. N. *The Intellectual Tradition in the Old Testament* (Berlin: W. de Gruyter, 1974).
———. *Wisdom in Proverbs* (London: SCM, 1965).
Wilckens, U. *Weisheit und Torheit* (Tübingen: Mohr, 1959).
Zimmerli, W. 'The Place and Limit of the Wisdom in the Framework of the Old Testament Theology'. *Scottish Journal of Theology* 17 (1964).

God
    Father, Son, Spirit,
    Creator, Redeemer, Sustainer,
    Holy Trinity, fizzing with life and love.

Preserve us from the desire
    to win at all costs
    to be right all the time
    to be dominant
    to believe for just a second
    that the universe revolves around us.

In your mercy
    enfold us in your otherness
    in ways of knowing that confound us
    in depths of understanding that
    disturb, open, deepen and provoke
    our limited grasp
    of experience and hope.

In your grace
    drench us in wisdom,
    keeping us in good company with you
    that we will fully live and love
    as Christ fully lived and loved,
    the Word of life, the Word made flesh,

6

The Way of Practical Modesty

Brian Haymes

One is often bewitched by a word. For example, by the word 'know'.
Ludwig Wittgenstein (1974: para. 435)

The editors of this volume of essays honoring Ernest Lucas have kindly invited me to 'explore the theme of *epistemology* especially in the debate between science and theology'. This is a wide enough brief for anyone so I propose to focus on the question, asked with absolutely no sense of impertinence at all but with much affection and gratitude, 'Does Ernest Lucas know what he is talking about?'

In some respects the question is easily and I suspect uncontroversionally answered. For example, Lucas has a doctorate in biochemistry awarded by a British university. As such, the necessary research work would have been open to investigation by other scientists, closely examined by acknowledged specialist experts in the field who judged Lucas worthy to be counted among their number. Unless one were prepared to argue that the whole field of biochemistry is in error and that the recognized universities and learned societies are perpetrating an intellectual hoax then we have every good reason to assert that, as biochemist, Lucas knows what he is talking about. This is the case even if at some time in the future the whole area of biochemistry were to be reconsidered by some new fundamental experimental knowledge which called into question the value of all earlier work.

This same argument can be applied to Lucas's work as a biblical scholar. Again, another doctorate, this time in the study of Hebrew texts. The work has been examined and approved by recognized scholars. Lucas has shown himself to be expert in biblical languages and their interpretation. As a biblical historian and exegete, he knows of what he speaks.

Religion and knowledge

However, the question has at least one further dimension and it is with this that my essay is concerned. Lucas is a confessed religious believer, a Christian no less. He shares publicly in acts of Christian worship; he prays to God; he preaches and commends what he believes to be the good news of God; he engages in and supports Christian mission. Those who know him personally are aware of how serious and important this commitment to God is in his life. It is in this regard that my question can be pressed; does he know of what or of whom he speaks? It is not enough to go to his fellow believers to ask them. They will bear witness to Lucas's integrity, his willingness to live and work for Christ. But they would say that, wouldn't they? By contrast, there are strident voices asserting that Lucas and his fellow believers are, in fact, deluded and that, in propagating their religious beliefs, they seriously mislead people. In what has been termed 'the New Atheism'[1] the charge is that all forms of religious belief are dangerous and irrational. As such, Christian believers, like Lucas, are self-deceived and do not know what they are talking about in worship, prayer and preaching, because there is nothing or no one beyond the empirical world explored by science to know.

I take this assertion of delusion and irrationality to be a very serious charge. Christians claim to 'know' God and such claims occur in different forms in the Bible.[2] Moreover, within the tradition of Christian theology some fine intellects have worked to produce insights and reasoned philosophies of beauty and perception, of immense power and practical worth, into the human condition. It is hard to imagine that they were all deluded and their lives' work consisted in so much superstition. I acknowledge that this is logically possible, hence the seriousness of the charge which is never going to be settled by dogmatic claims to divine revelation. I am also aware that the terms 'reason' and 'rationality' are notoriously difficult to define and that no little confusion arises when the terms are used differently in various discourses. However, I propose to argue that religious believers are not irrational simply by holding religious beliefs. I acknowledge the help I have received in this from the Baptist scholar and minister, the philosopher William Donald Hudson.[3]

Religion and belief in God

To sharpen my argument let me say that I take it to be the case that religious beliefs are, by definition, about 'God'. I am aware that other beliefs may be held 'religiously', meaning that they are scrupulously and conscientiously practised. But religious belief I hold to be about 'God' and that is what makes it a religious belief. 'God' is another term given wide use and therefore carrying various meanings. Here I shall assume a traditional Christian approach such that when I speak of God I mean Transcendent Consciousness and Agency. God is transcendent in that God, although fundamentally related to creation, is other than all that is. I do not mean 'wholly other' because if that were the case then we could know nothing of God, not even that God is wholly other. God is other than the world, even as God nonetheless relates to the world. By

Consciousness I mean mind and purpose. By Agency I mean that history is the sphere of God's activity. This is a form of traditional theism, a position which invites many philosophical objections and refining arguments. I shall also assume that although the Bible speaks in many impersonal metaphors of God, such as rock and fortress (Ps. 18:2), it is significant that the primary metaphors are personal and relational.

Religious language, like the language of any intellectual discipline, shares words in common with ordinary speech but does not always employ them with the same sense and meaning. Both the physicist and the poet may use the word 'world' but will, quite likely, mean different things by it. Typically in science we use words and symbols to identify and explain. But this is not the only use to which words and symbols are put. The meaning of a word is the use to which it is put in any universe of discourse. This is why careful attention must be given to the language we use and it can only bring confusion if we assume always a static 'dictionary definition' of meaning. Moreover, it is the sentence, not the isolated word, that carries sense and meaning.[4] The employment of language is multifarious. It always requires careful attention.

Religious beliefs and delusion

Given its long intellectual history, why should anyone argue that holding religious beliefs is irrational? I suggest that behind this argument lie three basic and related assertions:

1 First, that religious belief is delusional and irrational because its assertions, by definition, cannot be verified or falsified. As such, they lack evidence.
2 Second, that religious beliefs brook no argument. They are commonly held by those who are, on these matters, closed-minded. The implication is that religion must always, in some sense, impose itself. As such, it is anti-intellectual.
3 Third, religion trades in superstition. It involves belief in the alleged 'supernatural'. Science, the most productive and currently dominant way to knowledge, is by contrast rational and evidence-based. Scientists, appealing to reason, can show that they know what they are talking about. Religious believers are unable to satisfy any criteria for knowledge claims in the public world.

How might a Christian believer reply to these charges? I shall take each one in turn.

First, the appeal to evidence. The recent centuries have seen the rise of modern scientific inquiry to the immense benefit of us all. While various methodologies are employed as befits the subject matter, essential to scientific learning is evidence. On this understanding, claims for what counts as knowledge must meet three together necessary and sufficient conditions:

- that what is claimed is true. It hardly makes sense to say we know what is untrue. We cannot 'know' that Paris is the capital of Germany. Of course we may be mistaken in our beliefs but recognizing this is an admission that we did not know what we claimed to know.
- that the claimant believes in and is sure of the claim. Again, it would be odd to say, 'I know Paris is the capital city of France but I am not sure that it is.'
- that reasons can be given for the claim which amount to more that the assertion that 'I really believe it'. Where evidence can be cited appropriate to the claim then the claim is justified.

In bald terms, knowledge is justified true belief, therefore evidence is essential to genuine claims to knowledge.[5] If any claims to knowledge are made which do not meet the tests of evidence—claims which can be neither verified nor falsified—then they fail as knowledge claims. Religious believers sometimes speak of an event as an act of God in the sense that God caused it to happen. But nothing is taken in science to be a cause or effect unless it can be in some clear sense identified. The appeal is to evidence and demonstration in the public world. This is nowadays asserted as the rational approach and becomes the way by which reasonable people seek to understand the world we inhabit and the universe (universes?) we can only tentatively explore at present. All this has been at the heart of the great scientific endeavour of empirical research which has brought so much benefit to humankind.

God and knowledge

Clearly, if by 'God' we mean what Christians have taken God to be and if by 'knowledge' we mean justified true belief secured by empirically tested evidence, then there can be no knowledge of God. God is not part of the world, open to investigation by scientific methods. God cannot be put under a microscope, dissected or measured. In other words, God does not exist as identifiable things exist. Who or what the religious believer means by God is not available to such inquiry and study. To imagine this is the case would be a clear blunder in the understanding of language and logic.

Epistemologically, it has long been understood that the search for knowledge is a rich and demanding intellectual adventure more than a matter of routinely proceeding through an agreed programme. We cannot avoid circularities in our arguments here. For example, whatever the subject matter, we have to believe in what may not yet be demonstrable in order to understand, and to understand in order to believe. Again, how we come to know anything is related to the object we seek to study, and the nature of the object shapes the forms by which we come to know. All epistemological forms have these limitations and it explains why Newton's great work is surpassed and must be surpassed if we are to understand more of the universe.[6]

'God' may not be open to study in the way the universe invites our questions and exploration but does that mean that all talk of knowing God is delusional? It would be if it is the case that all knowing is scientific in the sense that it requires appropriate testable evidence. But then this is close to asserting that anything is delusional that is not scientifically demonstrable. Such a bold claim needs substantiation. I shall return to this issue later.

The truth revealed?

I am aware that some Christians would want, at this point if not earlier, to speak boldly about evidence for God. Without attempting any descriptions of how it might have happened or be happening, they would assert that God stands behind all that is as its Creator. They would take the beauty and order of the universe as evidence of a creative mind (Ps. 19). They might refer to what seems to be a widespread aspect of human experience, namely of some spiritual depth to life, a longing for God (Ps. 42). Some would be eager to tell of personal experiences which they take to be, without doubt, experiences of God. Christian believers, in particular, would want to speak of Jesus, the prophet from Nazareth in Galilee who was crucified in the time of Pontius Pilate. They would speak of their conviction about his being raised from the dead. They would want to record their experiences in worship and prayer, experiences which they would claim relate to the activity of God the Spirit. This list could be much further expanded.

Scientifically, none of this counts as evidence at all because it cannot be tested, falsified or verified to scientific standards. Some aspects may be open to the usual methods of historical study but God remains beyond that. The fact, if it is a fact, that the tomb is empty does not logically entail the assertion that God raised Jesus from the dead. There might be other explanations for its emptiness. We may be left with a puzzle but science will not take us beyond the evidence. There is always a logical gap between any such claims and the public world of testable evidence. Even if someone were to die for these beliefs that would prove nothing for they might be deluded even in the offering of their life. Martyrdom is an extraordinary act of witness to beliefs strongly held but the question of proof and the truth or falsity of the claim is not settled by the martyr's death alone. It would be important, however, to note that the martyr's death only is so described as martyrdom because it fits within a particular narrative, otherwise it might better be described as suicide or murder.

Internal and external questions

But here it is important to recognize a significant distinction. It is one drawn, among others, by Rudolph Carnap (1950: 20–40.[7] It is between what he called external and internal questions. Internal questions are those that arise within the framework of a given conceptual system, such as science. These questions are settled by applying the criteria the system supplies. External questions are those relating to the reality or existence of the framework itself. Internal questions may find answers within the conceptual framework in which they are set. In this sense the notion of evidence is applicable and the claims testable. But external questions cannot be settled in this fashion because external questions are about the framework itself. For example, the question, 'Do material objects exist?', considered as an external question, is not one that can be answered straightforwardly by reference to evidence. It is a question of whether there is to be a system of rules or a framework concerning the concept of 'material object'. However, the question, 'Does my laptop computer exist?', considered as an internal question, is answerable in terms of the system rules governing the use of material-object questions.

This does not mean that the 'existence' of any framework thereby establishes the reality of what the framework involved because using the language involved in the framework does not imply the ontological reality of the entities in question. Indeed, Carnap challenged those who claimed that the ontological status of an entity must be settled before we can talk about it meaningfully and rationally. He claimed that an entity can be talked about if we chose to follow the linguistic forms but this is a practical and not theoretical question as far as he is concerned. A choice is to be made but:

> The acceptance cannot be judged as being either true or false because it is not an assertion; it can only be judged as being more or less expedient, fruitful, conducive to the aim for which the language is intended. Judgements of this kind supply the motivation for the decision of accepting or rejecting the framework. Thus it is clear that the acceptance of a framework must not be regarded as implying a metaphysical doctrine concerning the reality of the entities in question. (Carnap, 1950: 31–32)

All this is highly germane to the question of evidence. Anyone making what might be called an 'internal assertion' is obliged to justify it by providing evidence but what counts as evidence will be determined by the linguistic form being used, the framework in operation. Thus both a scientist and a Christian believer might have what they take to be evidence for their assertions. To ask for evidence of the framework itself, however, is to ask another kind of question, perhaps an impossible question because where could one ever go for an answer? Such questions are asked, nonetheless. It is not that they are not proper questions in the sense that they are not formed grammatically, but there is no conceivable way of answering them. Either the questioner chooses to entertain the proposition foundational to the framework or system of language or he does not. The justification of the choice is practical and not theoretical and being practical means it can be justified only in its own terms. Thus for example, Reinhold Niebuhr understood the Christian faith as offering an insight into 'the nature and destiny of man' as a context for the appropriation of empirical knowledge for the contemporary world (so Rice, 2009: 8). He did not set out to 'prove' the foundational assertions of that faith. John Howard Yoder claims that 'the confessing community is unembarrassed about the fact that its confession is not ultimately subject to irresistible verification (or falsification) from outside its own system. The quality of confirmation or validation that the community does claim is the inherent coherence of the several elements of confession and experience among themselves and their reciprocal confirmation among the several members of the body' (2010: 67).

Evidence and truth

Evidence for any assertion implies verification or falsification conditions and procedures. What would have to be the conditions under which we would know that or have good reason to believe that the assertion is true? It is one thing for the assertion to be conceivably the case. It is quite another thing for us to know that it is true. In this sense, every assertion has its price and part of that price is the indicating of what counts as evidence. But is it really the case that should any assertion not have means of verification it is necessarily meaningless? The truth conditions of any statement are not the same as verification conditions. A statement may be meaningful to us even though we do not know how to test it for truth or falsity. But then, what would it mean to believe in God in this world if there is nothing in this world that would make the believer disbelieve in God? I shall return to this question in a moment. Here I want to examine the issue in terms of the practical relevance of an unscientific belief.

We might well wonder about the integrity or even sanity of a scientist constantly performing many tests of his hypothesis, having decided beforehand that none of the results are ever going to count against the hypothesis. What is the point of his work? It has no relevance. One might even suggest he is deluding himself.

What, however, is the case with religious belief? A religious believer will assert that if you believe what she believes, and if you believe it seriously, then the difference between the believer and an unbeliever will not be that the unbeliever is prepared to conduct enquiries by the light of evidence and the believer is not but that the believer is committed to certain ways of action, to certain ways of interpreting life, as the unbeliever is not, which makes all the difference in the world between the two of them. The commitments we make, the ways of interpreting life one adopts, are highly relevant to life in the sense that they do make a great deal of difference to the way we live.

Religious believers do not hold their beliefs in the way scientists hold to convictions about their hypotheses; which is to say that religion is not science and that appeals for evidence may not always be appropriate. But that does not mean that holding religious beliefs is irrational or delusional. To advance such an argument is scientific positivism and overlooks the various forms of knowing that go with our humanity and for which appropriate reasons may be given. 'Knowing' amounts to more that proving by empirical demonstration. It can entail acquaintance, direct experience, possibly intuition and certainly practice. The word 'know' is used in many different contexts with corresponding logical limitations and forms. It is indeed easy to be bewitched by the word 'know'. If rationality is limited to what can be proven scientifically, then what becomes of falling in love, or being moved to wonder at something seen, or by the intensity of a silence deep and full? Are such experiences really exhausted by scientific explanation as to cause?

Religious belief and criticism

I now move on to the second aspect of the charge that religious beliefs are irrational and delusional, that they brook no argument and are commonly held by those who are, on these matters, closed-minded. Religion, it is argued, must always, in some sense, impose itself. As such, it is anti-intellectual.

It is a matter of historical fact that there have been those ready to impose their religious beliefs on others. This has sometimes been in the form of personal threat—believe or you will be damned! At other times this has taken political form as religion and politics become intertwined either in common cause or as enemies. The Crusades, the Inquisition, the wars of Europe are sufficient examples, assuming such events were fundamentally about religious beliefs. In struggles for power there have always been those who have sought the support of religious institutions for political purposes, using dogmatic forms of religion to subdue populations.

There have also been forms of religion which insist upon obedience to the leadership. Those in power have sought to impose their beliefs, at times by cruel and inhuman methods. Attempts have been made to silence the scholars. Books have been burned and so have bodies in propagation and defence of the 'truth'. The religious believer cannot deny dark aspects of the church's history where the authorities brooked no dissent or argument. Beliefs have been imposed.

It is also embarrassing for a believer to have to admit that there have been some very strange ideas propagated in the name of God, ideas in sharp contrast to good common sense. At times such 'beliefs' have frustrated socially critical and beneficial scientific research, not least with medical implications.

Of course, these power struggles, impositions and threats can also be found outside of religion. A leader or a government does not have to be religious to be tyrannical. Religion may be employed to further tyrannical ends but this is a failure of both religious and political integrity. It offends the rights of intellectual, political and religious freedom. It is a matter of fact that, on theological grounds, such freedom has been argued and suffered for by religious believers of all kinds. Religion need not take the unpleasant forms it sometimes does. Sometimes religion supplies the grounds on which totalitarianism is challenged.[8]

All of which being admitted, I none the less argue that it is not necessarily the case that religious beliefs are held only by the closed-minded, the anti-intellectual and fearful. There is nothing in the Christian religion as such that requires these dire forms. Indeed, I suggest that the contrary is the case and that open-minded intellectual inquiry into the truth is a necessary form that loving God with all one's mind takes (Mark 12:30). That humankind is called to explore, develop, understand and care for creation is a feature of Jewish and Christian views of life. That both science and religion are part of human culture is something recognized within these faith traditions. The intellectual quest in all its dimensions is a significant feature of what it is to be human.[9]

The open mind

But are there limits? W. D. Hudson engaged in a debate on the concept of open-mindedness with the philosopher W. W. Bartley III (Hudson, 1974: 179–86). Bartley offered his definition of a rationalist:

> A rationalist [is] to be characterized as one who is willing to entertain any position and holds *all* his beliefs, including his most fundamental standards, goals and decisions, and his basic philosophical position itself, open to criticism; one who protects nothing from criticism by justifying it irrationally; one who never cuts off an argument by resorting to faith or irrational commitments to justify some belief which has been under critical fire. (Bartley, 1984: 118)

How is this definition to be taken, with logical or psychological force? Psychologically, there is a problem here for the kind of fundamental propositions Bartley may have in mind are often aspects of individual or corporate identity. Giving them up may entail more than intellectual struggle alone. What seem good reasons may be intellectually troubling but not in the end decisive. This is the case whether we are talking of religious convictions or some other fundamental propositions. Not a few Christian believers, for example, being brought up on a very doctrinaire literal understanding of the Bible as the Word of God, meeting the good sense of historical study, have found a deep psychological struggle going on long after the intellectual debate has been settled in their minds. This may indicate something about the psychological strength with which fundamental propositions are held. It may even indicate an aspect of the nature of religious belief. What I have in mind here is the kind of confession found in Job who, after many disasters which would test the faith of anyone, none the less confesses, 'Though he kill me, yet I will trust in him' (Job 13:15, NRSV margin). This is akin to the faith of the martyrs who have what to others looks like obvious reasons to deny their faith. It may be that it is very difficult to hold to Bartley's definition psychologically speaking. Still, people of strong convictions do change their minds and some believers recant. That undoubtedly happens.

Hudson was more interested in the logical possibility of such critical open-mindedness. Does this apparently rational confession of rationalism actually make sense? Working as he does with the inward and outward nature of frameworks in language, Hudson, being himself committed to open-mindedness, is cautious. It makes sense to think of reasons why someone might give up their religious beliefs but could these be religious reasons? Can a rationalist give up a commitment to rationalism on reasonable grounds? Could a Christian abandon Christian faith on Christian grounds? Hudson argues: 'a rationalist *in religion* will necessarily be someone who does so for what he considers good *religious* reasons. I suggest that *within* religion it is possible to hold *all* the beliefs, which as a matter of empirical fact one holds, open to abandonment or revision if one has, or thinks one has, good religious reasons for doing so' (1974:184). Reasons do not exist *in vacuo*. They belong with a framework of thought and practice. There are, it seems to me, good reasons why Christians must keep reflecting on their faith, bringing those convictions into debate with what else is known of our life in the world. Ways of speaking of God may, in these circumstances, undergo development and change. This would be the sign of a living rational faith. This is what Hudson argues for and I believe he is right.

I do not think this gives open permission for us to create any linguistic frameworks we choose and live by them without relating them to whatever else we claim to know. It seems to me that Christians, especially given what we say of God as the source of all truth and knowledge, should look for coherence in our understanding of ourselves and the universe. Thus every intellectual discipline is an expression of one common search for truth. If some assertions are self-contradictory, then it would be illogical and false to try to hold them together. That would be irrational. But that does not mean that one must be right and the other wrong. Reason keeps on with the search and I see nothing in this open-mindedness that prevents an intellectually honest approach to life and faith. Imposing beliefs of any kind, religious or otherwise, lacks respect for our humanity in this essential human quest. All forms of fundamentalism, religious or non-religious, are irrational. But then, fundamentalisms are ideological forms of a different kind from both science and religious beliefs precisely because they deny that open-mindedness which is a necessary feature of being rational. Theologically speaking, in their absolutism they are idolatrous.

Supernatural beliefs

The third charge of irrationality is closely related to the other two in that it claims that religion trades in superstition and belief in the 'supernatural'. Science, by contrast, is rational and evidence-based. Scientists, appealing to reason, can show that they know what they are talking about. Religious believers are unable to satisfy any criteria for knowledge claims in the public world.

I see no reason why anyone should defend superstition which amounts to ungrounded irrational credulity. I am thinking here of fingers crossed, touching wood, lucky charms and sports players always putting on their socks and shoes in a precise order lest their performance in the game be jinxed. It may be that in the past some of these actions had a religious stimulus but today they are without much sense[10] and I see no reason why Christians should defend their practice since they have little or nothing to do with religious believing.

What of belief in the 'supernatural'? I am aware that not a few Christians glory in supernatural events, miracles and healings which they attribute to God. I am cautious about such language and such claims. I do not wish to be misunderstood here since I believe in God and in miracles. A major problem with miracles lies in defining what is meant by the word and for that we must look and see how it is used. Fundamentally, it is a religious term, relating to some event or action in history which came about because God caused something to happen which would otherwise not have so happened had not God so acted. Etymologically the word 'miracle' is related to 'wonder' and 'awe'. Such have remained stubborn and common features of human experience. They are not easily explained. Not every strange and remarkable happening is a miracle. It may simply be something for which we cannot yet give an explanation and here the god of the gaps does not help. But then neither does any suggestion that the 'supernatural' is, by definition, the 'contranatural'.

The reason why the third charge is false is that science can never give an exhaustive account of the nature of the reality we experience. It is a reductive approach to knowledge to suggest that we know only what we can empirically prove to be the case. That this has been the highly productive and successful approach of science we may readily thank God. But such an approach does not account for all human experience. It has limited explanatory power.

Let us contrast, for a moment, Lucas in his laboratory and Lucas at home. In the laboratory all concentration is on the object under scrutiny. It is dissected, placed under microscopes. The scientist is looking for the general, the observable, repeatable, empirical and testable. The object of the natural world with which he works may be brought to destruction by this task of 'taking apart'. When it has been used it can be discarded. No matter, another quickly takes its place for experiment. Should Lucas have any feelings towards these pieces of tissue or whatever they are is of no consequence, indeed it might prove to be a hindrance. This is importantly and necessarily a world of impersonal transactions, even though the scientist is a person.

The world of persons

But it is not like that when Lucas is at home. There he is with people and the quality of relationships is what matters. The way of life at home does not take an approach to people in general, a species to be examined and tested. At home Lucas lives in relationships of mutual trust and care. This is the world of persons which does not focus on the testing of hypotheses, nor dissection, nor detached observation. The knowing of persons is different from that of scientific proof.[11] However, I would not wish to suggest that by the world of the personal I simply mean personal relationships. This personal 'world' is the one world we all inhabit, which science explores by examination. But this world is also one where deep personal relationships of love are enjoyed, where there are moments of wonder, even awe. This happens to us because we are persons and because this world has surprising depth without which we would be less than the humanity we share. In such moments our minds are functioning more in synthetic than analytic ways. If we think of God in personal terms then we might still have faith in his hidden, quiet, persuasive presence, expressing God's own freedom and honoring ours. This may not have been the way people thought of God in the past but, in the light of our growing understanding of the world, it might be one way by which God is conceived now. It would be in keeping with the fundamental Christian conviction that God's self-revelation is most importantly in a person.

The world of persons, while open to scientific study and testing, is not exhausted by such work. The world of personal relationships, so precious and vital for many of us, suggests that the nature of reality may have depths and aspects not available to the scientific methods of detachment and objective examination alone. Words such as 'claim', 'will' and 'trust' come into play, as does 'love', of course. These are aspects of the *real* world which turn out to be more profound than scientific evidence suggests or presently knows.

All this is not to succumb to any suggestion of spirit–matter dualism. It is to suggest that in and through the natural world (the only world there is) moves the Eternal Personal, in whom and through whom all things live and have their being. It is to suggest that science describes one set of facts in one way but religion in another and because we describe the world differently we experience it differently. Theists and others believe that in our lived awareness of 'the personal' we are down to one of the 'ultimates' of reality which can only be described in its own terms. We do not enter into this 'world' by being a spectator, analysing and dissecting, but by engaging with the will and claim of others in relationships and with what we call 'nature'. 'Knowing' in this aspect of our living involves personal commitments. We know the depth of friendship only by making friends, the meaning of reconciliation by forgiving and being forgiven, the meaning of love by loving. The approach is practical but not simply utilitarian. As I have already argued, the fundamental propositions of the framework of language appropriate to the world of persons cannot be demonstrated outside of practice. It is no surprise that personal categories and metaphors have been used by many who speak of God.

It is in this one world, the 'world of persons', that many Christians speak of experiences of God; the experience of moral claim, sometimes of an absolute quality we cannot lay upon ourselves; of being addressed by an 'other' who calls for respect and honor; of contentment and joy before beauty and wonder. It is remarkable how widespread such experiences are and how varied. That there is variety is no surprise since we never do just have 'experience'. As Karl Popper argued, all experience is conceptually loaded and context-dependent. We 'make' our experience and our language frameworks have a great deal to do with that (Popper, 1959: 280). The language we use is a key to our interpretation of the world and what constitutes our experience of it. It is sometimes argued that we do not need religious language today because we have better explanations. It is certainly true that linguistic frameworks can lose their hold on people's lives, becoming obsolete and forgotten (Wittgenstein, 1972: I:23). Is this what has happened to first-order religious language in recent years with consequences for what we experience? We will not have religious experiences or appreciate the meaning of faith in God without using the language of God. And should anyone ask why we should want to do that, the answer will be practical, citing the rich way life may be interpreted in the light of God and because it rings true. Resting faith and its meaning on 'experiences' as some do is epistemologically unsound but to abandon that language limits the range of our interpretation of life and its meaning. We might lose more than we realize in calling religious belief delusional, as we would lose much by ignoring the language of beauty, wonder, morality and science. 'A rational life is one that integrates knowledge into a larger choreography of virtue, imagination, patience, prudence, humility and restraint. Reason is not only knowledge, but knowledge perfected in wisdom' (Hart, 2009: 236).

Thankful for science

I do not accept the charge that religious believers are involved in spreading a serious delusion. Living faith in trust of God is not the same as testing evidence in support of a hypothesis. Far from brooking no argument, religious believers are often engaged in reflecting seriously, even painfully, upon their faith. The history of the church shows how the Christian faith has undergone many different expressions and, when it has been true to itself, has never sought to impose its beliefs on others. No more have faithful Christian scientists sought to oppose religious and scientific convictions, let alone prioritize religion over science. It is one world in which we live and Christian believers are bidden to explore and partner God in this universe, loving God with all their minds. Lucas, after all, is only one in a long tradition of those whose lives embrace both faith and science in the search for truth in this amazing universe.

Jonathan Sacks argues that the important work of scientists, for whom there are special blessings in Jewish prayer books, is the task of explanation. Religion is concerned with interpretation. Science takes things apart to see how they work. Religion puts things together to see what they mean (Sacks, 2011: 284).[12] Atheists hold that there is no inherent meaning in our living and such meaning as might be discerned is our own creation. To seek meaning in and of the universe is to ask a question impossible to answer. Some will assert that a question impossible to answer is not a genuine question at all and those who think they have answers are seductive misleaders. They argue that there is no need for a god hypothesis.

I have already said this stands as a powerful argument but its scope is too limited. There is more to our living, our growing experience of the world, than that which can be proven. Some questions abide and come fresh with each new generation, not least the present one. Who are we? Why are we here? How shall we live? When all the scientific work is done, these questions nag away in our minds.

What counts and evidence, again

Does Ernest Lucas know what he is talking about when he speaks of God? There is no knock-down argument such as would convince those who see life only through the spectacles of scientific methodologies. This is not to say that there is no evidence for religious belief. It is to acknowledge that what counts as evidence relates to the Subject which means that evidence is internal to religious belief and language. The story of Israel, Jesus and the continuing life of the church figure considerably in Lucas's thought. They count as evidence but not in the sense of proving the Subject they affirm. But then 'God' amounts to more than an explanation.

However, let me suggest two tests that might be applied that do not of themselves require any prior religious commitment to be useful. Neither will prove God's existence but will, at least, give some indication of the believer's seriousness of intent and knowledge and what such believing means.

The importance of practice

The first is practical and I invoke the argument of Wittgenstein. I have already suggested that any framework of language (what Wittgenstein called a language game) is one with a corresponding life of practice (what Wittgenstein called a form of life). Some things we learn and come to know only by practice. We learn to swim by swimming, to pray by praying. Those who live only in theory will never get to know the heart of the matter. This is not to argue that we have to do some things in order to know, a kind of learning by doing. It is that the knowing is the doing and the doing is the knowing;. 'to imagine a language-game means to imagine a form of life' (Wittgenstein, 1972: para. 19). That is true of any fundamental proposition underlying any universe of discourse, even science.

> Suppose somebody made this guidance for this life: believing in the Last Judgment. Wherever he does anything, this is before his mind. In a way, how are we to know whether to say he believes this will happen or not?

Asking him is not enough. He will probably say he has proof. But he has what you might call an unshakeable belief. It will show, not by reasoning or by appeal to ordinary grounds for belief, but rather by regulating for all in his life. (Wittgenstein, 1970: 53–419)

Religious belief is not first a matter of having evidence. Holding such a belief is not like entertaining a hypothesis to be tested. It may not even entail a formal expression of this belief. It is religious. It regulates for life and should the declared belief make no difference then it is not a religious belief. In the language of the New Testament, 'Now by this we may be sure that we know him, if we obey his commandments. Whoever says, "I have come to know him", but does not obey his commandments, is a liar, and in such a person the truth does not exist; but whoever obeys his word, truly in this person the love of God has reached perfection' (1 John 2:3–5, NRSV).

Those who declare their faith in God, who show a deep respect for all persons, recognizing in them a sacred claim such that they are cared for with all that is, whose integrity of thought is a matter of honorable practice as they seek coherence in their understanding of their existence with others, such a life might well be taken to indicate a significant depth to their life others do not necessarily know. It is how any claimed knowledge of God might show itself.

There is a mystery here and I know I have not solved it. Indeed I do not think I can solve it. The mystery is that the notion of 'knowledge', apart from religion, seems to run out into the question of in what ways 'knowing how' and 'knowing that' relate and are held together; that is, how the fundamental propositions we believe and the rule by which we live relate. The mystery is that in some way the one is the other. This is something religious believers have always said.

Living before God

The second test I describe as modesty. Both scientific study and theological work have this in common in that neither can claim it has reached the end of the road in understanding. Science submits its findings to examination and the hypothesis, which may not be given up easily, will be abandoned or refined if evidence requires it. It is not that a prior understanding is wrong. It is that

Newton must give way to Einstein and Einstein to who knows what. Questioning is essential to the search for truth. Arrogant certainty is beyond us as the search goes on. There is something tentative, even uncertain, about all serious science.

But this is also the case in religious believing. Our understanding and belief in God undergo change as new factors come to light, as new possibilities are explored, as life is lived before the God who remains a mystery to us. There are forms of religious believing that are simply too confident to be true. The linguistic forms employed themselves become absolutes and so intellectual idols are created. There is a necessary tentativeness in religious believing, that lives with doubt, seeing as in a mirror, dimly (1 Cor. 13:12). Such modesty, honesty and openness is a test of genuine religious belief.

Twice in these closing paragraphs I have used the word 'mystery'. I am, however, cautious about its use. Too easily and quickly, when Christians have been pressed hard about the meaning and sense of their faith they can invoke the notion of 'mystery'.[13] This may be used as a 'get out clause' and represent no more than a form of intellectual laziness. But those who press on with the intellectual quest, not seeking to avoid the hard and threatening questions, come nearer to the genuine mystery at the heart of all; that is, the mystery some call God, elusive yet fundamental to all things. True faith is always faith seeking understanding, but modestly as befits the Subject.

Christians speak of the knowledge of God. When they do so they employ a wide range of meanings of the word 'know', indicating a rich concept as I have tried to show elsewhere (Haymes, 1988). Ernest Lucas comes to his studies in life using different approaches as relate to the subject matter under reflection, as scientist and theologian. As a religious believer he tries to see all things before God. I think he knows what he is talking about.

Notes

1 The term is used of the writings of, among others, Richard Dawkins, Daniel Dennett, Sam Harris and Christopher Hitchens. I shall not be engaging with their work in detail in this short essay, although I hold that their challenge is very significant and that there is no doubt but that their work reflects a growing and widespread mood.
2 I have attempted to outline the logical form of these several claims in *The Concept of the Knowledge of God* (Haymes, 1988).
3 W. D. Hudson was prepared for ministry at the Manchester Baptist College. From 1944 to 1960 he served two pastorates in the north of England before becoming Lecturer, later Reader, in Moral Philosophy at the University of Exeter. A fine teacher and expositor in the analytic tradition, he was a specialist in the work of Ludwig Wittgenstein. His most sustained reflections on religion and rationality are in his Whitley Lectures published as *A Philosophical Approach to Religion* (1974).
4 This is but to simplify the arguments of, among others, Ludwig Wittgenstein (1972) and J. L. Austin (1962).

5 This is a very bald statement of what is much disputed. The early forms of logical positivism have given way before later reflections but the case is so stated here because, in general terms, it is so often uncritically assumed.
6 See the discussion by John Polkinghorne in the Gifford Lectures of 1993–94 (1996: ch. 2).
7 I am drawing here on my discussion of Carnap (Haymes, 1988: 165–66).
8 An obvious example of what I have in mind here is Thomas Helwys, the leader of the first Baptist Church on English soil whose book *A Short Declaration of the Mystery of Iniquity* included an early plea for religious liberty for all (1611). For more contemporary illustrations and discussion see Cavanaugh (1998).
9 This case is vigorously put by Sacks (2011).
10 Always preparing for a game, even dressing, in a particular way may be helpful as a means of focusing confidently on the task.
11 I readily acknowledge in exploring this theme my debt to the writings of H. H. Farmer.
12 Sacks works with the difference between left- and right-brain thinking.
13 I recall the taunt of an atheist student who came to the manse in our days in the Exeter pastorate who would express his exasperation when the appeal to mystery went up. He would sing, 'Mystery, mystery, we all fall down!'

Bibliography

Anscombe, G. E. M. and G. H. von Wright, eds. *On Certainty* (trans. Paul Denis and G. E. M. Anscombe; Oxford: Basil Blackwell, 1974).
Austin, J. L. *How to Do Things with Words* (ed. J. O. Urmson; Oxford: Oxford University Press, 1962).
Bartley III, W. W. *The Retreat to Commitment* (London: Open Court, 1984).
Carnap, Rudolph. 'Empiricism, Semantics and Ontology'. *Revue Internationale de Philosophie* (Bruxelles: 1950).
Cavanaugh, W. T. *Torture and Eucharist; Theology, Politics, and the Body of Christ* (Oxford: Blackwell 1998).
Hart, David Bentley. *Atheist Delusions: The Christian Revolution and Its Fashionable Enemies* (London: Yale University Press, 2009).
Haymes, Brian. *The Concept of the Knowledge of God* (London: Macmillan, 1988).
Hudson, W. D. *A Philosophical Approach to Religion* (London: Macmillan, 1974).
Polkinghorne, John. *The Faith of a Physicist; Reflections of a Bottom-Up Thinker* (Minneapolis: Fortress Press, 1996).
Popper, Karl. *The Logic of Scientific Discovery* (London: Hutchinson, 1959).
Rice, Daniel. *Reinhold Niebuhr Revisited; Engagements with an American Original* (Grand Rapids: Eerdmans, 2009).
Sacks, Jonathan. *The Great Partnership: God, Science and the Search for Meaning* (London: Hodder & Stoughton, 2011).
Wittgenstein, Ludwig. *Lectures and Conversation on Aesthetics, Psychology and Religious Belief* (ed. Cyril Barrett; Oxford: Basil Blackwell, 1970).
———. *Philosophical Investigations* (trans. G. E. M. Anscombe; Oxford: Basil Blackwell, 1972).

Yoder, John Howard. *A Pacifist Way of Knowing: John Howard Yoder's Nonviolent Epistemology* (ed Christian E. Early and Ted G. Grimsrud; Eugene, OR: Cascade Books, 2010).

God
> you invite us
> ignite us
> entice us
> into scaling the contours of
knowledge.

Make our minds
> as sharp as flints
> as expansive as night skies
> as free as eagles.

And, as we drill deep for truth,
give us hearts humbled by grace,
made modest by mercy

7

The Environment and the Developing World

Elaine Storkey

As both scientist and theologian, Ernest Lucas embodies Christianity's rejection of a dualist world-view. It is significant that, for him, science does not simply meld with faith, but grows from faith and reinforces belief in a Creator God. Whether in the detailed empirical work of analyzing aspects of the world we live in, or 'big picture' debates in cosmology or biology, Ernest has been committed to integration, rejecting any clumsy dismissal of theology by scientists, or of science by theologians. So it seems appropriate that this chapter focuses on a topic where this integration occurs at both a practical and a theoretical level: the environment and the developing world. When we look at ecology and the Global South it usually involves issues studied by a large number of scientific disciplines: atmospheric physics, ecology, biology, meteorology, economics, agronomy, entomology, hydrology, to mention a few. But for the integrating scholar, we are also drawn into theology, hermeneutics, ethics, pastoralia and missiology. For these areas open up some of the most fundamental aspects of the relationship between human life and the rest of creation. It is here, then, where I want to begin.

Whose environment?

The term 'environment' implies that the 'natural world' is the context for our human life. And so it is. Yet, wherever we look in biblical revelation, we are reminded that 'nature' is God's world. More accurately, 'nature' is 'creation' and God is the author of the whole of creation in its intricacy and diversity. From the earliest books in the Bible, God is identified as the originator of life and the one who brings creation into being. In the first two, quite different, chapters of Genesis, God is disclosed as Creator of the heavens and earth, the planets, the stars, the land with its vegetation, the waters teeming with living creatures, the birds flying across the expanse of the sky, the land animals, livestock, and human life. In succinct prose and dramatic narrative we are taken into the world-view of divine purpose, authorship and thought and hear God's reflection on all he had made—that it was very good.

It is therefore not unreasonable to begin our exploration of the environment and the developing world with some reflections about the Creator God revealed in the Scriptures. We find God is both creative and imaginative, personal and relational. The universe is an ordered whole, with interdependence built into its very structure. Everything is in relationship. What is more, relationship exists within the Godhead itself—a relationship of dynamic inter-personality between divine persons that we have come to call the Father, Son and Holy Spirit. This interpersonal Triune God is defined by love, indeed is the origin of love, and that love reaches out from God to embrace the world God has made. The mystery of creation's dependence on God is expressed exquisitely in Paul's letter to the Colossian church. He describes Jesus Christ as the 'image of the invisible God' and then slowly draws us into his cosmic significance as the one who is 'before all things' and the one in whom 'all things hold together'.[1]

Biblical revelation is a wonderful source for glimpsing the relationship between God and creation. The detailed care and delight which God expresses for the world he has made is expressed by the psalmists and the prophets in so many graphic images. We note it in the prophet Isaiah: 'It is I who made the earth and created mankind upon it. My own hands stretched out the heavens; I marshalled their starry hosts.'[2] Or in Jeremiah: 'God made the earth by his power, he founded the world by his wisdom and stretched out the heavens by his understanding ... He makes clouds rise from the ends of the earth. He sends lightning with the rain, and brings out the wind from his storehouses.'[3]

It is there in the imageric questions that God fires at Job:

Who shut up the sea behind doors when it burst forth from the womb ... ?
Have you ever given orders to the morning, or shown the dawn its place ... ?
Have you comprehended the vast expanses of the earth? ...
Who cuts a channel for the torrents of rain, and a path for the thunderstorm, to water a land where no one lives, a desert with no one in it?[4]

And in the fulsome exuberance of the psalms: 'The heavens are telling the glory of God and the skies proclaim his handiwork';[5] 'In the beginning you laid the foundations of the earth, and the heavens are the works of your hands'.[6]

Sometimes, the language is both tender and intimate when the psalmist presents God's connectedness with the world he has made: 'Every animal of the forest is mine, and the cattle on a thousand hills. I know every bird in the mountains, and the creatures of the field are mine.'[7]

Nor are these reminders of God's relationship with creation confined to the Hebrew Scriptures. In the gospels too, Christ himself recalls how God feeds the ravens, clothes the lilies, tends the grass and cares for the sparrows that we sell two for a penny. And since God cares so deeply for such basic living things, how much more does he care for us, who are made 'in his own image'?[8] That question is answered throughout the gospels, not least by pointing us to the ministry, death and resurrection of Christ.

Although we humans are also creaturely, sharing the fundamental structure of much of the rest of creation (more than 98 per cent of our DNA is apparently found in higher primates and 33 per cent of our DNA is in bananas!) the difference between us and our fellow creatures is very significant. God creates us with moral responsibility, freedom to choose, and with spiritual awareness, and welcomes us into relationship as sons and daughters. It is to us and not to the primates or lions that the guardianship of the rest of creation is given. It is we, not the elephant or ants, who will be held accountable before God. And in our stewardship of God's world we are required to treat it with honor, and not usurp its power, or destroy its beauty. We are called, in effect, to reflect the love God shows to us and to the rest of creation. For that love is the central dimension through which the world was made and the key structure for us to live by. When love is violated, the consequences can be dire. It has often been said that we need to love if we want to be happy. But increasingly we are realizing that we need to love if we want to survive.

The theme of creation is therefore central to the biblical story of our relationship with God, each other and the natural world. Yet, as we know, it is not the only story which unfolds in God's revelation. The Bible also refers to the way these relationships have been corrupted by sin—and its expression in our lack of love, our self-centredness, violence and abuse. Paul's letter to the early church at Rome speaks of the whole creation being subjected to sin, groaning, like a woman in childbirth.[9] It is a picture of brokenness and anguish, pain and struggle. Yet this is also a hopeful image, for it points us to new beginnings, to redemption, and renewal. It shows us creation waiting to be released from bondage through the children of God. This amazing passage was written centuries before the measurements of science, or before any concept of climate change or habitat loss had become an issue for the planet. And yet in its sombre, prophetic note it reminds us of the urgency of our human responsibilities—both for the initial stewardship of creation and for the work of redemptive change.

Since this responsibility for the environment is so clearly ours, it seems important to ask, then—how are we doing?

Ecological crisis

The answer to that simple question is not encouraging. Our appalling failure has become very public—the subject of reports from scientists even more than from theologians. More than a decade ago, in its publication of 2001, the United Nations Intergovernmental Panel for Climate Change (IPCC) called attention to the need for lifestyle changes if we were to steward the earth responsibly. Noting that rises in the earth's temperature had been higher in the 1990s than in any other decade on record this report warned that 'Greenhouse gas forcing in the 21st century could set in motion large-scale, high-impact, non-linear, and potentially abrupt changes in physical and biological systems over the coming decades to millennia, with a wide range of associated likelihoods'.[10]

It also predicted that some impacts of anthropogenic climate change may be slow to become apparent, and some could be irreversible if measures were not taken. The IPCC was clear what those measures should be. We should reduce greenhouse gases in the atmosphere. The rise of carbon dioxide emissions had to be stabilized or reversed: 'The stabilisation of atmospheric CO_2 concentrations at 450, 650 or 1000ppm would require global anthropogenic CO_2 emissions to drop below the year 1990 levels ... Eventually CO_2 emissions would need to decline to a very small fraction of current emissions.'[11]

The data, graphs and tables which the IPCC produced are now part of the archives of climatology. We are familiar with the graphs which present the variations in the earth's temperature over the last 140 years, and over the last thousand years. Particularly striking were the tables which showed the changes over the last thousand years alongside the projections into the year 2100. A rapid increase in average global surface temperature of 0.5 to 1°C has taken place in the last twenty years and a rise of 1.4 to 5.8°C is to be expected by 2100.

Although the IPCC publication was widely discussed, it did not bring any overnight rush in governmental policy decisions, or indeed in public resolve to meet the challenge. Valuable time passed as people questioned the urgency and debated the predictions. From the beginning there was a reluctance among some politicians and scientists, particularly in the United States, to accept the data. In the UK too, opponents articulated their scepticism. By 2005, the Royal Society felt it necessary to issue a document to address the controversy. This publication, 'A Guide to Fact and Fiction about Climate Change', was authored by a group of scientists which included Sir David Wallace, treasurer of the Royal Society and Sir John Houghton, one of the former chairs of the Intergovernmental Panel on Climate Change's Scientific Assessment Working Group. They examined twelve misleading arguments put forward by the opponents of urgent action on climate change, arguments challenging the evidence for global warming, and alleging that the IPCC was politicized.

Although some years later the Royal Society reviewed the tone of some of its earlier documents, it has never deflected from its position that evidence points definitively to rises in the Earth's temperature which cannot be explained without reference to human activity.

Interpretation and impacts of global warming

The idea that climate change could be explained entirely by natural cycles of life on the planet had been subject to scrutiny for many years. No one doubted that there were fluctuations in the Earth's temperature over time, and that these fluctuations were influenced by natural processes including solar and volcanic activity. Yet the consensus was that these could not explain the rapid rises in temperature measured in the last two decades of the twentieth century and beyond. Tables characteristically compared the temperature fluctuations that might be reasonably assumed without anthropogenic involvement with what is actually the case.

The widespread agreement among scientists is that what is indicated in these graphs cannot be explained by 'natural' cycles, but that human 'intervention' plays a significant part. Anthropogenic burning of fossil fuels, use of chemicals in manufacture and production, emission of greenhouse gases, all contribute to the warming of our planet. We should be aiming to limit our output to ensure that we keep the concentration of CO_2 below 350 parts per million. The data updated in 2010 by the Hawaii Observatory shows our failure in stark terms, with CO_2 reaching a concentration of between 385 and 395 parts per million.

The Fourth Assessment Report of the Intergovernmental Panel was published in November 2007. The tone was definitive and many of the earlier qualifications were no longer articulated. Its summary left little room for the uncertainties formerly expressed: 'Today, the time for doubt has passed. The IPCC has unequivocally affirmed the warming of our climate system, and linked it directly to human activity. Slowing or even reversing the existing trends of global warming is the defining challenge of our age.'[12]

The indications were that the situation was worse than envisaged in 2001. The report suggested that 29,000 observational data series from 75 studies showed significant changes in physical and biological systems which are more than 89 per cent consistent with effects from global warming. They pinpointed many interrelated factors. Some of these relate to water as drought-affected areas increase, and heavy precipitation leads to high rise in floods and flood risks, especially in the mega-deltas of Asia and Africa. Along with this goes a decline of water stored in glaciers and snow cover, acidification of oceans, negative impacts on marine shell-forming organisms, disappearance of coral reefs and serious disturbance of ecosystems. Linked with these issues is the further problem of coastal erosion where the sea level rises and coastal wetlands decline as they become starved of sediment. Inevitably this has effects on agriculture and forestry and on those communities who live along the shore line.

Loss of species and biodiversity in the environment has also been put under the spotlight. In 2004 researchers on five continents surveyed the ecosystems covering 20 per cent of the Earth's surface and found that if surface temperature rose even to the middle of the expected range, between 15 per cent and 37 per cent of the world's species will become extinct by 2050. Biologists like Stephen Hubbell, of the Smithsonian Tropical Research Institute, believe this will rise even higher as the century progresses. Human beings are already using 40 per cent of all the 'plant biomass' produced by photosynthesis on the planet—very disturbing when we consider that most life on Earth depends on plants. He points out that some three-quarters of all species thought to reside on Earth live in rain forests, and they are being cut down at the substantial rate of about 0.5 per cent per year. Hubbell speaks of this 'sixth documented mass extinction' on the surface of the Earth as unique, in that the other five were caused by physical processes, whereas this is strongly related to climate change and habitat loss due to human activities. His summary of the situation is stark: 'The present extinction crisis is very serious. With no change in the rates of habitat loss and with expected climate change now on the horizon we could lose anywhere from 20% to 50% of all species in the next 100 years.'[13]

The Royal Society was prompted to publish its own statement in 2010, urged on 'in view of the ongoing public and political debates'. Implicitly it addressed the ongoing scepticism voiced among a minority of critics. A working group chaired by Professor John Pethica, vice president of the Royal Society, produced *Climate Change: A Summary of the Science*. Its aim was to outline the current scientific evidence on climate change, highlighting the areas where the science is now well established, where there is debate, and where uncertainties remain. The report concluded: 'Climate change science has advanced markedly over the past 20 years, as a result of many factors. These include improved methods for handling long-term climate data sets, the ever-lengthening record of climate observations, improved measurement techniques, including those from satellites, better understanding of the climate system, improved methods for simulating the climate system, and increased computer power.'[14]

Significantly, these advances had increased, not dented the confidence of the Royal Society in the findings of the IPCC with regard to anthropogenic global warming: 'One indication of these advances is the increasing degree of confidence in the attribution of climate change to human activity as expressed in the key conclusions of IPCC Working Group 1 (WG1) in its assessments.[15]

The environment and human life

The hundreds of environment research projects conducted over the last few years across the world have increased concern not simply for the health of our planet and its loss of species, but for the well-being of those who live on it. In almost every study of water, glaciation, food production, public health, deforestation, freak weather conditions, floods, hurricanes, droughts, animal welfare, insect-borne diseases the results have been sobering. We have become used to reports like one in 2005, from researchers from University College,

London, and the Met Office, which told us that 'the Amazonian forest is currently near its critical resiliency threshold'. They pointed out that 'with just a small degree of warming 'the interior of the Amazon Basin becomes essentially void of vegetation'.[16] The Fourth IPCC report suggested that observational evidence from all continents and most oceans showed that many natural systems are now affected by regional climate change. They gave examples of increasing ground instability in permafrost regions, rock avalanches in mountain regions, along with changes in Arctic and Antarctic ecosystems.

Although the science of climate change is conducted in university departments across the world, the impacts of climate change have become the business of everyone. Back in 2007, Sir John Holmes, British diplomat, and then the United Nations under-secretary-general for humanitarian affairs, pointed to a growing problem in the record number of floods, droughts and storms around the world that year. Few of these floods had made headlines in any UK newspaper but collectively they told a powerful story. He explained his concern: 'All these events on their own didn't have massive death tolls, but if you add all these little disasters together you get a mega disaster . . . We are seeing the effects of climate change. Any year can be a freak but the pattern looks pretty clear to be honest.'[17]

In fact, the UN Office for the Co-ordination of Humanitarian Affairs (OCHA) issued 13 emergency 'flash' appeals from January to October 2007 for international disasters—more than three times the record held two years earlier. And of these 13 emergency appeals, 12 were deemed to be climate-related. Weeks later OCHA put out another flash report as 80,000 people were hit by floods in Southern Africa. Sir John Holmes' warning that more appeals would be likely had sadly come true.

Overall, the United Nations Disaster Assessment and Coordination teams (UNDAC) carried out 14 missions in 2007, 70 per cent of them in response to hurricanes and floods, giving us in the words of John Holmes a 'curtain raiser' on the future. He claimed that nine out of every ten disasters are now climate-related.[18] In 2011 the UNDAC review claimed: 'The combination of urbanisation, environmental degradation and the apparent effects of climate change are significant factors contributing to the impact of disasters, such as the 2010 Haiti Earthquake and Pakistan floods. It is predicted that by 2015 around 375 million people will be affected by climate-related disasters every year.'[19]

In the view of Lord Paddy Ashdown; 'We are caught in a race between the growing size of the humanitarian challenge, and our ability to cope; between humanity and catastrophe. And, at present, this is not a race we are winning.'[20]

The developing world

The 'humanitarian challenge' has particular significance for communities which already face hardship. Tragically, it is those who live closest to the margins of poverty and poor health who suffer the most lethal consequences of climate change and environmental degradation. Of the world's population of seven billion almost three billion live on less than two dollars a day. Poverty is not simply economic, however, but multiple. These same low-income people are also likely to be subject to hunger, malnutrition, high infant and maternal mortality rates, disease and epidemics, low access to fresh water, few health provisions, poor educational opportunities, limited access to information, transport, and financial services, illiteracy, indebtedness, global exclusions, powerlessness and, increasingly, vulnerability to climate change. As IPCC Chairman Rajendra Pachauri predicted, 'It is the poorest of the poor in the world, and this includes poor people even in prosperous societies, who are going to be the worst hit.'[21] Even the World Wildlife Fund showed its concern for the burden of the poor in its statement of 2006: 'Global warming is already happening. Its impact is being felt most by the world's poorest people. Food production, water supplies, public health, and people's livelihoods are all being damaged and undermined. Global warming threatens to reverse human progress, making the United Nations' Millennium Development Goals for poverty reduction unachievable.'[22]

The unequal weight of the burden of climate change is something which humanitarian agencies have known for many years. In February 2003 the United Nations Environment Programme (UNEP) warned in Nairobi that one result of global warming would be rising levels of disease, famine and poverty in Africa. In those parts of Africa that became dryer, agriculture was bound to decline. The sheer vulnerability of food systems would be evident when arable land was lost as a result of declining ground-water levels and rising sea levels. For then, land no longer becomes suitable for cultivating crops. The increasing levels of saline lead to aridity of soil. Small fresh-water lakes also disappear with swelling seas, and there is a reduction in fish stocks.

Rising sea levels inevitably mean a shortage of fresh water. Both the IPCC and the World Meteorological Association have alerted us to this danger. In Africa's large catchment basins of Niger, Lake Chad and Senegal, total available water has already decreased by 40 to 60 per cent, with subsequent rising levels of drought and the spread of deserts, including the Sahara. In fact, as the problem is replicated in many vulnerable areas across the globe, the number of people likely to suffer water stress in the next two decades has been put at more than a hundred million.

The impacts of all this on human health were identified in the IPCC Report in 2007 and are now well documented.[23] Those living in the Global South are particularly at risk. Illnesses related to rising temperatures multiply. Witness the increases in cardio-respiratory diseases due to higher concentration of ground-level ozone. Vector-borne diseases have increased too, as mosquitoes thrive in warmer temperatures and new strains of pathogenic microorganisms develop. There have also been subsequent increases in malaria, diarrhea, cholera, river blindness and a cluster of associated complaints. We could take any one of these problems and see how its distribution is grossly disproportionate. For example, nearly half of the world's population is infected by vector-borne diseases, which bring high morbidity and high mortality, yet the overwhelming impact is felt in developing countries. When we add the perennial problems of multiple poverty, outlined above, we begin to understand the incredible burden on the world's poor.

The effects of climate change, in the erratic nature of the weather, does not help either. A short spell of drought or a wetter than usual rainy season bring problems, but not insurmountable ones. Yet changes in precipitation are not merely about increasing or decreasing rainfall. They can mean that the rainy seasons begin much later, or earlier than normal, or that sudden rain spells can hit a region when it is supposed to be dry. These changes and the increase of heavy, monsoon-like rains and higher temperatures have a much greater impact on life in vulnerable areas. They can mean that the river beds dry up, or that the harvest is washed away. And not only do they affect crops, farming, cattle and livelihood, but they promote the spread of a host of diseases like malaria, dengue fever, yellow fever and encephalitis. With global warming, mosquitoes and other disease-carrying insects are now found in areas where they were once absent.

Sir John Holmes reinforced all this in 2009 when in an address to the British parliament lunchtime meeting, he pointed out that climate change was becoming a major driver of humanitarian need, and likely to become a huge factor in future forced displacement. 'The point is that climate change is not just a future threat. It is an actual danger to millions of people, including many of the most vulnerable groups in the world. And this is bound to get worse.'

In fact, he suggested that our response to disasters themselves is becoming out of date, and increasingly difficult to manage. It is less relevant to define humanitarian action by reference to trigger events such as natural disasters or conflicts than to recognize that in many areas drought, flooding and sea-level rise now become the norm. His conclusion was that 'climate change threatens to overwhelm the current capacity of the humanitarian system to respond effectively and to impose new models of prevention, preparedness and response'.[24]

This is recognized by many who work with humanitarian efforts across the globe. Ten years of work in development can be wiped out by one flood, but long-term environmental change inevitably imposes an ongoing burden on the world's poor. The Christian relief and development charity, Tearfund, of which I am president, now finds it must respond to climate change issues not just in its disaster and emergency work, but in addressing the new 'normal' needs of communities. Many of our partners in sub-Saharan Africa and South Asia are struggling with more severe droughts and desertification; farmers can work all year but reap no harvest. Failed harvests, food insecurity and water scarcity afflict communities who are already vulnerable because of poverty; malnutrition, diseases and poor health are never far behind. Consequently, along with many other NGOs, our own work has had to include adaptation:

ensuring that communities can adapt to the current and future consequences of climate change that we know to be already inevitable.

The terrible irony is, of course, that although the poor of the world face the consequences of climate change so severely, they themselves contribute little to its existence. We have known this too for a long time. In 2000 our own government declared: 'On a global and national level, the poor are not usually the major cause of environmental degradation. They consume too little, contribute little to pollution and waste, and have too little access to soils, forests, fisheries and freshwater to be a major source of degradation.'[25]

Even the diet of the poor in the developing world conveys this truth. Unlike the heavy meat consumption of most of us in the West, a grain and vegetable diet is the mainstay of those in poor communities. Whereas our cattle consume tons of grass and grain in a lifetime, their goats, pigs or poultry graze around the huts in the compound, and obligingly fertilize the ground. Furthermore, pound for pound, beef production generates greenhouse gases that contribute more than 13 times as much to global warming as do the gases emitted from producing chicken. For potatoes, the multiplier is 57.[26]

That is why adaptation in the developing world cannot be the main response to climate change, and why as Christians we also need to be active in advocacy and mitigation, addressing the responsibilities of the richer nations. Over the last few years Christian development organizations have begun to work and campaign together to increase our effectiveness in advocacy, putting our collective weight behind measures to reduce rapidly the levels of greenhouse gas emissions, especially in developed countries. While poorer countries need access to clean energy solutions to help them develop without high emissions, richer nations need to adopt sustainable development. Low-carbon living, where we do not rely on burning fossil fuels, must be embraced not just as a one-off strategy, but as the way of future living.

Christian responses: initiatives and sceptics

Given all that we know, it is therefore very evident to many Christians that the need to address climate change and its effects on human life and environment must be one of the central aspects of our Christian calling today. And many have taken this seriously. As long ago as 2002 the Catholic Church pointed out that 80 per cent of the world's resources are commandeered by the richest 20 per cent of the world's population, and much of the consumption of the rich becomes waste almost immediately. Meanwhile, 20 per cent of humanity remains destitute, lacking even basic necessities. Their statement sums up why we need to respond: 'A way of life that disregards and damages God's creation, forces the poor into greater poverty, and threatens the right of future generations to a healthy environment and to their fair share of the earth's wealth and resources, is contrary to the vision of the Gospel.'[27]

The gospel in fact underlines key principles which make up both our theology of human personhood and our theology of justice. In offering good news to all people, it teaches us the equal significance of every human being before God. The crippled Bangladeshi widow, struggling with poverty and AIDS, is as valuable in God's eyes as the wealthiest and most powerful media tycoon in the West. Our attitude and social policies must reflect her worth. In acknowledging the universal condition of sin, it teaches us to stem the urge towards self-righteousness, and to recognize with penitence our own sins of negligence towards other people. We cannot ignore the suffering we create, simply because we are able to ignore it. In inviting us to love our neighbours as ourselves, it disallows partiality and self-serving, urging us to protect the vulnerable and seek the common good.

When we share a common understanding of the implications of the gospel it is possible for Christian agencies to work together in advocacy for the environment and to alleviate the hardship experienced by the world's poor. This is what is now happening as CAFOD (the Catholic relief agency), Tearfund and Christian Aid work together in joint campaigns to implement a Christian vision for justice, as illustrated by the 'Creation Care' and 'Whose Earth?' campaigns of 2011 and 2012. Many other Christian environmental organizations have also sprung up over the last few decades, keen to take the integration of Christian faith and action seriously. Consequently, environmental and climate issues are being addressed in a large number of contexts: in education with the John Ray Initiative; in simpler lifestyles with Breathe; in hands-on creation care with A Rocha; in lifestyle, liturgy and campaigning with Operation Noah; in partnerships and advocacy with Christian Ecology Link. Hundreds of churches, national groups and eco-congregations have taken on carbon fasting commitments, recycling waste or fostering green energy use. Consequently, Christians from many walks of life are making both an impact and a witness, showing that we have responsibility for God's creation, and the poor of God's world.

Yet this still is not the case universally. There are also pockets of Christian resistance which have been both vocal and effective. Often this opposition comes when proclamation and social action have not been integrated in a biblical worldview. Opponents often argue that the Christian task is not to concern itself with social, environmental or justice issues, but to concentrate on preaching and evangelism. When we do turn our attention to ethical issues, it must be only to emphasize traditional morality which has always been at the heart of Christianity. This is expressed succinctly in a letter posted by James Dobson where he expresses disapproval of the interest in global warming, shown by Rich Cizik of the National Association of Evangelicals in the USA. He even sees some conspiracy behind this: 'We have observed that Cizik and others are using the global warming controversy to shift the emphasis away from the great moral issues of our time, notably the sanctity of human life, the integrity of marriage and the teaching of sexual abstinence and morality to our children.'

The remarks highlight differences in Christian attitudes towards environmental issues, particularly within the evangelical wing in North America. Dobson's comment received a swift response from Jim Wallis, founder of Sojourner's, who sees no biblical reason at all for refusing to be involved in this area. He questions what counts as a 'great moral issue': 'Is the fact that 30,000 children will die globally today, and every day, from needless hunger and disease a great moral issue for evangelical Christians? How about the reality of 3 billion of God's children living on less than $2 per day? And isn't the still-widespread and needless poverty in our own country, the richest nation in the world, a moral scandal?'[28]

In fact there is no 'either/or' in the sanctity of human life, sexual morality, creation care and justice for the poor. The call of the gospel is surely 'both-and'. We pray, preach and proclaim the call of Christ, recognizing that he is indeed the one who offers good news for the poor, freedom for captives and release for the oppressed. Putting all that in action is part of our own thankfulness for Christ's redeeming love.

Sadly, many of those who do oppose involvement in climate change legislation or resist measures to reduce emissions of CO_2 are influenced more by politics than by Christian theology. They often have a strong commitment in the so-called 'free market' and hold avowedly right-wing libertarian views. Consequently there is an incipient fear that climate science and policy measures are a covert way for liberal environmentalists and governments to diminish freedom for individuals; that green jobs, renewable energy and climate legislation 'engineer' the market and hinder economic progress in the affluent world. And even though other Christians feel that these political assumptions do not sit easily with a biblical world-view gleaned from the prophets and the gospels, the assumptions themselves still exercise a powerful grip on the minds of those who hold them.

Our prophetic calling

I want to conclude this chapter as I began, with a call to heed what the Bible has to teach us about God's relationship with the world he has made and about our own responsibility for both stewardship and justice. In this, it is important to acknowledge the voice of the prophets. For they were those who spoke the oracles of God to their culture—warning others who could quite easily find out for themselves, that things are not as they should be. The prophets acted as eyes that penetrated below the surface, ears that noticed the hypocrisy and justifications that people use to excuse doing what they want, tongues that were willing to speak to disturb complacency and inertia. The prophets were rarely popular for they brought people up against the reality of how they were living. They spoke to ways of life which were actually ways of death, and spelled out the consequences of continuing in those ways.

This is so evident in one of the prophecies of Isaiah, when he speaks into a worshipping and observant community with the challenge of God's word in Isaiah 58. As far as the people were concerned, they were doing everything necessary to warrant the blessings of God: observing the law, fasting, practising humility and ritual penitence. So why, they wanted to know, were they not being blessed? Why was God ignoring their worship? The response of God through Isaiah cuts into every refusal to see worship, prayer, work and justice as a seamless whole. God's reply is a strong rebuke: their idea of a fast is simply hollow. His concept of fasting is much deeper—involving loosening the chains of justice, paying fair wages, alleviating hunger, sharing with the poor and abandoning self-interest. Only when these are an integral part of our worship can we be said to be living an authentic life of faith, and may we expect the fruit of blessing.

Just as the prophets of old spoke God's word into human failure of their day, so today we have prophets who draw us into a bigger vision of our lives together on this planet. They take seriously the parables of Jesus—the rich man and Lazarus, the sheep and the goats, the rich fool, the vineyard workers. They recognize, like Rowan Williams that '[w]e stand before God's judgment on these matters. In life we have to make moral choices over our sex life and over our domestic and financial affairs. We make choices of moral significance and our relation to the environment is no exception.'[29] They understand, like Sir John Houghton, the danger of turning our backs on our responsibility for change. 'As a climate scientist who has worked on this issue for several decades, first as head of the Meteorological Office, and then as co-chair of scientific assessment for the UN intergovernmental panel on climate change, the impacts of global warming are such that I have no hesitation in describing it as a "weapon of mass destruction".'[30]

We must both heed the prophets and be ready to join them in rebuking the governments of the world for past failures and asking them to enact future policies that will protect and enhance life on our planet. For the call to a sustainable future, where there is greater justice for the vulnerable and greater care of creation, will remain a key challenge for the affluent world. To bring the whole of life, including consumption lifestyles and economic activity, under the will of God requires sacrifice, urgent action and a fundamental change of attitude. Yet, if the creation is to be conserved and the poor released from the hardship of paying for our self-indulgence it is the only way forward. And for Christians, the call to prophetic witness, scientific work, prayer, loving action and justice-seeking must take its full place in the life of our churches as we walk obediently in God's grace, and seek to love his world.

Notes

1 Col. 1:15–18, NRSV.
2 Isa. 45:12, NIV.
3 Jer. 10:12–13, NIV.
4 Job 38 8, 12, 18, 25–26 NIV (adapted slightly).
5 Ps. 19:1–2, NRSV (adapted slightly).
6 Ps. 102:25, NIV.
7 Ps. 50:10–11, NIV.
8 Matt. 6:28, 10 29; Luke 12:24.
9 Rom. 8:22.
10 IPCC. *Climate Change 2001. Synthesis Report*: Summary for Policy-makers (2001): p. 14.
11 IPCC, *Climate Change 2001*, pp. 19–22.
12 IPCC, 2007.
13 UCLA Institute of the Environment and Sustainability. Interview with Stephen Hubbell, 2011 <http://www.environment.ucla.edu/news/article.asp?parentid=11796>.
14 Royal Society, *Climate Change: A Summary of the Science*, September 2010 DES1929 sections 51/52.
15 Royal Society, *Climate Change*.
16 Sharon A. Cowling et al. 'Contrasting Simulated Past and present Responses of the Amazonian Forest to Atmospheric Change'. *Philosophical Transactions of the Royal Society* 359 (29 March 2004): pp. 539–47.
17 Julian Borger, 'Climate Change Disaster is upon Us, Warns UN'. *The Guardian* (5 October 2007).
18 Opening Remarks: DIHAD 2008, United Nations Office for the Coordination of Humanitarian Affairs (OCHA), 8 April 2008.
19 Humanitarian Emergency Response Review (HERR), DFID 2011, quoted in *United Nations Disaster Assessment and Co-ordination Team Review* (December 2011): p. 13.
20 Lord (Paddy) Ashdown (2011), Forward to the *Humanitarian Emergency Response Review*.
21 Rajendra Pachauri. 'Climate Change Impacts, Adaptation and Vulnerability'. Working Group II Contribution to the Intergovernmental Panel on Climate Change Fourth Assessment Report on Climate Change (2007).
22 World Wildlife Fund. Factsheet: 'Global Warming and Poverty' (2006): p. 1.
23 See, for example, J.P. Majra and A. Gur, 'Climate Change and Health: Why should India be Concerned?', *Indian Journal of Occupational and Environmental Medicine* (April 2009): pp. 11–16; Priva Shetty, 'Climate Change and Insect-Borne Diseases: Facts and Figures', *Science and Development Network* (September 2009).
24 Sir John Holmes. 'The Humanitarian Implications of Climate Change'. Speech (18 March 2009).
25 DIFD. 'Achieving Sustainability: Poverty Elimination and the Environment' (October 2000): p. 20.
26 Nathan Fiala. 'How Meat Contributes to Global Warming'. *Scientific American* (February 2009).
27 The Catholic Bishops Conference of England and Wales 2002. *The Call of Creation. God's Invitation and the Human Response* (London: CAFOD, 2008)

28 Jim Wallis. 'Dr Dobson, Let's Have a Real Debate'. *Huffington Post* (6 March 2007).
29 Rowan Williams. *Sunday Times* (23 July 2006).
30 Sir John Houghton. *The Guardian* (28 July 2003).

No more hand-wringing prayers,
> words that are content to express mild dissatisfaction
> and lukewarm regard of the suffering of others.

No more nestling in to a well-worn acknowledgment of regret,
> words that betray the 'but what can we do' tone of our
> > hearts
> and 'not really my problem' whine of our souls.

No more, God, no more.

The brokenness of the world
is borne on the backs of the poor,
while the rich sigh and go shopping,
larding out on over-consumption
and hollow hoarding.

For your sake, God, no more!

Drive us to action
channel our anger
detach us from small preoccupations
and unite us in Christ, crucified and resurrected,
who calls us to follow,
radically, prophetically, sacrificially, justly,
to build a shalom-filled world

8

Hopeful Disciples in a Time of Climate Change

John Weaver

In this chapter we will engage with the current concerns over climate change and, focusing on the nature of God, find hope for living hopefully in God's world. This is a theme which is addressed by Ernest Lucas in some of his writings. He has explored the link between salvation and a redeemed creation; living out our belief in God; and hope that is founded in the coming kingdom of God.

As a scientist Ernest has maintained an interest in the issues of climate change through his involvement with the John Ray Initiative,[1] which seeks to explore the relationships between Christianity, science and the environment. Ernest has been a member of the JRI Board and is currently its publications editor.

We will use these aspects of Ernest's work to shape the rest of this chapter, but first we consider some of the features of the current state of concern for the environment.

The current debates about climate change and the global environment

The United Nations Climate Change Conference (COP 17), Durban 2011, delivered a breakthrough on the international community's response to climate change. In this the second largest meeting of its kind, the negotiations advanced in a balanced fashion with the implementation of the Second Kyoto Protocol, the Bali Action Plan, and the Cancun Agreements. The outcomes included a decision by parties to adopt a universal legal agreement on climate change as soon as possible, and no later than 2015—the 'Durban Platform'. A policy 'roadmap' was secured, leading to a legally binding agreement by 2015, and implementation by all countries to reduce carbon emissions by 2020. But we may note that many hopes and fine words were expressed after the previous climate change conferences in Copenhagen, 2009, and Cancun, 2010. Prevarication and disagreements have continued to mark the responses of many.

Sadly the UK Government's commitment to addressing climate change is weakening. In the twentieth-anniversary edition of the *Big Issue* in October 2011, fourth in their twenty issues facing Britain was climate change. Green MP, Caroline Lucas, writes:

> I am deeply concerned about the government's obvious lack of commitment to environmental policy. Whether it is scrapping the Sustainable Development Commission, reforming planning laws, developers proposing a forest sell-off, offering too weak proposals on energy efficiency, or failing to properly capitalise the Green Investment Bank, these are not the actions of a government overly concerned about its green credentials.
>
> A green economy offers a compelling vision for the future: policies to address the climate crisis can help create hundreds of thousands of jobs in clean industries and help lift us out of economic stagnation. (2011)

In fact Sir Nicholas Stern, who earlier this century was commissioned by the UK Government to make an economic assessment of climate change, made a similar observation. His report, published in November 2006, dealt with the economics of climate change and presented some dire warnings concerning the results of inaction in addressing carbon emissions and a 2°C rise in average global surface temperature.[2] By the time of the Copenhagen climate change conference in February 2009, Stern warned that governments should prepare for a 4°C rise. Climatologists stated that such a rise would lead to the loss of 85 per cent of the Amazon rainforest. Stern referred to climate change as 'the greatest and widest-ranging market failure ever seen', but noted that addressing climate change offered a return on investment and an improvement to the UK's economic situation.

But with no sign of the world governments taking action to reduce humanity's carbon footprint, Sir John Houghton (President of JRI and former head of the Intergovernmental Panel on Climate Change's scientific assessment working group) considers that average global surface temperature is most likely to increase by between 3°C and 4°C above the pre-industrial revolution temperatures during this century, rather than the more optimistic 2°C that had been hoped for in 2006. The causes of inaction include the global financial crisis—we can't afford to deal with climate change—and sceptical views concerning the reality of climate change and its human causation. The results of inaction may be catastrophic.

There is uncertainty in these scientific predictions, but not of the sort that the sceptical voices suggest. Global temperatures are following the predictions of the scientific models, but scientists recognize that there is an uncertainty factor of two; for example, we might predict certain climate measurements by 2040, which with a factor two uncertainty will mean those events arriving in 2030 or 2050.

We can study local events, such as floods in Oxford in 1898, 1947, 2000, 2003, 2007, and ask if they are the result of climate change. These are rare events, but we can observe that they are becoming more frequent. Generally we can predict that northern-hemisphere winters will become wetter and African and Indian winters will become drier.[3]

We can also consider the effect of climate change on the occurrence of freak weather events; for example, the exceptional rainfall and ensuing floods in Cumbria in November 2009. We can state that the probability of such events increases but this does not mean that it is certain. Explanation is the key, for while we (a) cannot pin an individual weather event on climate change, we (b) can state that this is the sort of event that can be expected with global warming. But these two views when expressed by two different scientists may suggest disagreement where there is none. Science can demonstrate that these freak weather events would have been less likely if human interference with climate had not taken place.

Some right-wing politicians and businessmen are against climate change because they fear top-down legislation which would damage a free-market economy. Thus, because recognition of human-induced climate change interferes with their planned development and may affect their wealth creation, they may claim that it is a false theory.

For the rest of this chapter we will explore how Christians can and should respond. The situation is not without hope, when we focus on the nature and promises of God.

Defining hope

In his letter to the Christians at Colossae, Paul spells out the hallmarks of the work of God and the basic description of a true disciple as faith, love and hope, which are marked by spiritual fruit, truth and fullness. Paul gives thanks for the fruitful lives of these young Christians, he assures them of the truth of the gospel they have accepted, and prays for their growth in spiritual wisdom and power. He gives thanks for the marks of true Christian disciples: they have faith in Christ which is a genuine spiritual work; they have love for all their fellow sisters and brothers in Christ—a sacrificial love which is a mark of the Spirit (cf. Gal. 5:22–5); and they have hope laid up in heaven, which is their ultimate future—confident of their assured acceptance before God in Christ.

These are the marks of consistent faith; committed love; and certain hope. A genuine Christian is marked by faith, love and hope, and a genuine Christian experience places Christ, Christian fellowship and heaven as objects of faith, love and hope respectively.

This truth is living, growing, bearing fruit—when it is understood and it transforms lives—it is the grace of God at work, and its proof is seen in the life of love in the Spirit (Col. 1:8).

Brian Walsh and Sylvia Keesmaat rewrite the opening verses of the letter (in the form of a Jewish *targum*) and include the following section on hope:

> But your hope is not the cheap buoyant optimism of global capitalism with its cybernetic computer gods and self-confident scientific discovery, all serving the predatory idolatry of economism. You know that these are gods with an insatiable desire for child sacrifice. That is why your hope is not in the shallow optimism of the 'Long Boom' of increased prosperity. Such optimism is but a cheap imitation of hope. Real hope—the kind of hope that gives you the audacity to resist the commodification of your lives and engenders the possibility of an alternative imagination—is no human achievement; it is a divine gift. This hope isn't extinguished by living in 'the future of a shattered past', precisely because it is a hope rooted in a story of kept promises, even at the cost of death.

Also

> You didn't get this hope from cable television, and you didn't find it on the Net. This hope walked into your life, hollering itself hoarse out on the streets, in the classroom, down at the pub and in the public square, when you first heard the good news of whole life restoration in Christ. This gospel is the Word of truth—it is the life-giving, creation-calling, covenant-making, always faithful servant Word that takes flesh in Jesus, who is the truth. So it is not surprising that the Word of truth is no detached set of objective verities committed to memory and reproduced on the test. No, this Word of truth is active, bearing fruit throughout the cultural wilderness of this terribly scorched earth. From the beginning blessing, 'Be fruitful and multiply', God has always intended that creation be a place of fruitfulness. Now the Word of truth is producing the fruit of radical discipleship, demonstrated in passion for justice, evocative art and drama, restorative stewardship of our ecological home, education for faithful living, integral evangelism, and liturgy that shapes an imagination alternative to the empire's. . . . You see, friends, because we are not subservient to the empire but subjects of the kingdom of God's beloved Son, we have the audacity to say to the darkness, 'We beg to differ!' We will not be a pawn to the Prince of Darkness any longer, because we owe him no allegiance, and by God's grace, through our redemption and forgiveness, our imaginations have been set free. (Walsh and Keesmaat, 2004: 39–41)

Here is our hope. It is focused and centred in God.

Martin and Margot Hodson explore Colossians 1:15–20, where Christ is seen as the agent of creation, the sustainer of creation and, as redeemer, the one who holds creation together, and suggest that 'if Christ is the source of every element in the universe, then no part should be treated dismissively. Our role should be to interact with the world to enable all to flourish' and 'if Christ, the redeemer, is the source of all things and is chief over creation, it means that redemption is built into the fabric of creation' (2011: 19).

They observe that the negative effects of climate change can lead to despair, but if we accept that redemption is for all creation, 'then we should meet these difficulties with a purposeful hope'. Their response is to offer an environmental ethic based on Colossians 1:15–20:

> A world-view that places Christ at the heart of creation ... generates a distinctive set of values. The intrinsic value of all elements of creation comes from Christ's creating role. Christ as redeemer and his holding all things together provides a context of hope for any Christian engagement with the world and affirms interconnectedness. Christ as image of the invisible God is a reminder that humans are made in God's image. Christ's roles as supreme over all things and head of the church give a dynamic responsibility to be co-creators and make his Kingdom visible on earth as in heaven. (Hodson and Hodson, 2011: 23)

With such a hope we live as purposeful disciples.

Paul prays that the Colossian Christians might have knowledge, wisdom and understanding that the Spirit gives (Col. 1:9). Christians are called to live in this truth. Walsh and Keesmaat maintain that truth 'is a decidedly personal, social and relational concept in the Scriptures. To know the truth, and to be known in truth, is fundamentally a matter of covenantal faithfulness, manifest in the concreteness of daily life within a particular community at a particular time.' They observe that 'Steadfast love, truth, righteousness and shalom are all inextricably related in a biblical worldview. And when God restores covenantal shalom to the land, then truth, or faithfulness, will permeate life so deeply and fully that it will seem as if truth springs up from the ground' (Walsh and Keesmaat, 2004: 45).

Biblical truth is embodied or incarnated in the life of the community in the land and when truth 'dies' the socio-cultural and ecological consequences are disastrous. In Christ there is a new creation, but as ever in the New Testament, there is a now-but-not-yet aspect. There are the first fruits of the Spirit, but still creation groans as it waits for God's human creatures to reach their perfect humanity in Christ (Rom. 8:18–23).

Our true humanity is to be located in Christ, and when we locate ourselves outside Christ we find ourselves in disharmony with God's purpose for the well-being of creation (Houston, 2005: 88–89).

God and creation

As a biblical scholar looking at the current environmental situation, Ernest Lucas notes that the Old Testament with its emphasis on land and an agricultural economy says a great deal which has relevance to modern environmental issues. However, while noting that environmental matters were not a central concern in New Testament writings, he identifies a number of passages where Jesus' teaching reflects the Old Testament teaching on the environment (for example, Matt. 6:25–30) (Ernest Lucas, 1999: 93).

Luke 4:18–19 gives the programmatic statement of Jesus' ministry, where Jesus inaugurates the year of the Lord's favor with its links to Jubilee and Sabbath (cf. Isa. 61:1–2; 9:1–9). The parallel passages in Mark 1:15 and Matthew 4:17 present Jesus' calls for repentance in the face of the kingdom's presence. The two commands to love God and to love neighbour reflect core kingdom ethics which include the environment.

When Jesus responds to John's disciples (Matt. 11:1–6) Ernest recognizes an allusion to Isaiah 35, which speaks not only about the healing of humans, but the wider renewing of creation, with the desert blooming. Ernest maintains that this Old Testament background enables us to see that Jesus' announcement of the coming kingdom of God has ecological implications, and Jesus' healing miracles can be seen as signs of the coming renewal of the whole created order. 'In his work as Redeemer Jesus is forwarding God's work as Creator' (Ernest Lucas, 1999: 94).

Often we are tempted to begin any discussion about the state of the planet with a discussion about the role of human beings. When we do this our hope diminishes. It is better to begin with God: God's view of creation, and God's assessment of and desires for humanity, for in God's promises we find hope renewed.

In Genesis 1 we have a picture of a world with which God is pleased, and human beings in God's image, reflecting the nature of God.

Genesis 2 shows us the relationships God desires in a world that is good: human relationships with God, with each other, and with the environment.

But in Genesis 3 we find that human rebellion and self-centredness lead to the breaking of these three relationship and God's judgment on humanity and the world.

Genesis 1–11 presents us with the picture of God the creator and covenant-maker. The Psalms express creation's praise and revelation of God the creator (cf. Ps. 19; 104). The Prophets describe human rebellion in breaking the covenant and the resulting destruction of creation (see Isa. 24).

But our true hope is in God's covenant with all creation. Genesis 8:21–22 assures us that lasting change will depend on God's activity in the face of human wickedness. God will not destroy the earth, but in God's grace the cycle of day and night and of crops and seasons will continue. It is clear that hope is based on God's grace alone, and God's promise never again to flood the earth.

From the Old Testament we understand the nature of God's involvement with creation in the gift of the rhythm of time and in the Sabbath. Chris Wright notes that Jubilee was intended to protect the small householder and also 'served to establish an economic practice for redeeming the land and the people', (2005: 58); and Peter Carruthers suggests that Sabbath and Jubilee give three principles for farming and food production: sharing—with the poor; caring—for the earth; and restraint—of power and wealth. But there are imbalances in the world food system, there is unfair trading, and a growing industrialization of agriculture, which is destroying the environment. Instead of keeping the Sabbath we have a 'Sabbath-less society' (Carruthers, 2005: 74).

One of the great gifts that the Judaeo-Christian tradition can give to the environmental movement is the concept of Sabbath. Not just a pause for breath before carrying on consuming, and not just for humans. In Genesis 1, we find that the crown of creation is not humankind, created on the sixth day, but the Sabbath, instituted on the seventh day, when God took a rest, and God did not do so because of personal tiredness. The Mosaic covenant commands regular Jubilee seasons when debts are forgiven, families reunited, and land left fallow. We wear ourselves, and the land, out by constantly rushing. There is nothing that works against a green lifestyle more than being in a hurry. Too much of a hurry to ponder shopping choices. Too much of a hurry to walk rather than drive. Too much of a hurry to cook. Too much of a hurry to grow food. Too much of a hurry to turn off their TV and play with our children. Too much of a hurry to sleep properly and give the world a rest from our self-important busyness.[4]

Finally, perhaps, too much of a hurry to have noticed the damage we have done to the planet, before it is too late. We need to step back and take the time to look, to learn about what we see, so that we can appreciate in more and more astonishing detail the beauty of what we see, and we can love it, if we but give ourselves the time.

The technical control of time (departing from the natural God-given rhythms) is human-centred and takes our times away from a relationship with the Creator. 'The Sabbath reflects on faith in the creator-redeemer, who is Alpha and Omega, the beginning and the end. As God consummates the work of creation, so God will complete God's purposes in redemption as the incarnate Lord' (Houston, 2005: 95). Jesus declared the Sabbath and Jubilee principle at the beginning of his ministry (Luke 4:18–19) and we are called to live as Sabbath-keepers within the new covenant in Christ (Rom. 8:18–21).

In discussion of Daniel 9, Ernest Lucas explores the symbolic meaning of 'seventy years' (9:2) and 'seventy sevens' (9:24). He recognizes a possible allusion to Leviticus 25:8 pointing to a symbolic understanding in terms of jubilee and sabbatical periods (see also the verbal links between Daniel's prayer and Lev. 26:27–45). In Leviticus 26 'the people are warned that their *covenant disloyalty* will result in *desolation*, but that if they *confess* their sins Yahweh will remember the covenant and the Promised Land. Daniel follows this pattern. He admits Israel's covenant disloyalty, which has brought about desolation, and confesses the nation's sin, appealing to Yahweh's mercy' (Ernest Lucas, 2000: 15).

Ernest believes that such action as the Jubilee 2000 campaign have made people aware of the biblical concept of Jubilee as a time of release and restoration, and is a way in which God acts.

William Willimon helpfully observes that Sabbath-keeping was a public recognition of trust in God's care and ordering of creation, and maintains that Christians:

> believe that Sabbath has been fulfilled and forever changed through the Resurrection. Jesus was raised on the 'eighth day', the day when creation was brought to fulfilment, initiating for us a new world, giving us back time in a way we would not have had without God's raising Jesus from the dead. Just as God entrusted the Sabbath to Israel, so that the world might know God's intentions for creation, so Christians worship on the day of the Resurrection, thereby signalling that God's promise to Israel has gone to all the world. (Willimon, 2002: 329)

Michael Northcott reminds us that the Old Testament prophets criticized the people for breaking the covenant through their unjust treatment of the poor and the vulnerable, and through their failure to care for the land, such as God's warning given by Isaiah (Isa. 24:5–6) (2001: 221–22). The exclusion of the poor and the degradation and exhaustion of the environment are seen as the results of ignoring God's care of creation and God's justice expressed in the covenant. Margot Hodson observes that in Isaiah 24:3–5 'the full consequences to the earth of human transgression are outlined. This section of Isaiah resonates with Genesis 3 and the impact of human disobedience at the Fall, and also Deuteronomy 28 and the consequences of not keeping God's covenant' (2011: 9).

We can also note that Isaiah presents the alternative covenantal way of life (Isa. 24:4–12; cf. Isa. 5:1–7; 19:9; 32:14–20; 41:18–19; 55; 58:13–14), which brings peace and fruitfulness as opposed to the destruction that comes through foreign gods, and political, economic and military alliances. In Deutero-Isaiah hope is presented when relationships are restored between God and humanity, and the earth is restored to fruitfulness and harmony (Isa. 55:10). Ultimately the earth will be full of God's knowledge and glory (11:9; 6:3) and will be made new (65:17).

In further consideration of Isaiah of Jerusalem, Margot Hodson notes that 'There are two major threats to fruitful cultivation of the earth: the devastation of the land through war (14:17), and drought (24:4). These are associated with desertification, and are seen as a direct result of human rejection of God' (2011: 9).

She suggests that desertification may be the result of overfarming with iron ploughs of the thin limestone soil, poor agricultural methods, overgrazing and drought. This might be the result of ignoring the Sabbath year, when the land is given rest.

In summary she maintains that the dominant thread is a message of judgment and failure transformed into rejoicing and fruitfulness. Nature is seen as the victim of the first because of human sin but the beneficiary of the second because of human repentance. The benefits of restoration are not only for humans but also for the rest of nature in its own right.

Walsh and Keesmaat present a similar conclusion, suggesting that throughout Israel's history:

> themes of creational fruitfulness and social justice become the grounding rhythm for Israel's life before God. In every period of its history and in every genre of its literature, there is a witness to God's fruitful blessing in creation and the practice of an alternative social ethic that images God in redemption and care for creation and neighbour. The alternative social ethic of the practice of jubilee envisioned in Leviticus 25 will result in faithfulness and peace. (2004: 73) (See Lev. 26:3–6)

Similar themes appear in the book of Revelation as explored by Simon Woodman (2008). Woodman observes that in the sequences of seals, trumpets and bowls, John depicts scenes of environmental devastation, which culminate in the pouring out of the bowls triggering the death of every living thing in the sea, the poisoning of all waters, burning from an intensified sun, and a time of darkness (Rev. 16:2–12) (2010: 179–95). He sees a powerful ecological parable here, noting that these visions of environmental destruction are interspersed with scenes of judgment on humanity, with the entire created order depicted as suffering the effects of humanity's rejection of God.

He draws on the work of Bauckham, who observes that in John's own time, the Syrian elephant was hunted to near-extinction to supply the trade in carved ivory (2005: 99), and Howard-Brook and Gwyther (2001), who note that the Roman system of *latifundia*[5] pressurised land into non-productivity through intensive farming, as well as forcing peasant farmers to the brink of starvation (2001: 248). This situation was so severe that Pliny the Elder (AD 23–79) commented on these large-scale farms: '[W]e must confess the truth, it is the wide-spread domains [latifundia] that have been the ruin of Italy, and soon will be that of the provinces as well' (Woodman: 2010).

Woodman observes that empires which take dominion over the earth frequently engage in ecological violence. He notes that the environmental judgments of Revelation are not personally targeted punishments aimed at those who deny the lordship of Christ, but rather are images evoking the inevitable end-results of the human capacity for empire and exploitation. He maintains that the environmental call of Revelation is for the church to discover its vocation as witness to an alternative, non-exploitative expression of humanity, focused around the lordship of the one on the heavenly throne (Woodman, 2008).

In discussing the Pauline material, Ernest Lucas notes that the created order reveals something of the nature of God (Rom. 1:20), and that being in Christ and being a new humanity give us the sense of our material bodies being renewed. He suggests that Romans 8:18–25 implies that 'the redemption of humans by Christ is the central part of a wider redemptive work, involving the whole created order'. In Christ all things are reconciled (Col. 1:15–20); Christians have been given the ministry of reconciliation (2 Cor. 5:18–20); and there is both a continuity and a transformation, where the resurrection of the body presents the same model as the renewal of the whole of creation (1 Cor. 15). He sees that the resurrection of Jesus' transformed body, scars and all, is a sign of what the renewal of creation might mean (Ernest Lucas, 1999: 95).

Ernest concludes that the New Testament does not allow any separation between God's purpose in creation and in redemption; that the destiny of the non-human created order depicted in the New Testament is not that of a throwaway container which God will discard when Christ finally comes to consummate the salvation of humans. Rather, the final salvation of humans is part of a wider renewal of the whole creation through transformation. He also concludes that the Incarnation shows that Christianity has no place for a strong spirit–matter dualism that denigrates the material world, and that the doctrine of resurrection shows us that God will take up the material and transform it, not discard it. (Ernest Lucas, 1999: 98).

The beginnings of hope

Moving on to consider our hope focused in the coming kingdom of God it is helpful to examine Ernest Lucas's thoughts on Daniel 7. He suggests that the animal imagery reflects Babylonian creation myths, such as *Enuma Elish* (cf. similar imagery in other Hebrew texts—see Job 26:12–13; Pss. 74:12–14, 89:9–11; Isa. 51:9). For Jews living in exile these images would be evocative of the themes of chaos and creation, and the question of which god is able to transform chaos into cosmos-ordered creation. In addition the imagery of the throne scene (Daniel 7:9–14) reflects Canaanite culture—the Ancient of Days and the one coming with the clouds of heaven would have strong numinous associations (see also Ezekiel 1).

In Daniel 7:13 there is emphasis on the human-like nature of the figure who receives the ultimate kingdom over against the bestial nature of the historical kingdoms. Ernest believes that the use of a Hebrew phrase *bar' ^{e}nosh*, which evokes Psalm 8, and through it also Genesis 1:26–28, indicates that:

> this is a vision about the consummation of Yahweh's purpose in creating the world. At the same time it is a vision about Yahweh saving his people from oppression. This is explicit in the interpretation in vv 21, 25–27. This vision, therefore, brings together the two great biblical themes of

creation and salvation. Through his saving acts Yahweh brings to completion the purpose he had when he created the world. (Ernest Lucas, 2000: 7–8)

Ernest recognizes that there is an integral relationship between God's purposes in creation and salvation, which has particular relevance in the light of the ecological crises threatening the world today. 'Salvation embraces the renewal of the whole of creation, not just the saving of individual human beings. Therefore to work for that renewal now is to provide a sign of the kingdom of God, in the same way that working for justice in human society provides such a sign' (Ernest Lucas, 2000: 8–9).

Ernest helpfully links redemption with the coming of the Son of Man (see Daniel 7) when God steps in to establish his kingdom as the completion of his creative purpose. The coming of the kingdom does not mean the abolition of God's creation, but the restoration and fulfilment of creation (cf. Matt. 19:28, where the coming of the Son of Man in glory is linked with the renewal of all things. See also Acts 3:21).

For Ernest the renewal of creation at the coming of Christ is also to be found in the Johannine material. The kingdom of God is replaced by eternal life in John's writing, but the new Jerusalem of Revelation 21–22 is established on a renewed earth. Revelation 21:5 (cf. Isa. 65:17) suggests a renewal of the old by a radical transformation. So the redeeming work of Christ is not separated from the achieving of God's creative purpose; 'God is concerned with the renewing of creation, not with saving humans alone and discarding the rest' (Ernest Lucas, 1999: 96).

We recognize that in the book of Revelation John offers his theological assertion that systems of oppression and destruction will themselves ultimately face judgment, something which he vividly depicts in the vision of the destruction of the great whore and the great city (Rev. 17–18) (Woodman, 2010).

Yet there is both judgment and hope beyond catastrophe. While the breaking of covenant inevitably leads to judgment, Woodman maintains that John also presents a positive role for creation. John evokes the Noahic covenant, recalling God's promise to remain faithful to creation in his description of the rainbow around the divine throne (Rev. 4.3; cf. Ezek. 1.28; Gen. 9.13–16), and the whole of creation is seen to participate in the offering of worship to the one seated on the divine throne (Rev. 5.13; cf. Phil. 2.10) (Woodman, 2010).

Eugene Peterson challenges us to consider the way in which we experience creation. Each new day presents us with a world we did not make. We perceive it in every sight, sound, smell; around us, above, below, inside, outside; every experience. It is, he observes, the sheer 'is-ness' of color, shape, sound, texture (2005: 51).

Jesus is the key to our understanding of creation as illustrated in Hebrews 11:3; John 1:1–14; Colossians 1:15–20. Recognizing that creation is God's creation we submit to what God will do, has done and is doing. 'We are not spectators of creation but participants in it. We are participants first of all by simply being born, but then we realize that our births all take place in the defining context of Jesus' birth. The Christian life is the practice of living in what God has done and is doing' (Peterson, 2005: 54).

In Jesus, God is a participant in creation, totally committed and personally present (Heb. 4:14–16; John 1:14; 3:16).

It is God's grace which is our ultimate hope, and we thus move on to explore God's redemptive mission. In the New Testament we read of Christ as co-creator and as redeemer of creation (John 1; Col. 1). The post-resurrection church lives in the power of the Spirit (Eph. 1:20; 3:14–21) and is called into God's redemptive activity (Rom. 8:18–25). Christians have resurrection life now (John 11:25–26), which is eternal life (John 6:34ff.; 10:10) or life in Christ (Rom. 6:3,11; 8:1) or experience the presence of the kingdom in their midst (Luke 10:9,11; 11:20; 17:21). We are called to live as kingdom people, who regularly pray 'Thy kingdom come, Thy will be done, on earth as in heaven'.

Considering those who find themselves in dark places, Alan Jamieson expresses some important thoughts on our hope in God (2004). He explores hope and trouble (Rom. 5:2–5) and helpfully introduces the reader to Ricoeur's 'knot of reality'. This is a move to Ricoeur's second naïveté created through forming a knot of realities—'the reality of pain, suffering and despair that lies within and around us tied to the reality of a deep faith in God'—which brings hope in despair (Jamieson, 2004: 31).

We can imagine a reef knot which bears all the stress that we place upon it; the realities of life being intimately intertwined with the promises and reality of God. The witness of the three men in the burning furnace fire (Dan. 3:16–18, noted by Ernest Lucas, 2002, which will be discussed in the next section) is an example of such faith, or Job's testimony in his suffering: 'I know that my Redeemer lives' (Job 19:25–6). Living by faith will mean living with uncertainty (Rom. 8:24–25; Heb. 11:1–2), but nevertheless living in hope (Rom. 5).

But how is there hope in the midst of despair? The image of Ricoeur's knot reminds us that we cannot ignore either the reality of the environmental situation and human greed or the reality of faith in God's promises and purposes.

There is little hope without God as all our good intentions often lead nowhere as a result of selfishness and self-centredness. Without God we find that there is no way forward, no purpose or motivation for living, in fact no hope. We can see this as an apt reflection on the lack of results, thus far, from the various UN climate conferences.

Is the situation is hopeless? Eat, drink and be merry for tomorrow you may die (cf. Eccl. 1:12—2:26); or as today's hedonists might say: 'Fly, drive and consume for tomorrow you may die.'

Walsh and Keesmaat suggest that many people believe that the future is bleak. This leads the authors to comment that 'if the guiding narrative of our culture breeds suspicion, not confidence, then history-forming action is paralyzed' and 'the progress myth of democratic capitalism that promised economic prosperity and social harmony strains under the weight of economic contraction, ecological threat, and an ever-widening gap between the rich and the poor' (Walsh and Keesmaat, 2004: 23). They observe that 'International tensions have increased over the last one hundred years, the environment continues to be raped, and the rise of prosperity for the wealthy has been accompanied by increased poverty, starvation, homelessness and misery for the majority of the world's population. There is something wrong with this story (2004: 30).

We recognize the need of a meaning beyond ourselves to give direction, accountability and hope to our lives. We find this in the purposes and promises of God. This is a theme that is explored in some detail by Brian McLaren in his book, *Everything Must Change* (2007). McLaren asks: If Jesus is going to change the world, what sort of community will his followers have to be? Not an institutional church fussing over its organization and doctrine, but something much more radical, rampant, risk-taking—he suggests a 'divine peace insurgency', 'God's unterror movement', a 'global economy of love', 'God's sacred ecosystem'. These metaphors offer us an image of the subversive and redemptive potential of a community of grace.

He suggests that the central 'missional' argument of Scripture is that we are called out of the world to be an alternative humanity in the midst of the nations and cultures of the world—a redeemed, renewed, transformed community who stand as a prophetic witness to how God intended creation to be.

In a later work (2010) McLaren emphasizes the gospel message as 'repent, the kingdom of God is at hand' (Mark 1:15). In the face of Caesar the early Christians declared the treasonous statement: Jesus is Lord. Such a cry was a witness to the striking contrast between two competing kingdoms and their lords—one who would gladly torture and kill to establish dominance through the *Pax Romana*, the other who would willingly suffer and die to establish reconciliation via the *Pax Christi*.

Jesus did not come to establish a new religion, but a new kingdom, which would have room for many religious traditions within it. This is the kingdom that the letter to the Colossians proclaims, a kingdom which is radically different from the violent absolutism of the empire.

But at the time of Colossians the myth of *Pax Romana* remained—peace, prosperity and fertility comes by means of the empire, blessed by the gods. Festivals honoring the emperor become part and parcel of this myth. The Roman Empire exercised its control through an efficient military structure financed by taxes and tributes from the regions under her control, echoing McLaren's description of the modern western world as a global suicide machine.[6]

Walsh and Keesmaat observe that modern globalization is driven by the progress myth. We now have *Pax Americana*, in which the 'empire' finds salvation in economic progress and global control, and 'through mechanisms such as the World Bank and the International Monetary Fund, powerful nations in the North are able to dictate the economic terms by which the South is kept firmly ensconced in the cycle of international debt and development aid. There are images of consumer affluence, for example Disney, Coca-Cola and McDonalds.' The authors comment that just as in the ancient world the images of peace and prosperity masked the reality of inequality and violence, so the contemporary images projected by advertising mask the reality of sweatshops, inequality, and domestic and international violence created by our lifestyles (Walsh and Keesmaat, 2004: 60–63). The environmental crisis with global climate change, pollution and the exhaustion of natural resources bear testimony to the truth of this observation.

In his letter to the Colossians, in the face of the dominant empire, Paul claims Jesus as the true image of God (Col. 1:15) and calls the Colossian Christians to bear the image of Jesus in shaping an alternative to the empire. For Christians today this will include the way in which we approach God's good creation.

Hopeful disciples

In Ernest Lucas's studies of the book of Daniel (2002) we can identify the theme of living as hopeful disciples.

Discussing Daniel 1:8 (Daniel's vegetarian diet in the Babylonian court) he noted that we should be wary of the way in which we interpret biblical texts. There is no mandate for our eating habits as such in this passage; what is important is an individual's belief in God.

Thus we see that Daniel—believing certain things about God, and given his situation, as an exile in a pagan land—behaved in a particular way. The application for us is that believing the same things about God, and given our particular situation, we must behave in a way appropriate to the reality of God and the reality of our situation. Ernest maintains that Daniel 1:8 is about being loyal to the God of Israel in a pagan land. Daniel's life in the Babylonian court is best described as 'principled involvement'—he is a 'light' by being faithful to Yahweh, while doing a good job in the pagan court (2002: 54–55, 57–59; 2003).

A similar picture emerges in Daniel 3, where in the story of the three men in the blazing furnace, the emphasis is on their faith in God. The three men have no doubt in God's ability to save, but they don't worship God because he is powerful but because he is good. We can note that in the furnace the three men sing a song in praise of the Creator, who is also their saviour (*Jerusalem Bible* Daniel 3:52–90 and LXX). This hymn of praise, largely based on Psalms 103 and 148, is inserted after Daniel 3:23 (Ernest Lucas, 2002: 91–97; 2003).

The central 'missional' argument of Scripture is that a people are called out of the world to be an alternative humanity in the midst of the nations and cultures of the world; a prophetic witness to how God intended creation to be. So the question for us is: How we are to be involved in our situation in a principled way?

Walsh and Keesmaat note that the Old Testament prophets call Israel to be countercultural to the empires around it. In the covenant Israel is called to be a people of Jubilee, where slaves are released and life renewed, in contrast with the slavery and death of empire. Israel is called to care for the stranger, the widow and the orphan—the marginalized. So that while the empires of other nations are frantically caught up in the management of production and consumption, 'Israel is called to a sabbath keeping that acknowledges the gift character of its life in the land' (Walsh and Keesmaat, 2004: 66).

Israel is to be an alternative society—not like the nations around—but they do just this and find that they are under God's judgment in exile. But even here God's call through Jeremiah is that they should be a blessing, witnessing to an alternative society (Jer. 29:5–7; cf. Gen. 1:28–29). Even as exiles they are to live out of the vision and hope of Genesis. Even under the oppressive rule of Babylon, Israel is called to build a faithful community, living under a different kingship, which we have seen in Ernest's discussion of Daniel 1 and 3.

Can there be a theology of hope? Can our sinful actions thwart the purposes of God? The promise of the first covenant, with Noah, is that while human sinfulness and self-centredness will continue so will God's gracious promise 'never again' to destroy the earth (Gen. 8:21–22).

God promises to be present with us in the realities of life (Ps. 23; Isa. 43:1–5; Matt. 28:20), and encourages us to hold onto hope in the face of uncertainty. We learn from both Amos and Jeremiah that the false prophets promised hope without catastrophe, while God's prophets offer hope beyond catastrophe. We can speak of the hope of judgment; that there is accountability for our lack of care of the poor and of the environment. Our hope is based on God and God's justice and grace, which are not thwarted by human sinfulness.

In Romans 5:1–5 there is a link between hope and endurance; hope is the motivation to keep on going. We are faced with a failure and crisis in politics and public opinions, in regard to climate change. The situation for the poor in the developing world is reaching crisis proportions and at the same time we see a public weariness with the green agenda. There is no sign of governments reducing their carbon footprint. As a result of scepticism and the economic recession people claim that addressing climate change cannot be afforded, yet all the while consumption levels are rising in an unsustainable way.

Ultimate hope is in God and is eternal, while human hope is temporal and uncertain. Christians are called to a hopeful discipleship in the light of our ultimate hope in God's promises and purposes. We live as those who are created in the image of God and cooperate with God's transformative action in and for the world. As James Hunter suggests, 'to be a Christian is to be obliged to engage the world, pursuing God's restorative purposes over all of life, individual and corporate, public and private. This is the mandate of creation' (2010: 4).

Any tendency toward dualism—the division between secular and sacred, public and private, objective and subjective—is toxic and must be rejected.

The mandate is not for a few but for all—'*all* are participants, *all* are enjoined to participate in ways framed by the revelation of God's word in the creative and renewing work of world-making and remaking. Every person is made in God's image and every person is offered his grace and, in turn, the opportunity to labor together with God in the creation and recreation of the world' (Hunter, 2010: 93).

Hunter argues for Christians to be a 'faithful presence' in the world. He defines a theology of faithful presence as that vocation of the church to bear witness to and to be an embodiment of the coming kingdom of God. Such faithfulness works itself out in the context of complex social, political, economic and cultural forces that prevail in a particular time and place.

Christianity needs to produce a thorough critique of the modern world. We can explore Romans 5–8 as a key creation text, where following on from the resurrection we find creation suffering as it waits, waiting in suffering, waiting in hope. Christians should be living and acting prophetically; faithful rather than successful; confident in God's power to overcome and our hope in Christ (Eph. 3:14–21; 1:20).

We bring together resurrection and redemption. While ultimate hope lies in God and God's consummation of creation, present hope within God's world is found as Christians realize their discipleship as kingdom people, finding their role as co-redeemers in Christ's mission in and for the world.

Christians have a contribution to make. God created and entrusted the earth, and will redeem the whole of creation (Rom. 8:19–21). In Christ there is a new creation, but as ever in the New Testament, there is a now-but-not-yet aspect. There are the first fruits of the Spirit, but still creation groans as it waits for God's human creatures to reach their perfect humanity (Rom. 8:18–23). To believe in Christ in this world is to believe against reality—Christ is risen, but we live in a world of suffering, pain and destruction. It is hope, because now we see salvation for all creation appearing only in outline. But this cannot be a cheap hope, human beings must act in hope—the Spirit gives us the possibility to be what we are to become—the children of God. We find the same message in Colossians 1:15–20: 'For God was pleased to have all his fulness dwell in him, and through him to reconcile to himself all things, whether things on earth or things in heaven, by making peace through his blood, shed on the cross' (Col. 1:19–20, NIV).

Paul places the redemption of human beings in the context of the redemption of the whole creation, and creation is brought back into relationship with God through the cross. This takes place as human beings find their restored relationship with the Creator, through the cross; living as hopeful disciples. God is deeply and passionately involved in his world; God is no absentee landlord, but indwelling, accompanying, incarnate, and present as Holy Spirit. There are important implications for our relationship both with the Creator and with creation. Moltmann maintains that 'There can be no redemption for human beings without the redemption of the whole of perishable nature. So it is not enough to see Christ's resurrection merely as "God's eschatological act in history". We also have to understand it as the first act in the new creation of the world. Christ's resurrection is not just a historical event. It is a cosmic event too' (1995: 83; quoted in Liht, 2008: 38–41).

The call of Christ is expressed as 'Whoever wants to be my disciple must deny themselves and take up their cross and follow me' (see Mark 8.34). This is a different sort of life, a Christ-like life, a life that is 'in Christ'. It is to deny self—move away from a selfish materialistic lifestyle; take up the cross-shaped life of sacrificial love—sharing God's good gifts of creation with all; and follow Jesus—in his compassion for others and for the world. The call is to join in Christ's redemptive mission.

So to be involved in Christ's redemptive mission—for Christ's redeeming love to flow through us, in the power of the Spirit we must:

- *Deny self:* live more simply, use less of the world's resources; treat the created order with care.
- *Take up the cross:* live sacrificially for the sake of others; give up our greed; sacrifice our wants
- *Follow Jesus:* see the created world as an expression of God's order and love; see everyone as equally valued by God; take special care of the poor and the outcast; and love our neighbour as ourselves.

We must avoid the self-centred individualistic ideas of happiness and consumption, where growth is seen as a virtue expressed in consumerism and personal satisfaction. Hope requires a broader perspective of a worldwide community and nature's renewal. We need to reverse the broken relationships of the 'fall'. Our hope is set on that which is above, but brought into the present through transformative living on the part of the people of God. We seek to plant seeds of transformation (Jer. 29) in the here and now—political, economic, ecological and social seeds. There is something appealing about Brian McLaren's vision of a community of followers who:

> develop practices of spiritual formation so they and their children for generations to come would be able to learn, live, and grow as part of the solution, not part of the problem; as agents of healing, not as carriers of the disease; as revolutionaries seeking to dismantle and subvert the suicidal system of power and control, not as functionaries seeking to serve and preserve it. (2007: 292)

In Christ we are called into Christ's mission in and for the world, but what sort of community will Christ's disciples be? Walsh and Keesmaat ask how we are to confess with integrity that Christ is Lord of the cosmos when global economics and the cybernetic revolution seem to demonstrate decisively that economic determinism fuelled by information technology is sovereign over the affairs of the world. (2004: 97). They quote from Wendell Berry who suggests that we must secede:

> From the union of self-gratification and self-annihilation,
> secede into care for one another
> and for the good gifts of Heaven and Earth. (1998: 162–63)

This is an excellent comment on the current situation, where global multinational companies encourage climate change scepticism, and governments prevaricate in the light of UN climate change conference undertakings. Walsh and Keesmaat observe that the American way of life (to which we might add western Europe) and national security serve to legitimate the escalation of global warming through withdrawing from the Kyoto Accord, an action which they see as an act of anticreational and unneighbourly violence. In a western context of global consumerism the moral world is represented by the shopping mall. Here economic efficiency, consumer desires, repressive labor policies and ecologically unsustainable environmental practices come together (Walsh and Keesmaat, 2004: 165–66).

We look for Christian disciples to embody an alternative narrative, sovereignty and hope. If the problem with the empire was idolatry (Col. 3:5), then the alternative kingdom is the renewal of the image of God (Col. 3:10). In Christ we live as hopeful disciples, restored to our full humanity as God's stewards of creation, embodying the image of God, who has declared creation good and calls on human beings to exercise a godly care.

Walsh and Keesmaat ask: Why should the Christ-following community strive for an ecologically responsible way of life? Their answer: 'Because it is a worshipping community that joins its song with all of creation. When it is renewed in knowledge according to the image of the Creator, this community knows that its worship must both be in harmony with the rest of creation and must facilitate and make possible the free praise of our creaturely kin' (2004: 199–200).

Conclusion—working with others to bring this about

Christians are aliens in the world (1 Pet. 1:1; 2:11), but nevertheless their purpose in the world is to declare the one who has brought them out of darkness (1 Pet. 2:9). Hunter, following Miraslov Volf, maintains that Christian difference is not the presence of something new from the outside breaking into the old, but the bursting out of the new within old order. He can speak of a dialectic between affirmation and antithesis. The affirmation of God's good creation with beauty and truth, where life has significance and worth, and where all people have the ability to live in harmony with God's purposes as gifts of God's grace (whether they are Christian or not), even if this is a fallen world. So the accomplishments of non-believers are to be celebrated because they are gifts of God's grace.

He states that:

The task of world-making has a validity of its own because it is the work that God ordained to humankind at creation. Since all are created in his image, world-making is an expression of our divine nature. Though what we produce is fundamentally flawed at its best, it always possesses the potential and can, in fact, serve the good of all. It too is a place of grace. (Hunter, 2010: 231-33)

Christians may be involved in world-building but we are not building the kingdom of God on earth, but rather we are living as kingdom people in an alien kingdom. The establishment of the kingdom is an act of God's sovereignty and will find its consummation at the end of time. Hunter says: 'Perhaps it will be that God will transform works of faith in this world into something incorruptible but here again, it is God's doing and not ours.' Again he states that 'insofar as Christians acknowledge the rule of God in all aspects of their lives, their engagement with the world proclaims the shalom to come. Such work may not bring about the kingdom, but it is an embodiment of the values of the coming kingdom and is, thus, a foretaste of the coming kingdom' (Walsh and Keesmaat, 2004: 233-34).

This is the view of Ernest Lucas in his interpretation of Daniel 1 and 3, which we noted earlier. Hunter similarly uses the example of Jeremiah's words to the exiles. God has not abandoned the people in exile, but rather exile is the place where God is at work. As the people pursue shalom in Babylon, God will provide shalom for his people (Jer. 29:4-7).

In like manner Elaine Graham and Stephen Lowe (2009) challenge the church in the UK to address questions of citizenship and regeneration, culture and globalization, poverty and justice within an increasingly urban society. Graham, as one of the authors of the Anglican report, *Faithful Cities* (2005), offers further encouragement as she identifies the powerful influence of faithful capital in the long-term presence of people and networks of faith in our most deprived urban areas. Not only are faith communities in our cities physically present; they are also actively, dutifully and sometimes passionately engaged in caring and campaigning for those who need care most—sometimes people whom wider 'society' has forgotten. Christians have a philosophy of life, faith or worldview which includes a commitment to something beyond serving one's individual needs.

Paula Clifford (2009) believes that it is important to move away from a problem-solving approach to global climate change and recognize that we have to live with and respond to the challenges of climate change. Understanding that this is a global problem necessitates, I believe, a global approach. The Christian church is a worldwide community making up some one third of the world's population and as such is in a unique position to take up the challenge of restoring and renewing creation. Hope comes through a change of lifestyle as a mark of Christian discipleship—being the new covenant community in Christ, who live as hopeful disciples.

But our ultimate hope is always in God. This is hope beyond chaos and catastrophe. It is a hope that includes accountability and judgment. This is hope in God, who is Creator and Redeemer, and who will ultimately make all things new.

Notes

1 John Ray Initiative website: <http://www.jri.org.uk>.
2 Stern presented the following key points among others: carbon emissions have pushed up global temperatures by 0.5°C; if no action is taken on emissions, there is more than a 75 per cent chance of global temperatures rising between 2–3°C over the next fifty years, and a 50 per cent chance that average global temperatures could rise by 5°C; melting glaciers will increase flood risk; crop yields will decline, particularly in Africa; rising sea levels could leave 200 million people permanently displaced; up to 40 per cent of species could face extinction; extreme weather and rising temperatures could reduce global output by 10 per cent with the poorest countries losing the most. According to the report, a rise of 4°C would put between seven million and 300 million more people at risk of coastal flooding each year, there would be a 30–50 per cent reduction in water availability in southern Africa and the Mediterranean, agricultural yields would decline by 15–35 oer cent in Africa, and 20–50 per cent of animal and plant species would face extinction.
3 I am indebted to Miles Allen who is Head of the Climate Dynamics group at Oxford University's Atmospheric, Oceanic and Planetary Physics Department, who presented these comments at a JRI Conference in Oxford on 19 November 2010. See also the website: <http://www.climateprediction.net>.
4 These thoughts were presented in the Radio 4 sermon on 3 October 2010 given by Claire Foster, Chief Executive of the Ethics Academy and Senior Adviser at the St Paul's Institute for 21st Century Ethics, London, and a former National Policy Adviser in Science, Medicine, Technology and Environmental Issues to the Archbishops' Council of the Church of England.
5 *Latifundia*—the development of large estates with an industrial approach to both arable and pastoral farming, which were designed to work the land for the greatest profit.
6 McLaren describes three sub-systems that make up a global suicide machine: the prosperity system, which fulfils our desire for more and more happiness, which is achieved by consuming more and more. But there isn't enough for everyone and so there will be jealousy and violence. So we need protection. Although we can't protect ourselves from the panic of the money markets.

The security system protects our prosperity system with weapons, intelligence, border controls, police and surveillance, for which we need personnel and weapons, at a significant cost. This cost must be shared. But it is impossible to protect ourselves from random acts of violence.

The equity system shares the cost of the security system making sure that everyone has the possibility of happiness. But this is not equality and the few have the greatest chance of growing in prosperity. And even when we have our wealth and security it is no guarantee of happiness.

Bibliography

Bauckham,R. 'The New Teaching on the Environment: A Response'. In *A Christian Approach to the Environment* (ed. R.C.J. Carling and M.A. Carling; 2005, London: The John Ray Initiative, 2005.)

Berry, Wendell. *The Selected Poems of Wendell Berry* (Washington DC: Counterpoint, 1998).

Carruthers, Peter. 'Creation and the Gospels'. In *Caring for Creation, Biblical and Theological Perspectives* (ed. Sarah Tillett; Oxford: Bible Reading Fellowship, 2005).

Clifford, Paula. *Angels with Trumpets: The Church in a Time of Global Warming* (London: Christian Aid/ Darton, Longman & Todd, 2009).

Faithful Cities: A Call for Celebration, Vision and Justice. (Published jointly by Methodist Publishing House and Church House Publishing, 2005).

Graham, Elaine and Stephen Lowe. *What Makes a Good City? Public Theology and the Urban Church* (London: Darton, Longman & Todd, 2009).

Hodson, Margot R. *Uncovering Isaiah's Environmental Ethics*, Ethics Series E161 (Cambridge: Grove Books, 2011).

Hodson, Martin J. and Margot R. Hodson. *Climate Change, Faith and Rural Communities*. (Worthing: Verité for the Agriculture and Theology Project, 2011).

Houston, James. 'Creation and Incarnation'. In *Caring for Creation, Biblical and Theological Perspectives* (ed. Sarah Tillett; Oxford: Bible Reading Fellowship, 2005).

Howard-Brook, W. and A. Gwyther. *Unveiling Empire: Reading Revelation Then and Now*, (New York: Orbis, 2001).

Hunter, James Davison. *To Change the World: The Irony, Tragedy, and Possibility of Christianity in the Late Modern World* (Oxford: Oxford University Press, 2010).

Jamieson, Alan. *Journeying in Faith: In and Beyond the Tough Places* (London: SPCK, 2004).

Liht, Helle.'Restoring Relationships: Towards Ecologically Responsible Baptistic Communities in Estonia', unpublished MTh dissertation, IBTS, Prague, 2008.

Lucas, Caroline. '20 Issues facing Britain, number 4 Climate Change'. *Big Issue* (October 2011).

Lucas, Ernest. *Decoding Daniel: Reclaiming the Visions of Daniel 7—11*, Biblical Series B18 (Cambridge: Grove Books, 2000).

———. Edwin Stephen Griffiths lecture, given at the South Wales Baptist College (11 March 2003).

———. 'The New Testament Teaching on the Environment'. *Transformation: An International Journal of Holistic Mission Studies* 19 (1999).

———. *Daniel*, Apollos Old Testament Commentary (Leicester: Apollos, 2002).

McLaren, Brian D. *Everything Must Change: Jesus, Global Crises, and a Revolution of Hope* (Nashville, TN: Thomas Nelson, 2007).

———. *A New Kind of Christianity: Ten Questions that Are Transforming the Faith* (London: Hodder & Stoughton, 2010).

Moltmann, Jürgen. *Jesus Christ for Today's World* (London: SCM Press, 1995).

Northcott, Michael. 'Ecology and Christian Ethics'. In *The Cambridge Companion to Christian Ethics* (ed. Robin Gill; Cambridge: Cambridge University Press, 2001).

Peterson, Eugene H. *Christ Plays in Ten Thousand Places: A Conversation in Spiritual Theology* (London: Hodder & Stoughton, 2005).

Stern, Nicholas. *Stern Review on the Economics of Climate Change* <http://www.hm-treasury.gov.uk/stern_review_final_report.htm> (2006).

Tillett, Sarah. ed. *Caring for Creation, Biblical and Theological Perspectives* (Oxford: Bible Reading Fellowship, 2005).

Walsh, Brian J. and Sylvia C. Keesmaat. *Colossians Remixed: Subverting the Empire* (Downers Grove, IL: InterVarsity Press, 2004).

Willimon, William H. *Pastor: The Theology and Practice of Ordained Ministry* (Nashville, TN: Abingdon Press, 2002).

Woodman, Simon. *The Book of Revelation*, SCM Core Text (London: SCM Press, 2008).

———. 'Can the Book of Revelation Be a Gospel for the Environment?' In *Bible and Justice: Ancient Texts, Modern Challenges* (ed. M. J. Coomber; London: Equinox, 2010).

Wright, Chris. 'Sabbath for the Land and Jubilee'. In *Caring for Creation, Biblical and Theological Perspectives* (ed. Sarah Tillett; Oxford: Bible Reading Fellowship, 2005).

God our loving Creator
    who fashioned all things into being
    and took delight in their goodness,
    we need your help
    because we are killing your world.

Where we have replaced your concern
    for the prospering of all people and all creation
    with the worship of market forces and short-term gain,
    forgive us and heal us.

Where we have usurped your vision
    for a creation at peace and living justly
    with a shrug-shouldered acceptance
    of the ways of violence and greed,
    forgive us and heal us.

Where we have forgotten your rhythm of Sabbath,
    its gift of unhurried time and rich rounded living,
    with the idol of relentless work and busyness
    that separates us from you, each other and ourselves,
    forgive us and heal us.

Where we have wrenched ourselves away from Jesus,
    our strength, our song, our salvation,
    who is reconciling all creation to you
    in a work of glorious, wonderful, redemption,
    forgive us and heal us.

For we have nowhere else to turn.

We are made new in him;
forgiven and healed,

9

Take Ten: Scientists and Their Religious Beliefs

Robert S. White

On the 350th anniversary of the founding of the Royal Society in 1660, the Royal Mail released a set of ten commemorative first-class stamps, each featuring a Royal Society Fellow who had a major impact on science. As the world's oldest scientific academy in continuous existence, there were about 8,000 Fellows and Foreign Members from whom to choose. The Royal Society decided to split the 350-year history into ten 35-year periods and then to choose one Fellow from each period whose work had a significant impact globally.

The beliefs of these ten scientists played no part in their choice by the Royal Society. But it is striking that religious faith, or belief in the reality of spiritual or supernatural forces played a major part in the lives of the majority of these ten chosen solely for their seminal contributions to science and their impact on the world. Half of them were open in their writing about their Christian beliefs, and it is possible that others may also have described themselves as Christians, though we have little information about their beliefs. This certainly gives the lie to the popular notion that science fosters atheism, or that a scientific worldview renders faith irrelevant. It certainly does not lend support to statements such as that of Richard Dawkins who pronounced that 'Religious beliefs are irrational. Religious beliefs are dumb and dumber: super dumb' (2006).

Founding of the Royal Society

The founding of the Royal Society marks the start of the modern scientific method with its emphasis on studying the natural world through observation and experiment in order to understand how it works. That view is embodied in the Royal Society's motto: *Nullius in verba*. Roughly translated, it means 'take nobody's word for it'. It shows a determination to test ideas about how the world works against facts found by experiment. There is also a hint in the motto of the intellectual independence characteristic of many successful scientists which makes them question received wisdom. As the Nobel Prize-winner

Figure 1: Set of commemorative stamps issued to celebrate the 350th anniversary of the Royal Society

Richard Feynman put it: 'Science is organised scepticism in the reliability of expert opinion' (2007: 307).

The group of men (and they were all men initially) who first met together self-consciously decided that they could use that knowledge for the good of humankind. The official foundation date is 28 November 1660, when 12 men met at Gresham College after a lecture by Christopher Wren. They decided to found 'a Colledge for the promoting of physico-mathematicall experimental learning'.

King Charles II approved of this venture and gave it a royal charter in 1662, followed by a fuller charter in 1663 where the fledgling society was referred to as 'the Royal Society of London for improving Natural Knowledge'. The Royal Society is still governed by that charter today. Interestingly, the king wrote in the preamble that one of his reasons for giving it was so that he would always be recognized 'not only as the Defender of the Faith, but also as the universal lover and patron of every kind of truth'. This echoes a common understanding among scientists who are Christian believers that since God is the Creator of the cosmos, then investigating the material world could never throw up anything which disproves the existence of God. Both Christianity and science are in the business of truth-seeking. The king's statement in the charter is also reminiscent of the argument made a millennium and a half earlier by Tertullian (*c*. AD 160–225) that 'reason is a property of God', since there is nothing which God, the creator of all things, has not foreseen, arranged and determined by reason; moreover, there is nothing He does not wish to be investigated and understood by reason' (*De Paenitentia*, ch. 1).

Another aspect of the dual strengths of Christian belief and of scientific study is the 'two books' idea made popular by Francis Bacon (1561–1626). Charles Darwin quoted a passage extolling this view from Francis Bacon's *Advancement of Learning* opposite the title page of the first edition of his *Origin of Species*. He reproduced the excerpt: 'To conclude, therefore, let no man out of a weak conceit of sobriety, or an ill-applied moderation, think or maintain, that a man can search too far, or be too well studied in the book of

God's word, or in the book of God's works; divinity or philosophy; but rather let men endeavour an endless progress or proficience in both.' As it happens, Darwin omitted the two phrases following this extract where Bacon continued: 'only let men beware that they apply both to charity, and not to swelling; to use, and not to ostentation' (Bacon, 1605). That warning might dampen the hubris of some scientists who think that their scientific understanding is all that is needed to explain everything worth knowing. The 'two books' idea remains a helpful insight today: John Polkinghorne, for example, often uses a variant of it by referring to the depth of vision that the binocular vision of the eye of faith and the eye of science provide when used together to examine the world.

The 1663 charter of the Royal Society charter went on to declare explicitly that the society's 'studies are to be applied to further promoting by the authority of experiments the sciences of natural things and of useful arts, to the glory of God the Creator, and the advantage of the human race'. For many of the early Fellows of the Royal Society this dual aim of giving glory to God by using scientific understanding for the good of humankind fitted exactly with their religious and ethical perspective of the world.

In the remainder of this chapter we will look in turn at each of the ten scientists depicted on the commemorative stamps, treating them in chronological order.

Robert Boyle (1627–91)

The first of our men of science is Robert Boyle, who was at the inaugural meeting of the Royal Society, and was also part of its forerunner group of gentlemen who met together in Oxford. He is best remembered for the formulation of what is now known as Boyle's Law, which describes the relationship between the volume and the pressure of a gas. Although his roots were in the alchemy which was a feature of the age, his systematic studies of chemicals set him apart as one of the founders of modern chemistry. His book, *The Sceptical Chymist*, published in 1661, has come to be seen as a milestone in the field of chemistry, largely because it professionalized and systematized what had been a rather messy and smelly subject that hadn't hitherto been seen as fit for a university (Principe, 2011: 30–31).

Robert Boyle was also a devout evangelical Christian who generously supported Christian missionary work and the relief of poverty (Hunter, 2009). He also privately funded, among others, impoverished ministers in Ireland and Huguenots fleeing from repression on the continent. For many years from 1662 to 1689 he was a Governor of the New England Company, whose full title proclaimed its *raison d'être*: 'The Corporation for the Propagation of the Gospel in New England'. The company provided preachers and education for native Indian youths. It also set up a printing press for translations of the Bible and devotional works into Alonquian. That presaged his support for publishing

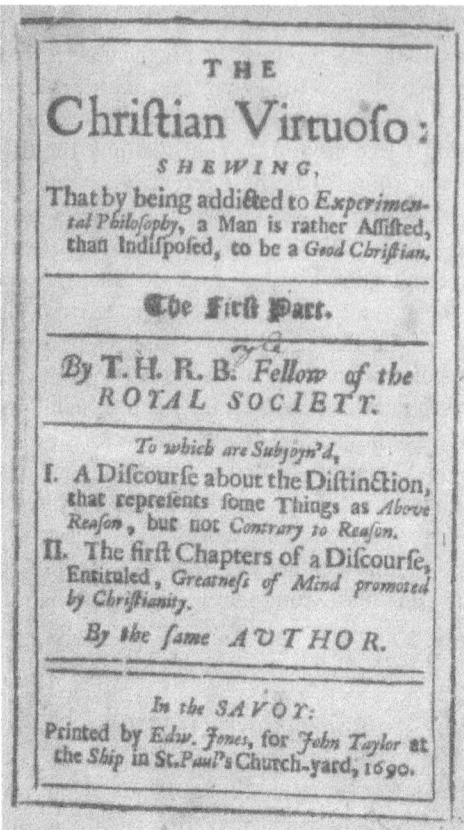

Figure 2: Robert Boyle's title page

the gospels into Malay in 1677 and his funding of a Bible translation into Irish, with the New Testament printed in 1682. The former interest came from his tenure as a Director of the East India Company. Though the company was set up for commercial reasons, Boyle characteristically used his position of influence to obtain donations to support Christian ministers working at converting and instructing native Indians. His concern for the Irish stemmed from the fact that he inherited considerable properties in Ireland, which were a major source of his wealth.

Boyle wrote a number of important books on philosophical theology, of which the main ones are his *Discourse of Things above Reason* (1681), *Disquisition about the Final Causes of Things* (1688) and *The Christian Virtuoso* (1690). Boyle thought deeply about the role of God in the world. He considered that there was no incompatibility between the study of nature and Christian belief. Indeed, the subtitle of *The Christian Virtuoso* succinctly sets out his view: 'That by being addicted to *Experimental Philosophy*, a man is rather assisted, than indisposed, to be a *Good Christian*'.

In these works Boyle reflected deeply on God's role in the world and the importance of the new experimental science in adding complementary insights to the truths of revealed Christianity set forth in the Scriptures. Boyle's view was that science and Christianity were profoundly complementary. Indeed, he considered that science could lead one to God, since it could act as 'a Bridge, whereon he may pass from Natural to Reveal'd Religion' (Hunter and Davis, 2000, vol 11: 303). He also thought that matters could work in the opposite direction, so that key truths about nature were only available from revealed (Christian) religion.

Nevertheless, Boyle was careful to make a distinction between science and theology. His view of the mechanistic nature of the world and his stress on the importance of collecting experimental evidence, with clear separation between facts and hypothesis, was influential in allowing subsequent scientists to adopt methodological materialism in their studies without also subscribing to Boyle's Christian faith. Another of the ironies of Boyle's strong espousal of the idea of a mechanistic universe to affirm God's sovereignty and his design of the universe is that it fostered deism. In the eighteenth century, deists would use the same idea of a clockwork universe to attack established religion (Brooke, 1991).

Michael Hunter has suggested that part of the experimental care which made Boyle such a great and pioneering scientist stemmed from the deep soul-searching in his spiritual life (2009: 205). He brought the same exactitude and refusal to be satisfied by facile explanations to his scientific experiments as his did to his spiritual quest.

A lasting legacy of Robert Boyle is the Boyle Lectures which he endowed in his will. His express wish was that prominent academics could use them 'to prove the truth of the Christian religion' against atheists and unbelievers. They were of great importance in the decades following the first lecture in 1692, but were delivered only sporadically during the twentieth century. In 2004 they were revived as annual lectures designed to address topics which explore the relationship between Christianity and our contemporary understanding of the natural world. So his profound interest between Christianity and the natural world lives on in those lectures.

Isaac Newton (1643–1727)

Isaac Newton's 1687 book *Philosophiæ Naturalis Principia Mathematica* (usually just called *Principia*) is considered by many to be one of the most influential science books written, laying the foundation for much of classical mechanics. In it, Newton described universal gravitation and his three laws of motion which dominated physical science for the following three centuries. They are still universally taught today in foundational physics courses. Like Boyle, Newton was a product of his times and was interested in alchemy. But he had his biggest impact in the fields of physics, mathematics and astronomy. The poet Alexander Pope considered his contributions to be so great that he wrote the well-known couplet intended as an epitaph:

Nature and nature's laws lay hid in night:
God said, 'Let Newton be!' and all was light.

Perhaps less well known is that Newton devoted more effort to theological study than to his scientific work, writing an estimated 2.5 million words on theology. Again like Boyle, Newton was a deeply religious man, far in excess of the norm for the conventional religiosity of his time. His list of sins written (in shorthand code) when he was 19, of which I show just the first 37, illustrates the depth of his piety (Table 1).[1] At the time his contemporaries thought of Newton as an orthodox Christian. But in fact, he was not entirely conventional. Newton's deep study of the Bible led him to realise that there was no reference to 'Trinity' as such, and so he began to reject Trinitarian views of the Godhead. Such rejection of the Trinity was illegal in England at the time and indeed remained so until as recently as 1813. So Newton wisely kept his heretical Unitarian views private except among his closest friends. There is a certain irony in the fact that he was a Fellow of Trinity College, Cambridge. It has been argued that it is possible that his iconoclastic views of Christianity were a reflection of the same revolutionary spirit that allowed him to break new ground in his science (Snobelen, 2009: 204–59).

For Newton there was absolutely no sense of conflict between science and religion (Brooke, 1991), which certainly contradicts a popular notion that science had liberated itself from theology by the end of the seventeenth century. Like Boyle, his convictions about the nature of God informed his understanding of how nature worked and vice versa (Brooke, 2012). Newton was happy to print Roger Cotes' statement in the Preface of the second edition of his *Principia* (1713) that 'the order of Nature was established by the will of God'.

Newton also added an appendix at the end of the second and subsequent editions of *Principia*, called the *General Scholium*. In this he spelled out his convictions about the nature of God and in particular set out the design argument, that the universe was so well set up that it must have been created by a single mind. He wrote that 'This most elegant system of the sun, planets, and comets could not have arisen without the design and dominion of an intelligent and powerful being' (Newton, 1999: 940). Newton would have felt right at home with modern-day discussions of the observation that the universe is astonishingly finely tuned for humans, and the metaphysical inferences we might make from this.

Newton inserted similar clear statements of his belief in a designer God into the second edition of his book on optics, where he wrote: 'How came the bodies of animals to be contrived with so much art, and for what ends were their several parts? Was the eye contrived without skill in Opticks, and the ear

**Table 1: Newton's list of sins
         Before Whitsunday 1662**

---

1 Using the word [God] openly
2 Eating an apple at Thy house
3 Making a feather while on Thy day
4 Denying that I made it
5 Making a mousetrap on Thy day
6 Contriving of the chimes on Thy day
7 Squirting water on Thy day
8 Making pies on Sunday night
9 Swimming in a kimnel on Thy day
10 Putting a pin in John Keys hat on Thy day to pick him
11 Carelessly hearing and committing many sermons
12 Refusing to go to the close at my mothers command
13 Threatning my father and mother Smith to burne them and the house over them
14 Wishing death and hoping it to some
15 Striking many
16 Having uncleane thoughts words and actions and dreamese
17 Stealing cherry cobs from Eduard Storer
18 Denying that I did so
19 Denying a crossbow to my mother and grandmother though I knew of it
20 Setting my heart on money learning pleasure more than Thee
21 A relapse
22 A relapse
23 A breaking again of my covenant renued in the Lords Supper
24 Punching my sister
25 Robbing my mothers box of plums and sugar
26 Calling Dorothy Rose a jade
27 Glutiny in my sickness
28 Peevishness with my mother
29 With my sister
30 Falling out with the servants
31 Divers commissions of alle my duties
32 Idle discourse on Thy day and at other times
33 Not turning nearer to Thee for my affections
34 Not living according to my belief
35 Not loving Thee for Thy self
36 Not loving Thee for Thy goodness to us
37 Not desiring Thy ordinances

---

without knowledge of sounds? ... and these things being rightly dispatch'd, does it not appear from phænomena that there is a Being incorporeal, living, intelligent?' (Newton, 1718: 344–35).

For Newton there could be no laws of motion without a divine legislator. Newton's bold principle of the laws of gravitation and of motion controlling the orbits of planets were made possible despite the absence of any mechanical

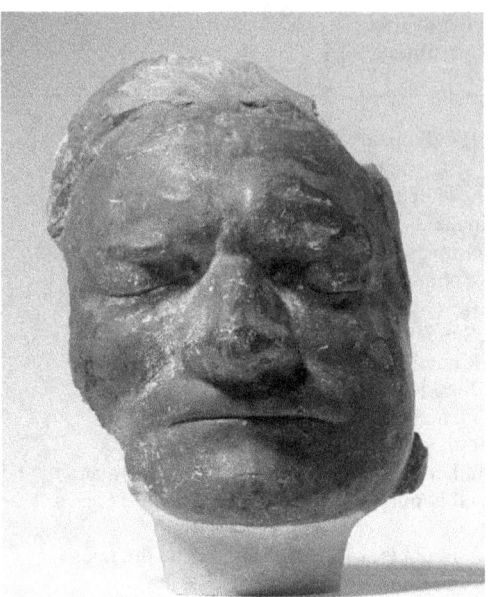

Figure 3: Isaac Newton's death mask

link between the bodies because he believed that God facilitated action at a distance and upheld the planets in their motions. As Newton wrote: 'there exists an infinite and omnipresent spirit in which matter is moved according to mathematical laws' (Brooke, 1988: 168–83). In fact he went further and postulated that periodic divine intervention was necessary to maintain the stability of the solar system. It was this view that led to argument with Leibniz, who maintained that an omnipotent God would never have made something so defective that it required intervention to keep it working properly. Nevertheless both Newton and Leibniz were committed to the view that science and religion were ineluctably intertwined. In the years that followed, Newton's view of a mechanical universe governed by God was widely used both to underpin the idea of a divine Creator and also as a bulwark against materialism and atheism.

Benjamin Franklin (1706–90)

Benjamin Franklin is well known as one of the Founding Fathers of the United States of America, and was active as a politician and diplomat as well as an author and scientist. His main contributions to science were his research and theories about electricity. Among other things, he invented the lightning rod and bifocals, many millions of which are still in use today.

Although Franklin grew up under Calvinist Christian teaching, he came under the influence of British deistic thinking and moved in that direction.

Figure 4: Benjamin Franklin National Memorial in Franklin Institute, Philadelphia, USA

Nevertheless he remained a member of the Episcopalian Church throughout his life. He maintained a lifelong belief in God and his sovereignty. In 1732 Franklin wrote a paper entitled 'On the Providence of God in the Government of the World' (1960). In this he affirmed 'the Existence of a Deity and that he is the Creator of the Universe'. When the Constitutional Convention was stalled for four or five weeks, he reminded the members that 'God governs in the affairs of men', and suggested that 'henceforth prayers imploring the assistance of Heaven, and its blessings on our deliberations, be held in this Assembly every morning before we proceed to business' (Hund and Scott, 1920).

Unlike the previous two scientists, Boyle and Newton, Franklin did not appear to agonize over his spiritual state. His was apparently a more pragmatic religion. As he wrote in a letter to his father dated 1738: 'I think vital religion has always suffered when orthodoxy is more regarded than virtue. The scriptures assure me that at the last day we shall not be examined on what we thought but what we did.' Franklin himself, with his deistic leanings, was certainly unorthodox. And he pungently commented: 'How many observe Christ's birthday! How few, his precepts! O! 'tis easier to keep holidays than commandments' (Franklin, 1743).

Franklin came closest to baring his soul in a letter to his friend Ezra Styles, the President of Yale, written a few weeks before his death at age 84. He wrote:

You desire to know something of my religion. It is the first time I have been questioned upon it. But I cannot take your curiosity amiss, and shall endeavor in a few words to gratify it. Here is my creed. I believe in one God, the creator of the universe. That he governs by his providence. That he ought to be worshipped. That the most acceptable service we render to him is doing good to his other children. That the soul of man is immortal, and will be treated with justice in another life respecting its conduct in this. These I take to be the fundamental points in all sound religion, and I regard them as you do in whatever sect I meet with them.

As to Jesus of Nazareth, my opinion of whom you particularly desire, I think his system of morals and his religion, as he left them to us, the best the world ever saw or is likely to see; but I apprehend ... some doubts as to his divinity; though it is a question I do not dogmatize upon, having never studied it, and think it needless to busy myself with it now, when I expect soon an opportunity of knowing the truth with less trouble. I see no harm, however, in its being believed, if that belief has the good consequences, as probably it has, of making his doctrines more respected and more observed (1904: 185–86).

Benjamin Franklin, renowned statesman and scientist, embraced belief in God as part of his world-view.

Edward Jenner (1749–1823)

Jenner is sometimes called the 'Father of Immunology', because he pioneered vaccination against smallpox. He was the eighth of nine children born to the Revd Stephen Jenner, vicar of Berkeley in Gloucestershire. Both his parents died in 1754. He was brought up largely by his aunt at Clapton Farm near Berkeley, and returned after training to general practice as a doctor in Berkeley, where he spent most of his life (Drewitt, 1931).

Jenner noticed that milkmaids rarely got smallpox and found that exposure to the bovine disease cowpox produced immunity to smallpox. In 1796 he used fluid taken from a cowpox sore on milkmaid Sarah Nelmes to inject the 8-year-old James Phipps. The boy did not subsequently get smallpox, despite repeated attempts by Jenner to infect him. It was an experiment which would be highly unlikely to get ethical clearance today!

Jenner's father and two of his closest collaborators (one his nephew) were Church of England vicars. Jenner himself apparently showed no more than conventional interest in religious matters, although he remained a regular worshipper in the Church of England. Nevertheless, he served as vice-president of Cheltenham Auxiliary Bible Society. He also became a Freemason and probably had deistic beliefs. In a letter to his friend Thomas Pruen he wrote:

Figure 5: Edward Jenner testing vaccination against smallpox. Note the cow at the door

'The weather may be inconvenient for the designs of man, but must always be in harmony with the designs of God, who has not only this planet, our Earth, to manage, but the universe. The whole creation is the work of God's hands. It cannot manage itself. Man cannot manage it, therefore, God is the manager.'

Charles Babbage (1791–1871)

Charles Babbage's main scientific claim to fame is originating the concept of a programmable computer. Like Newton, he held the Lucasian chair of mathematics in Cambridge. Babbage was a devout Anglican Christian who believed that 'the study of the works of nature with scientific precision, was a necessary and indispensable preparation to the understanding and interpreting their testimony of the wisdom and goodness of their Divine Author' (Buxton, 1978: 227). Indeed, in 1814, Babbage decided to become an Anglican minister. But although he applied for several vacancies in the Church of England, his applications were unsuccessful because church leaders were uncomfortable with his reputation as a liberal. Perhaps fortunately for us, he turned his talents to the problems of calculating machines instead and we all reap the benefit of that in the computers we use every day.

Our most detailed knowledge of Babbage's religious views come from the book he wrote in response to the Bridgewater Treatise series on natural religion. That series comprised eight volumes published by the Royal Society using an endowment from the Earl of Bridgewater. Their express purpose was to describe 'The Power, Wisdom, and Goodness of God, as Manifested in the Creation'. Babbage was not one of the authors chosen to write, so he published what he called *The Ninth Bridgewater Treatise, A Fragment* (Babbage, 1837). In it, he used his insights from calculating machines to describe God as a divine programmer who had set up complex laws to govern the behavior of the world. This included miracles, meaning that God did not have to intervene in the world to make a miracle happen. Rather, Babbage maintained that miracles are not the breach of established laws (meaning human laws) but indicate the existence of far higher laws (meaning God's laws).

Babbage thought that our mechanistic view of the world was not sufficiently complex to explain miraculous events. It was a call to work harder at science to develop a deeper understanding of God's laws which govern the natural world rather than abdicating understanding to divine intervention each time we cannot understand something (Lindgren, 1990). To an extent, Babbage was reacting against what we might call a 'God of the gaps' argument today. Anthony Hyman writes in his biography that 'Babbage came to believe that scientific method pursued to its uttermost limit was entirely compatible with revealed religion and he wrote his Ninth Bridgewater Treatise to prove the point' (1982: 14).

Figure 6: Part of Charles Babbage's analytical engine at the Science Museum, London

Babbage's beliefs went well beyond merely recognizing the compatibility of science and Christianity. As Buxton says, Babbage 'believed that the study of the works of nature with scientific precision, was a necessary and indispensable preparation to the understanding and interpreting their testimony of the wisdom and goodness of their Divine Author' (Buxton, 1978: 1986).

Alfred Russel Wallace (1823–1913)

Wallace was a British naturalist, explorer, geographer and biologist as well as a campaigning social reformer. It is interesting that the Royal Society chose him rather than Charles Darwin to represent the topic of evolution because history has largely eclipsed Wallace's contributions. In 1858 Wallace wrote to Charles Darwin from Malaysia where he was collecting specimens, setting out a theory of natural selection which was similar to Darwin's then unpublished ideas. Darwin had thought deeply about this topic for two decades, and Wallace's letter containing such similar ideas 'smashed' him (his own word) because he realized he might lose primacy and recognition for the considerable work he had done. Having taken advice from his friends, the botanist Joseph Hooker and the geologist Charles Lyell, Darwin honorably suggested the joint reading of his and Wallace's papers on evolution on 1 July 1858 at the Linnaean Society. As it happened, Darwin's 19-month old son had died three days earlier, so neither Wallace nor Darwin was at that meeting where the idea of natural selection was first presented, and it passed by with little comment (Moody, 1971: 474–76). Darwin was then spurred on to publish his own theory in a fuller book form the following year.

Soon afterwards, Wallace in 1861 wrote to his brother-in-law pointing out his own rejection of Christianity, though he did not reject all religion out of hand. Wallace wrote:

> I will pass over as utterly contemptible the oft-repeated accusation that sceptics shut out evidence because they will not be governed by the morality of Christianity. . . . I am thankful I can see much to admire in all religions. To the mass of mankind religion of some kind is a necessity. But whether there be a God and whatever be His nature; whether we have an immortal soul or not, or whatever may be our state after death, I can have no fear of having to suffer for the study of nature and the search for truth. (Marchant, 1916)

A few years later, Wallace turned to spiritualism and accepted it for the rest of his life. He repeatedly defended spiritualist mediums against accusations of fraud. He maintained that something in 'the unseen universe of Spirit' had interceded at least three times in history: to create life from inorganic matter; to introduce consciousness in the higher animals; and most importantly, and

Figure 7: Alfred Russel Wallace from
Popular Science Monthly **11 (1877)**

controversially, to generate the higher mental faculties in humankind (Wallace, 1889).

Wallace's public advocacy of spiritualism and particularly his belief in a non-material origin for the higher mental faculties severely strained his relationship with many leading scientists, including Darwin. Wallace believed that evolution suggested that the universe might have a purpose, and that certain aspects of living organisms might not be explainable in terms of purely materialistic processes. Indeed the very title of his 1910 book proclaimed that thesis: *The World of Life; a Manifestation of Creative Power, Directive Mind, and Ultimate Purpose* (Wallace, 1910).

Wallace's studies of evolution certainly did not turn him into an arch-reductionist like modern-day Richard Dawkins. Although not an adherent to an established religion, he believed strongly in a spiritual dimension which affected the reality we find around us. Like many other great scientists, he was unconventional and thought 'outside the box'.

I will leave the last word to Wallace, who wrote:

> I thus learnt my first great lesson in the inquiry into these obscure fields of knowledge, never to accept the disbelief of great men or their accusations of imposture or of imbecility, as of any weight when opposed to the repeated observation of facts by other men, admittedly sane and honest. The whole history of science shows us that whenever the educated and scientific men of any age have denied the facts of other investigators

on *a priori* grounds of absurdity or impossibility, the deniers have always been wrong.[2]

Joseph Lister (1827–1912)

Lister was an English surgeon who first promoted the idea of sterile surgery while working at the Glasgow Royal Infirmary. He introduced the use of carbolic acid as an antiseptic to sterilize surgical instruments and to clean wounds, which greatly reduced infections following surgery. Lister was brought up as a Quaker, in the faith of his parents, and went to the University of London because it was one of the few places which were then open to Quakers. After he married, he joined the Scottish Episcopal Church because his wife was not a Quaker, and remained a member through the rest of his life.

Lister's biographer Godlee, who was also his nephew and knew him well from having practised and spent a lot of time with him, described him as having 'a simple, it might be said a childlike faith in the Christian religion'. Godlee wrote that although Lister freely discussed spiritual matters with his relations and closest students in his youth and early adult life, he was more reserved in later life. That was perhaps a reflection of the more secular perspective then developing among scientists generally. After he became President of the Royal Society (1895–1900) he was asked his views on religious matters. Lister's answer was that 'I have no hesitation in saying that in my opinion there is no antagonism between the Religion of Jesus Christ and any fact scientifically

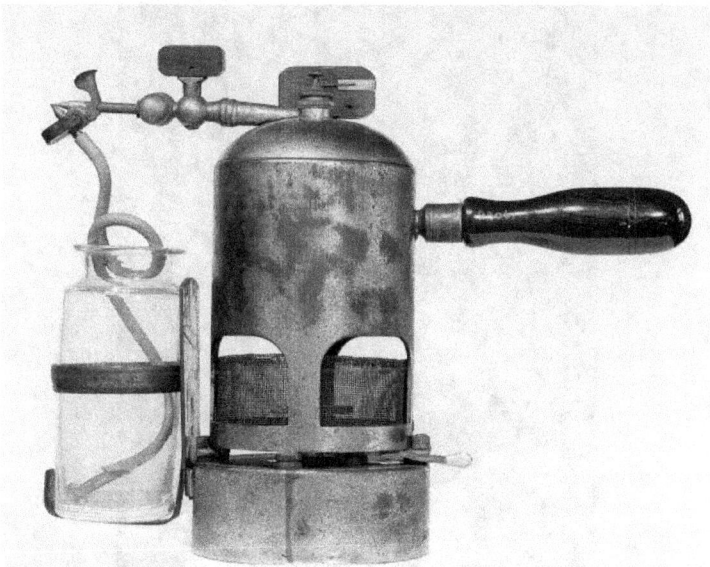

Figure 8: Joseph Lister's antiseptic carbolic spray

established', though he didn't allow this statement to be published until 1909. A fellow surgeon who knew Lister well confirmed this by writing:

> his life was, what is termed in theological language, a life of faith, even if he had never spoken a word to indicate his views. That he believed in the Divine Father of all, that he regarded the problems of life and death with simple faith and reverence, that he had firm faith in a personal immortality, I have no doubt, and I treasure as my greatest possessions, letters in which he has given expression to such faith and hope. (Godlee, 1924: 615–616)

Ernest Rutherford (1871–1937)

Rutherford became known as the father of nuclear physics, and was awarded the Nobel Prize in 1908 'for his investigations into the disintegration of the elements, and the chemistry of radioactive substances'. He is widely credited as splitting the atom in 1917 and leading the first experiment to 'split the nucleus' in a controlled manner by two students under his direction, John Cockcroft and Ernest Walton in 1932.

Rutherford had a Presbyterian upbringing, but apparently moved away from it in adult life, though he kept to its moral code. A colleague wrote of him: 'I knew Rutherford rather well and under varied conditions from 1903 onwards, but

Figure 9: Ernest Rutherford

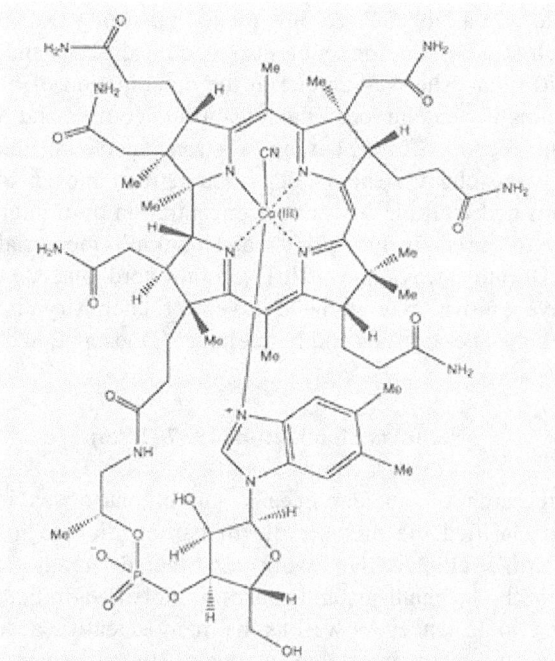

Figure 10: Molecular structure of vitamin B_{12} determined using X-ray crystallography

never heard religion discussed; nor have I found in his papers one line of writing connected with it' (Eve, 1939: 402). At the time there was a growing reluctance among younger scientists to be identified with any kind of metaphysical exercise, and Rutherford was typical of his age (Bowler, 2001: 61). Nevertheless, he was apparently happy to abide by the outward forms of Christianity. He was punctilious in always closing his laboratories on Sundays, and was renowned for wandering around the laboratory singing 'Onward Christian soldiers', if things were going well, or 'Fight the good fight' if they weren't.

In 1936 Rutherford was appointed to the newly reformed Papal Academy of Sciences, which was a strange distinction for a man who was known to be indifferent to religion. But he accepted the position because, as he told his Dutch colleague Professor Zeeman, he thought it might do something to ease the strain in 'International Relations' (Wilson, 1983: 596).

Dorothy Hodgkin (1910–94)

Hodgkin developed X-ray crystallography to determine the three-dimensional structure of biomolecules, measuring in particular the structure of cholesterol, penicillin, insulin and vitamin B_{12}. She was the first and so far remains the only female Briton to win a Nobel Prize. She picked up strong Quaker values from her mother, such as a passion for social justice, ethical issues and pacifism. Her biographer writes that 'she was unique in the combination of her authority in research, her humanity and her personal response to conflict and poverty'.

There is no record of her having a strong personal faith, though if interpretations were elusive, she would often retreat into an absorbed state, humming hymns and working with utter concentration until interrupted, or she became simply too tired. In his address at Hodgkin's memorial service Max Perutz said: 'Dorothy was more Christian in word and deed than many believers I have known. She radiated love: for chemistry, her family, her friends, her students, her crystals and her college' (Dodson, 2002: 179–219).

Nicholas Shackleton (1937–2006)

Shackleton's research on ancient oceans and climates was innovative and pioneering. He clarified the precise role of carbon dioxide in warming and cooling the Earth's climate. His work contributed greatly to our present understanding of the mechanisms and causes of global warming, a crucial topic of contemporary importance. As well as his many scientific accomplishments, he also excelled in another area, that of music. He was a very accomplished clarinet player and amassed what is almost certainly the largest collection of clarinets in the world, including 817 clarinets and basset horns. He used to lecture in the Music Department as well as the Earth Sciences Department in Cambridge.

I knew Nick Shackleton as a colleague. He never to my knowledge expressed any opinions on religious or spiritual matters and I am sure that he would have described himself as a secularist. He was supportive of and helpful to younger scientists and musicians worldwide, and gave freely of his time to discuss their results. Scientific research was the major interest in his life; music was a very close second. In his words: 'Both music and science are for me intensely human activities, and both have found me innumerable friends' (McCave and Elderfield, 2011: 435–62).

The final tally

The ten scientists depicted on the Royal Society anniversary stamp set line up as below if they are divided into categories. The *Religious* category includes those who aligned themselves with one of the mainstream organized religions. The *Spiritual* category is for those who believed in the reality of the supernatural, but often in a more personalized way than those who fall into the *Religious* category. *Secularists* are the remainder, who do not subscribe to any formal religious or supernatural views.

- *Religious* (50%): Boyle, Newton, Franklin, Babbage, Lister
- *Spiritual* (20%): Jenner, Wallace
- *Secularist* (30%): Rutherford (though he was not inimical to religion), Hodgkin, Shackleton

It could be argued that the religious practices of Lister, Jenner and Rutherford were simply a reflection of the cultural norms of their times, although at least in the case of Lister he seems to have had a definite personal Christian faith, and Jenner too believed in the presence of a deity and was a regular churchgoer. In any case none of these three saw any contradiction between science and religion. Even by the standards of their time, four of the remaining scientists (Boyle, Newton, Babbage and Wallace) were considered by their contemporaries to be overly enthusiastic in their espousal of religion or spirituality, and it played a major part in each of their lives.

There is perhaps a tendency to increasing secularization over the period since the founding of the Royal Society 350 years ago to the present, both in the beliefs of the ten scientists depicted on these stamps, and in society at large. But as I show below this split of eminent scientists over the past 350 years is, perhaps surprisingly, almost identical to the percentages of how present-day leading scientists categorise themselves.

The contemporary scene

After three-and-a-half centuries of scientific endeavour, in the course of which we have come to rely ever more heavily on the fruits of science and technology, the range of interactions between scientists and religion has remained surprisingly consistent. A recent survey of scientists in leading US universities (Ecklund, 2010) found that their adherence to religious views was essentially the same as that of the ten eclectic scientists chosen for the 350th anniversary stamp set.

Fifty per cent of the 2,200 scientists surveyed saw themselves as religious and regularly attended churches or other religious meetings. Twenty per cent considered themselves to be spiritual, but were not religious and didn't attend meetings, while the remaining 30 per cent considered themselves to be secularists. Scientists are not the arid reductionists, hostile to all religious or spiritual overtones, that some popular cultural views imagine. Indeed, those who thought of themselves as spiritual did so because they saw the individualistic search for truth of their spirituality as congruent with their scientific methodology (Ecklund and Long, 2011). Although a minority of scientists see religion and science as in conflict, the majority do not (Ecklund *et al*., 2011).

Among the 30 per cent of contemporary secularists, only a minority say that they are secularist because science won out over religion. For most, their secularism is a result of religion either being irrelevant or having let them down, and it being perceived as unable to answer the hard questions. Many were raised in homes where religion was seen as unimportant. Interestingly, of the 20 per cent of scientists who see themselves as spiritual, almost one quarter also say that they are atheists.

In 1916 James Leuba undertook a landmark study of 1,000 randomly selected scientists in the USA. He reported that 42 per cent believed in an afterlife and a personal God (defined rather narrowly by him as 'a God to whom one could pray in expectation of receiving an answer'). At that time he predicted that disbelief would increase as education spread (Leuba, 1916). Yet a repeat survey in 1996 gave almost identical results, with 40 per cent believing in a personal God and an afterlife, 45 per cent expressing unbelief in the definition of God proffered (though, intriguingly, one fifth of that group still believed in immortality), and the remaining 15 per cent agnostic (Larson and Witham, 1997). It seems that not much has changed in the 80 years from 1916 to 1996, nor apparently over the past 350 years.

Religion is alive and well among practising scientists today. There is a significant number who are prepared to declare publicly that they have a strong personal Christian faith, which affects their whole life (Berry, 2009). And there is a not insignificant number of people like Ernest Lucas who have moved from successful careers in science to researching and teaching theology. They perform an invaluable service acting as ambassadors for the coherence of science and faith, and encouraging those of us who have remained working in the scientific community to see both our science and our faith as part of our worship of God.[3]

Sources of illustrations

Figure 2: Robert Boyle's title page

Wikipedia: The Christian Virtuoso. This is a faithful photographic reproduction of an original two-dimensional work of art.

Figure 3: Isaac Newton's death mask

Royal Society

Table 1 and Figure 4: Benjamin Franklin

Wikimedia Commons. Benjamin Franklin National Memorial in the Franklin Institute, Philadelphia, Pennsylvania Category: Images of Philadelphia,

Pennsylvania. Photo by Michael Parker. James Earle Fraser, sculptor.

Figure 5: Edward Jenner testing vaccination against smallpox

Courtesy Science Photo Library

Figure 6: Part of Charles Babbage's analytical engine at the Science Museum, London

The Science Museum.

Figure 7: Alfred Russel Wallace

Wikipedia: *Popular Science Monthly* 11 (1877)

Figure 8: Joseph Lister's antiseptic carbolic spray

Copyright Wellcome Library, London

Figure 9: Ernest Rutherford

Wikipedia

Notes

1. A transcript of Newton's notebook listing 49 sins, of which I show the first 37 is online at www.newtonproject.sussex.ac.uk
2. Reprinted from an August 1893 essay presented to the Psychical Congress held in Chicago, a paper which became the most reprinted work during his own lifetime and was later incorporated into the Preface of the 3rd edn of Alfred Russel Wallace, *Miracles and Modern Spiritualism: Three Essays* (London, 1896).
3. I am grateful to Colin Bell for assistance with research for this chapter and to John Hedley-Brooke for comments on an earlier draft.

Bibliography

Babbage, Charles. *The Ninth Bridgewater Treatise, a Fragment* (London: J. Murray, 1837).

Bacon, Francis. *The Advancement of Learning* (Holborne: Henrie Tomes, 1605).

Berry, R.J. ed. *Real Scientists, Real Faith: 17 Leading Scientists Reveal the Harmony Between Their Science and Their Faith* (Oxford, UK: Monarch, 2009).

Bowler, Peter J. *Reconciling Science and Religion: The Debate in Early-Twentieth Century Britain* (Chicago: University of Chicago Press, 2001).

Brooke, J.H. 'The God of Isaac Newton'. Pages 168–83 in *Let Newton Be!* (ed. J. Fauvel, R. Flood, M. Shortland and R. Wilson; Oxford: Oxford University Press, 1988).

———. 'Newton, Science and Religion'. In *The Isaac Newton Guide-Book* (ed. D.R. Alexander; Cambridge: Faraday Institute, 2012).

Brooke, John Hedley. *Science and Religion: Some Historical Perspectives* (Cambridge: Cambridge University Press, 1991).

Buxton, H.W. *Memoir of the Life and Labors of the Late Charles Babbage Esq.* Unpublished, cited in *The Mathematical Work of Charles Babbage*, J.M. Dubbey (Cambridge: Cambridge University Press, 1978).

Dawkins, Richard 'Atheists for Jesus' (April 2006) at <http://richarddawkins.net/articles/20-atheists-for-jesus> (last accessed 7 March 2012).

Dodson, Guy. 'Dorothy Mary Crowfoot Hodgkin, O.M. 12 May 1910—29 July 1994'. *Biographical Memoirs of Fellows of the Royal Society* 48 (2002), pp. 179–219.

Drewitt, F. Dawtry. *Life of Edward Jenner, MD., FRS: Naturalist, and Discoverer of Vaccination* (London: Longmans, Green & Co., 1931).

Ecklund, E.H., J.Z. Park and K.L. Sorrell. 'Scientists Negotiate Boundaries between Religion and Science', *Journal for the Scientific Study of Religion* 50 (2011), pp. 552–69.

Ecklund, Elaine H. *Science vs Religion: What Scientists Really Think* (USA: Oxford University Press, 2010).

———. and Elizabeth Long. 'Scientists and Spirituality', *Sociology of Religion* 72 (2011), pp. 253–74.

Eve, A.S. ed., *Rutherford: Being the Life and Letters of the Rt. Hon. Lord Rutherford, O.M.* (Cambridge: Cambridge University Press, 1939).

Feynman, R.P. quoted by Lee Smolin, *The Trouble with Physics: The Rise of String Theory, the Fall of a Science and What Comes Next* (London: Allen Lane, 2007), p. 307.

Franklin, Benjamin. 'Letter to Ezra Styles, 9 March 1790'. Pages 185–6 in *The Works of Benjamin Franklin* (ed. John Bigelow; New York: Putnam's, 1904), vol. 12.

———. 'On the Providence of God in the Government of the World'. Page 264 in *The Papers of Benjamin Franklin* (ed. Leonard W. Labaree et al.; New Haven, CT: Yale University Press, 1960–, vol. 1); and online at <http://www.franklinpapers.org/franklin/framedVolumes.jsp Volume 1: 1706–34>.

———. *Poor Richard's Almanac*, 359 (1743) (originally published under the pseudonym Richard Saunders).

Godlee, Rickman John. *Lord Lister* (Oxford: Clarendon Press, 3rd edn, rev. 1924).

Hund, Gaillard and James Brown Scott eds. *The Debates in the Federal Convention of 1787: Reported by James Madison* (New York: Oxford University Press, 1920).

Hunter, Michael. *Boyle: Between God and Science* (New Haven and London: Yale University Press, 2009).

———. and Edward B. Davis eds. *The Works of Robert Boyle* (London: Pickering & Chatto: London, 2000).

Hyman, A. *Charles Babbage: Pioneer of the Computer* (Oxford: Oxford University Press, 1982).
Larson, Edward J. and Larry Witham. 'Scientists Are Still Keeping the Faith', *Nature* 386 (1997), pp. 435–6.
Leuba, James H. *The Belief in God and Immortality: A Psychological, Anthropological, and Statistical Study* (Boston, MA: Sherman, French & Co., 1916).
Lindgren, Michael. *Glory and Failure: The Difference Engines of Johann Muller, Charles Babbage and Georg and Edvard Scheutz* (Cambridge, MA: MIT Press, 1990).
Marchant, James ed. *Alfred Russel Wallace: Letters and Reminiscences* (London: Cassell, 1916).
McCave, I.N. and H. Elderfield. 'Sir Nicholas John Shackleton 23 June 1937—24 January 2006'. *Biographical Memoirs of Fellows of the Royal Society* 57 (2011), pp. 435–62.
Moody, J.W.T. 'The Reading of the Darwin and Wallace Papers: An Historical "Non-Event" '. *J. Soc. Biblphy. Nat. Hist.*, 5(6), (1971).
Newton, Isaac. *Opticks: Or, a Treatise of the Reflections, Refractions, Inflections and Colours of Light.* (London: W. and J. Innys, 2nd edn, 1718).
———. *The Principia: Mathematical Principles of Natural Philosophy* (new trans. I. Bernard Cohen and Anne Whitman with Julia Budnez; Berkeley, CA: University of California Press, 1999).
Principe, Lawrence. 'In Retrospect: The Sceptical Chymist'. *Nature* 469 (2011), pp. 30–1.
Snobelen, S.D. 'Isaac Newton, Heresy Laws and the Persecution of Religious Dissent'. *Enlightenment and Dissent*, 25 (2009), pp. 204–59.
Wallace, Alfred Russel. *Darwinism: An Exposition of the Theory of Natural Selection, with Some of its Applications* (London: Macmillan, 1889).
———. *The World of Life; a Manifestation of Creative Power, Directive Mind, and Ultimate Purpose* (London: Chapman & Hall, 1910).
Wilson, David. *Rutherford, Simple Genius* (Hodder & Stoughton, 1983).

You shall love the Lord your God
  with all your heart
  with all your soul
  with all your mind
  with all your strength
and your neighbour as yourself.
Do this and you will live.

God, alpha and omega,
  you have beckoned us into relationship with you,
  loving with every fibre of our being
  as you love—fully, totally, uncompromisingly.

You have given us
  hearts that hunger
  souls that seek
  minds that inquire
  strength that sustains
and the neighbourhood of the world
in which to live and move and grow
into the likeness of Christ.

Thank you for men and women
  who have patiently and riskily
  creatively and courageously
  sought to explore the workings
  of the universe
  and in the infinitely small
  discovered something of you
  which has expanded all our lives,
  all our hearts, souls, and minds,
  in the newly neighboured landscape

PART THREE

The Scriptures

10

The Evolving Agenda of Biblical Studies

Simon Woodman

This festschrift in honor of Ernest Lucas provides an opportunity to offer some reflections on the future of the academic discipline of biblical studies. Lucas came to biblical studies as an accomplished scientist, and his interest in the relationship between faith and science runs through a number of his publications. But more than this, he has engaged biblical studies not just as an academic, not just as a scientist, but also as a Baptist minister committed to the preaching and teaching of the Bible as the revelation of Jesus Christ. His publications track the collision of these three agendas as he brings academic rigour coupled with scientific integrity to the task of bringing the Bible to life for those who are seeking through its pages an encounter with the risen Christ.

Lucas has never confined himself to a narrow engagement with the ancient text; rather he has consistently brought the world of the text and the world of the contemporary reader to bear on each other in such a way as to allow the former to inform and challenge the latter. He states in the Author's Preface of his Apollos Daniel commentary that it 'is written primarily for those who have the responsibility of teaching and preaching the Bible, particularly those who do it in a Christian context' (Lucas, 2002: 9). By positioning himself at the conjunction of these three worlds of science, academic biblical studies and Christian faith, Lucas has put himself in a challenging and sometimes uncomfortable place. Yet it has been an endeavour that has borne much fruit. Just as the final editor of the book of Daniel brought the stories of Babylon to bear on the world of second-century BC Judea, so Lucas has brought the world of the Bible to bear on the contemporary world in ways that prophetically challenge dominant ideologies, while empowering and encouraging those who seek to live as faithful disciples of the God who calls them to live life differently.

The horizon of scholarly engagement with the text of the Bible is changing. From the early optimism of the quest to recover the events behind the text, to the focus on the redactional processes that gave shape to the text, to the scholarly reconstruction of the contexts of the recipients of the text, biblical scholarship through the twentieth century remained largely rooted within the first-century world. It sought to regain, recover and reconstruct the 'original' or 'authentic' voice of the text. Engagement with those who grappled with the meaning of the text for their own, later, generations remained the preserve of systematicians, doctrinal specialists and church historians.

However, a growing number of voices signalled a revolution, and the discipline of *reception history* emerged as a compelling feature on the biblical studies landscape. While recognizing the importance of investigating the way in which the biblical text was received by its initial readers, the horizon widened to include engagement with theatres of reception far removed, both in chronology and context, from the initial audience.

Crucial to this shift has been a value change as to what constitutes an 'acceptable' reading of the Bible. The traditional presupposition of biblical studies may be characterized as 'original is best'; in other words the pre-eminent 'original' meaning should function as a yardstick against which to measure other, later, interpretations. As a reaction against an ecclesial tradition which sought to restrict biblical interpretative diversity on doctrinal grounds, this emphasis on the 'original' meaning liberated scholarship from the controlling hand of traditional Christianity. However, as the monolith of Christendom relinquished its interpretative power so another monolith, that of Western academic biblical scholarship, emerged. Power passed from priest to scholar, and interpretative control became vested in a new scholarly elite, comprising those equipped to pass such judgments on interpretation.

However, the biblical text continued to be 'received' in contexts so diverse that many of them failed to cross the radar of academic biblical scholarship. The challenge to Western biblical scholarship in the latter part of the twentieth century came from the margins of the Western world, from the likes of feminist, liberationist, Marxist and post-colonial readings. These highlighted the extent to which biblical scholarship had remained a predominantly male, white, educated, wealthy endeavour, and brought to the academy a profound challenge: the new priesthood of scholars were challenged to look beyond themselves and their reconstructed historical contexts, and to take account of the way the text was being read by people with new, and challenging, agendas.

This trajectory has continued with the emergence of the discipline of reception history. From ecclesial and devotional to populist and secular, the Bible has continued to have an effect beyond the walls of the academy, and biblical scholarship has now woken up to this fact. The reception of the Bible has emerged as a valid object (or should that be subject?) of study, and the voices of those who have engaged the Bible from within their own context are now permitted to be heard within the academy. As W. J. Lyons asserts, 'Reception history . . . [opens] up a vast new area for study by historical critics . . . [it] offers real hope for New Testament studies' (2010: 217); cf. Crossley, 2012).

The term *Wirkungsgeschichte* (history of influence/effects) was coined by the German philosopher Hans Georg Gadamer (1900–2002) in his influential work *Wahrheit und Methode* (Truth and Method, 1960) (Knight: 2010: 137; Nicholls, 2005: 1, 5–6; Gadamer, 2004). Gadamer's influence on Western thought has been both far-reaching and profound, and his great challenge was to the philosophical perspective which located the quest for absolute truth within the correct application of rational method. For Gadamer, 'the idea that we can step outside our own cultural reference points to embrace timeless truth [was] a demonstrable fiction of modernist thought' (Lawn, 2006:1). It was in this context that Gadamer employed the concept of *hermeneutics*, borrowing a concept from the realms of biblical interpretation but using it to denote 'a more general procedure for understanding' (Lawn, 2006: 2; cf. Scheibler, 2000: 135). Gadamer thus spoke of the 'hermeneutical circle', denoting the non-linear and cyclical nature of interpretation. Rather than a journey towards a destination of ultimate truth, 'interpretation is sited within the mutual horizon of the interpreter and the thing to be interpreted' (Lawn, 2006: 2; cf. Gadamer, 1976: 38–42). Chris Lawn summarizes:

> for Gadamer hermeneutics is universal: what happens when we interpret a text is what happens when we seek to understand anything in our cultural social world be it the meaning of life or the more mundane interpretation of everyday events. Reading is interpretation, looking is interpretation, thinking is interpretation; interpretation is not a special activity confined to the unravelling of difficult texts it is an aspect of all forms of human understanding. (Lawn, 2006: 9; cf. Grondin, 2003: 143)

Gadamer thus engaged the concept of scholarly objectivity in historical study, so beloved of Western academia, and concluded that the 'horizon of understanding' available to the original readers of a text is irrevocably inaccessible to later readers, who must therefore approach the text from their own 'horizon of understanding' (Gadamer, 2004: 396.3; cf. Roberts, 2009: 35). By this account, the 'original' meaning of the text remains forever alien and inaccessible to the contemporary reader. Gadamer's solution was for readers to develop self-conscious reading strategies whereby they abandon any attempt at objectivity, and instead approach the text in the knowledge of their own historical 'horizon'. In other words, contemporary readers do to the text what the original readers did, which is to read it as themselves. The two horizons are thus fused, as the text continues to have an effect as readers continue to read it (Roberts, 2009: 36). The study of the relationship between reader and text, both contemporary and historical, is encompassed within the discipline of *Wirkungsgeschichte*. As Rachel Nicholls puts it: '*Wirkungsgeschichte* is not simply the sum total of interpretations of a text through history. It is not even the influence which past interpretations have on our present day work, whether we are aware of this or not. *Wirkungsgeschichte* is a description of our whole relationship to history which forms both the boundaries and the possibilities of interpretation' (2005: 6).

The repercussions of Gadamer's insights were first felt within the discipline of literary criticism, particularly at the University of Konstanz which was founded in 1965 as a 'reform university'.[1] Hans-Robert Jauss (1922–97), a former student of Gadamer at Heidelberg, taught there as professor of literary criticism and romance philology, and pioneered the concept of *Rezeptiongeschichte* (reception history) (Jauss, 1982). While his academic engagement with Marxism and formalism was of its time, the English translation of the term Jauss coined has, along with Gadamer's concept of *Wirkungsgeschichte*, come designate the emerging discipline of reception history (Knight, 2010: 139). John Sawyer comments: 'In many ways I prefer the term Wirkungsgeschichte 'impact history', coined by Gadamer, because it places the focus on the text rather than the reader, and on its power to influence people and events, rather than on the more passive process of reception . . . The term Reception-history, however, is much . . . more transparent than Wirkungsgeschichte, in English at any rate' (Sawyer, 2000).

Another academic from the University of Konstanz, Wolfgang Iser (1926–2007), helped to move the emerging discipline of reception history into a wider dialogue within academia, through his semi-foundationalist championing of reader-response theory (Iser, 1980). In this, Iser sought to locate the generation of meaning firmly within the world of the reader, rather than within the world of the text, suggesting that 'readers fill in the "blanks" and "negations" of the text through each act of reading' (Knight, 2010: 140). The 'work' of reading was thus to negotiate these gaps in the otherwise stable text. This challenge was taken further by the American literary theorist Stanley Fish (1938–), whose seminal work, *Is There a Text in This Class?* (1980), outlined his anti-foundationalist perspective whereby everything is interpretation. For Fish, 'meaning is what happens to readers during the reading process', leaving no objective textual foundation on which meaning can be constructed or adjudicated (cited in Sawyer, 2000: 2). Yet, Fish observes, communication still happens, and meaning is still shared; reality might evince interpretative diversity, but not interpretative anarchy. He points to the 'interpretive community' as the place where this occurs, commenting that 'the understanding achieved by two or more persons is specific to that system and determinate only within its confines' (Fish, 1980: 304; cf. Matlock, 1997).

From the 1980s onwards, the insights of reader-response theory began to make their presence felt within the academic discipline of biblical studies, with Fish being both hailed and reviled in equal measure (Knight, 2010: 140; cf. Thiselton, 1992: 541; Vanhoozer, 1998: 317–20; Hauerwas, 1993:19–28). However, it was Stephen Moore who articulated the possibilities for the reconceptualization of the discipline: 'Reader theory in literary studies is a Pandora's box into which we, infant literary critics of the Bible, have barely begun to peer. Opened more fully it might release some unsettling, but possibly timely, ways of reconceiving biblical interpretation' (Moore, 1989: 107).

The impact of discussions around the radical indeterminacy of texts has indeed generated new and controversial approaches to the biblical text. John Sawyer summarizes the result:

> What is also new is the notion that the reception of a text is more important than the text itself, and even that a text doesn't really exist until somebody reads it. 'The bare text is mute'. It is like the philosophers' old question: If a tree falls in the forest and no-one hears it, does it make a sound? A text without a reader has no meaning. It is the readers of a text that give it meaning. (Sawyer, 2000: 1; cf. Fowl, 1995)

The problem is that if meaning is generated in the interaction between text and reader, or more properly within the reader's interpretive community, then the basis on which to adjudicate between competing interpretations is also up for grabs. The biblical scholars' dictum of 'original is best' becomes as passé as any ecclesial claim to absolute authoritative control. The scholar can no longer stand objectively, observing the past from a position of academic isolation. Rather, 'we stand on the shoulders of centuries of conversations; our own positions are never independent of the reception history of these texts—ancient and modern—and our own work is woefully incomplete without a dialogic presentation of or response to those other responses' (Gowler, 2010: 204). Other criteria for arbitrating meaning are now required, which Sawyer notes may range from ethical to aesthetic, ideological to theological, historical-critical to academic (2004: 12–13). The unsettling aspect of these criteria, for some at least, is that they are dependent not on the objective entity of the text, but upon subjective opinions formed and informed by the human communities of which interpreters are a part. This unsettlement is however not a recent phenomenon, and finds its origins deep within the hermeneutical tradition. The philosopher Wilhelm Dilthey (1833–1911) noted the influence of the Reformation on biblical interpretation, tracing the emergence of modern hermeneutical theory to the Reformation conviction that 'texts are to be understood in their own terms rather than those of doctrine so that understanding requires not dogma but the systematic application of interpretive rules' (Warnke, 1987: 5; cf. Ermarth, 1978: 323; Dilthey 1976: 247–63). Dilthey's insight was to identify the meaning of a text with the 'subjective intention of its author', while understanding became an 'imaginative projection' on the part of the reader (Gadamer, 1976: xiii–xiv).

However, the emerging possibilities which these insights present to discipline of biblical studies are compelling as well as unsettling. Nicholls provides an evocative summary of Gadamer's insight into the relationship between the interpreter and the history of interpretation, suggesting that 'we experience our own historicity as a limit on our potential understanding, but it is also the means by which understanding is possible at all. There is no point in trying to deny our own historical finitude, any more than there is any point in defying gravity—the wise path is to work with it, not against it' (2005: 12).

In the light of this she suggests that 'perhaps we can learn from our own preunderstandings and gut reactions as they occur during the process of interpretation, rather than to try to bracket them out. These would include not only our own psychological disposition, but also our cultural and educational makeup and the communities which have formed us as a reader' (Nicholls, 2005:12).

While the appeal to the text may have diminished, the corresponding opportunity for exploration of the emergence of meaning within interpretive communities has increased.

The impact of reader-response theory within biblical studies has thus prepared the way for the rise of reception history as a significant factor within the discipline. Far from being 'biblical studies on holiday', as one anonymous critic once verbalized it, reception history raises the possibility of a breadth of engagement with the text unbound by dogmatic constraint, whether academic or ecclesial. As Robert Morgan explains, 'reception history includes in its purview both the broad spectrum of religious reception of the Bible and the wider and shallower cultural influence' (2010: 176). This widening of scope raises interesting possibilities for self-conscious scholarship, in which the horizon of the interpreter gives shape to the scope of their research. As Nicholls notes, 'it is our human finitude which provides both the limits and the possibilities for historical interpretation' (Nicholls, 2005:13).

It was the Swiss scholar Ulrich Luz (1938–) who pioneered application of the insights of Gadamer to a biblical studies agenda (Elliott, 2010: 162). While his main area of research has focused around the Gospel of Matthew, his methodological insights present far-reaching challenges for biblical scholarship more generally. For Luz, 'biblical texts do not simply have one set, closed meaning but are full of possibilities' (1990: 98). The intent of biblical studies, by his account, is not to restrict or control interpretative meaning, because 'one does not yet understand what the subject matter of the text *means* if one only understands what it *has meant*' (Luz, 1990: 98). Rather, a biblical studies agenda informed by reception history will note 'the problem of the contextuality of every interpretation. All interpretations and actualizations of biblical texts are contextual; their truth and power are valid only within those contexts' (Luz, 2005: 360). Envisaged in this way, a *Wirkungsgeschichte* biblical studies commentary, such as that written by Luz on the Gospel of Matthew, pays attention to 'the history, reception, and actualizing of a text in media other than the commentary, thus, e.g., in sermons, canonical law, hymnody, art, and in the actions and sufferings of the church' (Luz, 1990: 95). It is immediately clear that this represents a radical widening of the biblical studies agenda, in such a way as to encompass not only historical-critical engagement with the initial reception of the text, but also the way in which the text has been and continues to be received in a diversity of contexts, including the church. For Luz, the 'church' forms the primary community of biblical exegesis, construed as a variable entity both synchronically and diachronically.

It is therefore the church that defines the biblical canon, and the church that sets the parameters of biblical interpretation. Just as in, for example, the discipline of classical studies, the 'canon' of relevant literature is defined by the primary interpretative community, so for Luz the canon of the Bible is defined by the ecclesial community. Mark Elliott makes the point:

> The third thing to note, after his academic credentials and his championing of *Wirkungsgeschichte*, is Luz's conviction that the Bible is the book of the church . . . it is also the Bible which allows the church to be a community of openness yet alterity. It is this very ecumenicity that encourages him to look back down the centuries to the Bible's *Wirkungsgeschichte*, to trace what is the common inheritance of the church, widely conceived. . . . Thus the approach is that New Testament scholarship does not operate in a vacuum and has significance for those outside the academy to whom scholars should feel accountable. (2010: 163)

This fusion of horizons is radically generative of new possibilities. The horizon of original reception becomes the horizon of the contemporary interpreter; the horizon of the church becomes the horizon of the academy. Rather than restricting itself to the text and its original reception, biblical studies is liberated by reception history to encompass within its academic inquiry the diversity of biblical engagement within both the historic and contemporary worlds, whether such engagement be textual, artistic, musical or verbal. As Elliott rhetorically expresses it: 'Oral tradition became flesh, suffered under historical criticism, died and was buried and on the third day of the postmodern rose again' (2010: 167). Communities of engagement traditionally removed from the academy thus become of interest to those within; and the reception of the Bible within those groups becomes a legitimate discipline of research. Elliott notes that the scope of *Wirkungsgeschichte* in Luz's thinking extends to reception history within faith communities, including devotional readings: 'By making the *ekklesia* to be all those who are interested in the Bible, "meaning for today" is what the text says devotionally to individuals and perhaps small groups (fundamentalists, feminists, materialists and all permutations due to joint identity)' (2010: 172).

This notion that for Luz *Wirkungsgeschichte* and the hermeneutical strategies of faith communities are interrelated creates the context for research which is firmly grounded within the reading tradition of a specified faith community.

A range of scholars have followed in the path blazed by Luz, and have found in the discipline of reception history a fruitful way of engaging the text and its theatres of reception, from its original (implied) readership to the contemporary context. Mark Goodacre highlights the potential of *Wirkungsgeschichte* 'to draw together insights from different forms of scholarship, reminding us simultaneously that a text has a history, a history that begins after it has left the hands of its author'. Noting the way in which *Wirkungsgeschichte* straddles historical discipline and reader response, he suggests that 'it might even help to function as a useful control on some of the perceived excesses of some reader-response work' (Goodacre, 1997). Christopher Rowland has been one of the most prolific voices in championing the *Wirkungsgeschichte* agenda. He observes that *Wirkungsgeschichte* is 'a plea to be truly diachronic and appreciate the history of texts *through time* as a key to their interpretation and to see that exegesis should not be confined to written explication of texts which seek to relate their origins, purpose and reception solely to their original literary context, or to the views of a few academic exegetes who are preoccupied with this' (Rowland, 2009: 290; cf. Roberts and Rowland, 2010: 132). John Sawyer helpfully emphasizes the necessity for *Wirkungsgeschichte* to include analysis of the wider context of those who fall within its scope. He notes that 'if it is the case, as many believe, that the text without a reader has no meaning, and the Bible is "like a sheep that before its shearers is dumb", then it is its "shearers", the readers and interpreters that must be scrutinized, their presuppositions, their aims, and their methods, not only their readings and interpretations' (Sawyer, 2006: 5). The British New Testament Conference has instituted a 'Use and Influence' seminar, which has thrived alongside its more traditional counterparts, and other international biblical studies conferences have similarly embraced reception history, with seminars on the discipline being offered at both the Society of Biblical Literature and the European Association of Biblical Studies.[2]

These growing voices of engagement with *Wirkungsgeschichte* from within the mainstream biblical studies academy represent a sea change which is unlikely to be reversed. The discipline of reception history has thus moved in recent years to the forefront of the academic discipline of biblical studies. When Luz published his *Wirkungsgeschichte* commentary on the Gospel of Matthew, he set in place a methodological trajectory which includes the Blackwell 'Through the Centuries' Bible Commentary Series. The editors are David Gunn, Judith Kovacs, Christopher Rowland and John Sawyer, and the series preface notes that:

> The Blackwell Bible Commentaries series, the first to be devoted primarily to the reception history of the Bible, is based on the premise that how people have interpreted, and been influenced by, a sacred text like the Bible is often as interesting and historically important as what it originally meant. . . . Until quite recently this whole dimension was for the most part neglected by biblical scholars. (Sawyer, Rowland and Kovacs, 2004: xi)

This series represents a radical departure from the more traditional mode of biblical commentary. Gone is the synchronic reconstruction of the context of the original recipients, and in its place has emerged a diachronic trajectory of the reception of the text up to and including the present day. Readers are offered 'a representative sampling of material from different ages, with emphasis on interpretations that have been especially influential or historically significant' (Sawyer, Rowland and Kovacs, 2004: xii). Mark Knight points to Gadamer's ideas as the unifying theoretical thread which runs through the volumes of the series, and notes that they 'treat interpretation as an event in which the perspectives of past and present are indivisibly fused' with the effect that 'the resulting commentary draws liberally from fields such as politics and the arts' (2010: 143).

John Sawyer offers two key reasons in justification of the production of a series of commentaries focusing on reception history: 'The first is that the afterlife of the Bible has been infinitely more influential, in every way— theologically, politically, culturally and aesthetically—than its ancient near-eastern prehistory. . . . [The] second reason concerns the meaning of the text . . . to raise awareness of what these texts mean and can mean' (Sawyer, 2000; cf. Sawyer, 2004: 11).

This series, with the positive response it has received within the discipline of biblical studies, in many ways marks the 'coming of age' of reception history, and the commentary by Judith Kovacs and Christopher Rowland on the book of Revelation (2004) has become the landmark text in the application of reception history to this controversial and diversely received biblical text. Much as Luz's groundbreaking work in *Wirkungsgeschichte* was developed in the context of a commentary on Matthew, so analysis of the reception of the book of Revelation has provided a test case for further methodological and theoretical development of the discipline. For example, Kovacs and Rowland coin the term 'actualization' to describe the way in which the biblical text is actualized by those who engage the text. They explain:

> In one form the imagery of the Apocalypse is juxtaposed with the interpreter's own circumstances, whether personal or social, so as to allow the images to inform understanding of contemporary persons and events and to serve as a guide for action . . . [while the second] is the appropriation by visionaries, where the words of the Apocalypse either offer the opportunity to see again things similar to what had appeared to John or prompt new visions related to it. (Kovacs and Rowland, 2004: 9–10;[3] Lyons and Økland, 2009)

The December 2010 edition of the *Journal for the Study of the New Testament* focused specifically on the future of reception theory. In the introduction, Jonathan Roberts and Christopher Rowland assert that 'there is crucial work waiting to be done, as the variety and plenitude of biblical interpretation (orthodox and heterodox, from believers and non-believers alike) offers a way forward for biblical studies. Reception history, history of interpretation, call it what you will, is a subject whose time has come' (Roberts and Rowland, 2010: 132).

In the concluding article, W. J. Lyons offers a provocative re-visioning of biblical studies, in which he suggests that historical criticism developed tendencies to overreach itself based on too optimistic views regarding the possibility of achieving 'objective' historical knowledge. Lyons suggests that historical-critical methodologies should be reclothed using the terminology of reception history, thereby drawing into the interpretative process both audience and response. He presents this as the source of 'hope for a troubled discipline', and suggests that such an approach may be the only viable future for New Testament studies (2010: 216). To this end, he notes that:

> reception history ... rejects the division between original meanings and meanings in interpretive history, opening up a vast new area for study by historical critics. ... Historical criticism unchanged, however, offers no convincing argument, in my opinion, for its existence on its present scale. The broadening effect of adopting reception history's terminology offers real hope for New Testament studies, a discipline whose days at its current level may well otherwise be numbered. (Lyons, 2010: 217)

In an academic climate where the emphasis is increasingly placed upon academic scholarship to demonstrate its 'impact' in terms of 'economic and social benefits or outcomes',[4] the discipline of reception history offers a compelling research methodology which overcomes the historic division between the reception of the Bible within and beyond the academy. Not only are those within the discipline offered a mechanism for engaging those beyond, but also those beyond who have so often been resistant to the 'experts' from within are drawn into the debate as to the way in which the Bible has been received within their community. As Roberts and Rowland put it:

> Like a small nation that has yet to digest its loss of empire, biblical studies has yet to re-find its place in this world. To do so, it must relinquish its introspective, parochial and proprietorial urges, for unless it does so, the enormous potential for contribution of those of us who have spent a lifetime studying the Bible will be wasted, and our scholarly efforts will continue to have relatively little impact on the larger social, academic, ecclesial and religious cultures within which we live. (Roberts and Rowland, 2010: 136)

Lyons' proposal that reception history encompasses both original meaning and later meaning, both historical criticism and reader response, both original audience and later audience, provides an emerging methodological perspective from which to engage Ernest Lucas's contribution to the discipline. As Jonathan Roberts notes: 'The reception history of the Bible is the practice of making worldly records of those manifest and mysterious individual and corporate experiences of the biblical text. It is a recognition of the dynamic, living relationship between texts and readers, rather than an attempt to isolate and stabilize textual meanings from the mutability of life' (2011: 8).

I suggested earlier that Lucas's research has been located at the conjunction of three worlds: scientific enquiry, academic biblical studies and lived Christian faith. In this, he has brought an appropriate concern for the original context of reception to bear on a creative engagement of the text from the perspective of contemporary readers. This overt fusion of academic study of the Bible with current concerns surely represents the future of biblical studies, as the ancient text continues to be received within diverse and changing contexts.

Notes

1 <http://www.profil.uni-konstanz.de/en/university-portrait/history-of-the-university/> (accessed 23 Jan. 2012).
2 <http://www.bnts.org.uk/groups/8> (accessed 23 Jan. 2012). The 2011 Society of Biblical Literature International Meeting held in London included seminar streams on 'Bible and Its Influence: History and Impact' and 'Bible and Visual Culture'. <http://www.sbl-site.org> (accessed 23 Jan. 2012). The European Association of Biblical Studies includes a research group on 'The Biblical World and its Reception'. <http://www.eabs.net/rgroupDetails.aspx?id=34> (accessed 23 Jan. 2012).
3 This process of 'actualization' was further explored in the Interdisciplinary Colloquium on the Book of Revelation and Reception History, held in Bristol in 2006 as an explicit response to the Blackwell Revelation volume. The papers were subsequently published as an edited volume. Alongside worked examples of reception history as applied to the book of Revelation, this project served to further the methodological agenda and demonstrated ways in which the trajectory of *Wirkungsgeschichte* has generated new possibilities for scholarly engagement.
4 <http://www.hefce.ac.uk/research/ref/impact/REF_impact_pilot_guidance_on_submissions.pdf> (accessed 23 Jan. 2012).

Bibliography

Crossley, James G. 'An Immodest Proposal for Biblical Studies'. *Relegere: Studies in Religion and Reception* 2, no. 1 (2012): pp. 153–77.
Dilthey, Willhelm. 'The Development of Hermeneutics [1900].' In *W. Dilthey: Selected Writings* (ed. H. P. Richman; Cambridge: Cambridge University Press, 1976).
Elliott, Mark W. 'Effective-History and the Hermeneutics of Ulrich Luz'. *Journal for the Study of the New Testament* 33, no. 2 (2010): pp. 161–73.
Ermarth, Michael. *Wilhelm Dilthey: The Critique of Historical Reason* (Chicago: University of Chicago Press, 1978).
Fish, Stanley. *Is There a Text in This Class? The Authority of Interpretive Communities* (Cambridge, MA: Harvard University Press, 1980).

Fowl, Stephen. 'Texts Don't Have Ideologies'. *Biblical Interpretation* 3, no. 1 (1995): pp. 15–34.
Gadamer, Hans Georg. *Philosophical Hermeneutics* (trans. David E. Linge; Los Angeles: University of California Press, 1976).
———. *Truth and Method* (London: Continuum, 3rd edn, 2004 [1960]).
Goodacre, Mark. ' "Drawing from the Treasure Both New and Old": Current Trends in New Testament Studies'. *Scripture Bulletin* 27, no. 2 July (1997): pp. 66–77.
Gowler, David B. 'Socio-Rhetorical Interpretation: Textures of a Text and Its Reception'. *Journal for the Study of the New Testament* 33, no. 2 (2010): pp. 191–206.
Grondin, Jean. *The Philosophy of Gadamer* (trans. Kathryn Plant; Chesham: Acumen, 2003).
Hauerwas, Stanley. *Unleashing the Scripture: Freeing the Bible from Captivity to America* (Nashville, TN: Abingdon Press, 1993).
Iser, Wolfgang. *The Act of Reading: A Theory of Aesthetic Response* (Baltimore, MD: Johns Hopkins University Press, 1980).
Jauss, Hans Robert. *Toward an Aesthetic of Reception* (trans. Timothy Bahti; Minnesota, MN: University of Minnesota Press, 1982).
Knight, Mark. 'Wirkungsgeschichte, Reception History, Reception Theory'. *Journal for the Study of the New Testament* 33, no. 2 (2010): pp. 137–46.
Kovacs, Judith L. and Christopher Rowland. *Revelation*, Blackwell Bible Commentaries (Oxford: Blackwell, 2004).
Lawn, Chris. *Gadamer: A Guide to the Perplexed* (London: Continuum, 2006).
Lucas, Ernest. *Daniel* (Leicester: Apollos, 2002).
Luz, Ulrich. *Matthew 1–7* (Edinburgh: T. & T. Clark, 1990).
———. *Studies in Matthew* (Grand Rapids: Eerdmans, 2005).
Lyons, William John. 'Hope for a Troubled Discipline? Contributions to New Testament Studies from Reception History'. *Journal for the Study of the New Testament* 33, no. 2 (2010): pp. 207–20.
Lyons, William John and Jorunn Økland, eds. *The Way the World Ends? The Apocalypse of John in Culture and Ideology* (Sheffield: Sheffield Phoenix Press, 2009).
Matlock, R. Barry. 'Biblical Criticism and the Rhetoric of Inquiry'. *Biblical Interpretation* 5, no. 2 (1997): pp. 133–59.
Moore, Stephen D. *Literary Criticism and the Gospels: The Theoretical Challenge.* (New Haven, CT: Yale University Press, 1989).
Morgan, Robert. 'Sachkritik in Reception History'. *Journal for the Study of the New Testament* 33, no. 2 (2010): pp. 175–90.
Nicholls, Rachel. 'Is Wirkungsgeschichte (or Reception History) a Kind of Intellectual Parkour (or Freerunning)?' *British New Testament Conference* (2005).
Roberts, Jonathan. 'Decoding, Reception History, Poetry: Three Hermeneutical Approaches to the Apocalypse'. In *The Way the World Ends? The Apocalypse of John in Culture and Ideology* (ed. William John Lyons and Jorunn Økland; Sheffield: Sheffield Phoenix Press, 2009).
———. 'Introduction'. In *The Oxford Handbook of the Reception History of the Bible* (ed. Christopher Rowland, Michael Lieb, Emma Mason and Jonathan Roberts; Oxford: Oxford University Press, 2011).
Roberts, Jonathan, and Christopher Rowland. 'Introduction'. *Journal for the Study of the*

New Testament 33, no. 2 (2010): pp. 131–6.

Rowland, Christopher. 'The Interdisciplinary Colloquium on the Book of Revelation and Effective History'. In *The Way the World Ends? The Apocalypse of John in Culture and Ideology* (ed. William John Lyons and Jorunn Økland; Sheffield: Sheffield Phoenix Press, 2009).

Sawyer, John F.A., ed. *The Blackwell Companion to the Bible and Culture* (Oxford: Blackwell, 2006).

———. *The Place of Reception-History in a Post-Modern Bible Commentary*. (Nashville: Society of Biblical Literature, 2000).

———. 'The Role of Reception Theory, Reader-Response Criticism and/or Impact History in the Study of the Bible: Definition and Evaluation'. (2004) <http://www.bbibcomm.net/news/sawyer.html> (accessed 5 March 2011).

Sawyer, John, Christopher Rowland and Judith L. Kovacs. 'Series Editors' Preface'. In *Revelation* (ed. Judith L. Kovacs and Christopher Rowland; Oxford: Blackwell, 2004).

Scheibler, Ingrid. *Gadamer: Between Heidegger and Habermas* (Oxford: Rowman & Littlefield, 2000).

Thiselton, Anthony C. *New Horizons in Hermeneutics: The Theory and Practice of Transforming Biblical Reading* (Grand Rapids: Zondervan, 1992).

Vanhoozer, Kevin J. *Is There a Meaning in This Text? The Bible, the Reader, and the Morality of Literary Knowledge* (Grand Rapids: Zondervan, 1998).

Warnke, Georgia. *Gadamer: Hermeneutics, Tradition and Reason* (Cambridge: Polity Press, 1987).

Generous and gracious God
    we thank you for the Bible
    for the richness of its witness
    for its unsearchable wisdom
    for its revelation of salvation's story
    and its unmasking of the human heart.

    We thank you for the hard and hallowed work
    of grappling with the text,
    wrestling as Jacob with the angel
    to seek truth, to seek peace, to seek you,
    and then,
    touched
    by
    grace,
    discovering that
    when we take the Bible seriously,
    honoring scholarship and ancestral insight,
    or when we pick it up for the first time
    and experience its language, stories, contours,
    you are there, seeking us, calling us, converting
us.

    And we thank you that this task,
    this searching, this mining, this discovering,
    is not the stronghold of the few
    but belongs to the whole people of God,
    east and west, north and south,
    in every age and every place,
    as the living Word is encountered and known
    again and again and again and again.

11

Moving Towards a Theological Perspective on 'Place' in Mark's Gospel

Mike Pears

There is a lively and growing conversation in both the public and academic spheres about the nature of 'space' and 'place'. This so-called 'spatial turn' has its roots in the 1960–70s and from the 1990s onwards has gained significant momentum.[1] The 'spatial turn' is essentially a movement away from the treatment of place or location as a simple backdrop or blank canvas upon which are written the events of history, toward a newly conceived appreciation that every place 'at a basic level, is space invested with meaning in the context of power' and that the 'process of investing space with meaning happens across the globe at all scales and has done throughout human history' (Cresswell, 2004: 12).

My longer-term interest is to investigate marginalized urban communities within the UK by developing research methods which are derived from theological concepts of space and place. Over the last century in particular cities have become massively complex and dynamic organisms, and theories of space and place are providing a fascinating way of engaging with this complexity.[2] The aim of this paper is to develop some theological perspectives on space and place as a way of informing an approach to qualitative research into particular city-spaces.

My approach will be to critically engage with sources from within the discipline of social geography as well as theology. The first stage has been to investigate theologians who have sought to engage with theories of space and place being developed in the field of geography, with a particular interest in those who have attempted a spatial reading of New Testament texts. There are apparently only two people who have carried out this kind of study, namely Eric C. Stewart (2009) and Halvor Moxnes (2003); both authors pursue a reading of Mark's Gospel.[3] In the first part of this paper I will briefly summarize these two approaches and make some observations about the usefulness of their analyses to my own project.

The second step of my research has been to survey contemporary material on spatial theory within social geography in an attempt to find an approach which will open out possibilities for understanding contemporary city-space from a theological perspective and furthermore one which will suggest some research methodologies for investigating those places. Here I focus on the work of Tim Cresswell (1996) who develops a cultural-political notion of place. After summarizing Cresswell's work I will draw on his insights to engage with the works of Stewart and Moxnes and make some observations about how spatial readings of Mark might have relevance for the investigation of contemporary city space. This is essentially a hermeneutical task.

Drawing on theories of space and place as an approach to reading Mark's Gospel

I begin then by summarizing the works of Stewart and Moxnes. By drawing on somewhat different spatial geographies, each develops their own approach in distinctly different ways. Stewart's reference is primarily to geographies of agency and influence where place, and especially the relation of power to place, is discussed in terms of human activity, especially the influence of the elite. Moxnes on the other hand draws on geographies of structure. Here the relationship of power to place is predicated on key societal structures rather than human agency. By drawing on different geographies in this way, Stewart and Moxnes create different notions of place. I will engage with the issues this raises after a brief description of each of their approaches.

A summary of Stewart

Stewart's purpose is to inquire into 'ancient perceptions of space and place and how they underlie much of Mark's gospel', in particular attempting 'to understand the social nature of space in antiquity, addressing questions related to power and its dissemination in space as well as how Mark understands, accepts and subverts claims made by others to the space in which Jesus lived' (2009: 29).

Stewart argues that a spatial reading along these lines is significant for the interpretation of Mark's narrative. Jesus himself is portrayed as the new 'geographic centre' of the world with 'authority over a new spatial practice,' namely the kingdom of God. He creates the 'new space of the kingdom in gathering people around himself and sending them out in order to enlarge the space of that gathering' (2009: 218–19).

Stewart develops grounds for his enquiry by exploring 'critical spatial theory' (2009: 30–57), two aspects of which are of particular importance for the development of his argument. First, the recognition that space is socially produced such that 'space encodes social practices and power relations. Those who control space exert their control by means of particular spatial practices' (2009: 221). Second, 'texts represent space in a slightly different way from the way [it] is represented in the everyday social world' (2009: 57). Texts can be understood as mapping the world so as to present a static picture of space with fixed meaning. Stewart draws on Lefebvre's category of 'representational spaces' to describe the way a text creates space by ascribing certain fixed meanings to spaces which are otherwise socially produced and therefore always subject to change (Stewart, 2009: 57–61).

Having established grounds for his enquiry in relation to contemporary spatial theory, Stewart embarks on a detailed study of the spatial conceptions that Greek, Roman and Jewish authors brought to their own texts. Since scientific geography is little known in these traditions, the emphasis is strongly on the human aspect so that places are presented by 'alluding to mythical and "biographical" elements of each place. . . . Space in this type of geography is thoroughly imbued with the characteristics of its inhabitants while at the same time it endows those people with its own characteristics' (2009: 92).

Perhaps the most important concept for defining spatial awareness for these cultures is that of *oikoumene*, that is the notion of the inhabited world—'the extent of land in . . . which it was possible for people to live' (2009: 62). Greek, then Roman geography placed their own territory, by definition, at the centre of *oikoumene* and understood all other people and places in terms of their proximity to and relation with their own central position.

These geographical ideas are used in all forms of literary genre of the ancient world as the standard way of talking about and mapping the world; 'all used stock stereotypes in order to portray characters in their tales. So close was the relationship between geography and biography that to tell the history of a city one used the *bios* genre' (Stewart, 2009: 126). In addition, the geographical materials contained within these ancient texts 'encoded certain types of power relations. These power relations are presented as "inherent" in the land or in divine will. This manner of speaking about space offers a portrait of space that is arranged ideally in only one way. Describing space this way offers the opportunity to portray one's own culture as normative in spatial terms' (2009: 127). Thus Greek and Roman literature employed the language of 'geographical stereotypes . . . to discuss other "marginal" people at the edges of the earth', who from their perspective were deviating from normative lifestyle of those in 'civilized' society (2009: 127, 128).

Stewart moves on to show that 'these stereotypical ways of representing space', which encode power relations as part of the landscape, 'extend to other types of space as well' (2009: 128). Of particular importance is the understanding that cities function as the centre of a territory in such a way that the surrounding areas, including the villages, are defined by them (2009: 129). Here 'city' was not just a reference to size or population, but referred to people living together 'in a certain type of social arrangement' which was 'evaluated by its cultural similarity to Rome' and was also structurally embodied in its public buildings such as government offices, marketplace and gymnasium (2009: 130, 131). Furthermore:

cities and villages ... and the buildings contained within them, marked civilized areas from non-civilized. The spatial practice in these civilized areas, the way in which humans interacted with each other, the presence of religious institutions and the cultivation of the soil all distinguished these territories from those that surrounded them. Within these territories, distinctions were made among elites and peasants. Control over public space such as the temple and synagogues equated to being able to establish the norm of 'civilized' behavior in first-century Judea and the areas over which elite Judeans were able to exercise their influence. (2009: 142)

In contrast to the controlled city territories were the borderland spaces of wilderness and mountains. Here the lives of peasants were shaped by the particular characteristics of the boundary places; for example their religious and agricultural practices were shaped by the nature of living in areas that were unstable and unpredictable (see Stewart, 2009: 145–46).

Critically, while Stewart analyses territory in terms of the polarity of *oikoumene* and borderlands, he does not go on to adopt 'the traditional model of centre and periphery in which the centre dominates the periphery' so that 'social change occurs from the centre outward and change gradually transforms the peripheral or boundary areas of a society' (2009: 146). Rather he follows recent developments in anthropological studies in which borderlands are notably places in which the negotiation of identities occurs allowing for formation of new movements and alternative spatial practices. In arguing this Stewart states that:

borderlands, deserts and mountains are places in which normal patterns of social behavior do not apply. The lack of control of these places by human settlements encourages the negotiation of identity within them. The spatial practice of persons in civilized centres does not apply in these borderlands. Spatial practices in these areas vary from those found in the centres of civilization. Wilderness in these areas can imply either a heightened sense of observation of civilization or total lawlessness. (2009: 154)

Borderlands then were not well-defined political boundaries, they were fluid places where identities and practices were open to negotiation; they were on the one hand a threat to Roman (or Greek)[4] order and on the other a potential birthplace for new movements.

The hub of Stewart's argument is to engage the text of Mark's Gospel in the light of the spatial mapping of the ancient world which he has analysed. His contention is that Mark's approach to narrative is predicated on the same spatial mapping as the rest of the ancient world; that is he 'deals largely with the same geographical and topographical stereotypes' found widely in his culture (2009: 179–80).

Crucial to the narrative of Mark, according to Stewart, is that these geographical stereotypes are inverted in order 'to suggest a new type of space centred around the person of Jesus' (2009: 179). He thus creates a new representational place 'which stands in opposition to the civilized spaces of cities and the architectural spaces of synagogues and temple' (2009: 180). Synagogues in first-century Galilee, for example, represent the 'locus of a community's order' with institutional spatial practices organized around purity and Sabbath rules. Mark's narrative contests this representation in at least two significant ways. First, that Jesus consistently violates the spatial practices of the synagogues and does so with apparent impunity; the synagogue authorities seem powerless to prevent Jesus' activities and the crowds stand in wonder at his teaching. Second, by introducing synagogues as places inhabited by unclean spirits (Mark 1:21–27), Mark contests the very idea that they are places of purity and centres of community order. Stewart argues that demons are a 'locative category in antiquity' such that 'the haunts of demons are on the fringes of society'. They 'inhabit places where borders are not maintained' and are 'encountered where humans do not maintain social life' (2009: 193). Thus, Mark presents synagogues as places where civilized order has in fact broken down; these are places which, despite their claims, stand as if they were outside of *oikoumene*; they are not centres of purity but 'resemble peripheral territories' (2009: 192).[5]

Stewart's argument then is that Mark inverts the normal representations of space in the ancient world such that the Roman and Jewish elite space of temples and cities from which civilization emanates is now to be found as peripheral space.[6] Jesus becomes the new geographic centre of the world, forming around himself a community of followers by teaching, feeding and offering a purity not mediated by temple spatial practices but based on his own presence and power to cleanse from unclean demons (2009: 211). This idea that an individual might function as a geographic centre has precedent in the ancient world in figures such as the emperor or travelling philosophers. These would have been understood as a 'travelling centre' where territory is delimited by the bodily presence of a person (2009: 212, 171). Mark casts Jesus in this role as he describes the way that disciples and crowds 'gather' around him such that space around Jesus becomes the new meeting space in contrast to the architectural spaces of home, synagogue or temple.[7]

Stewart concludes that:

the Gospel of Mark's presentation of space is that it locates a new spatial practice centred around the exorcising, healing, and teaching Jesus. The cosmic perspective of Jesus' teaching concerning the return of the Son of man enables Mark's readers to understand the spatial practice of the temple/synagogue is coming to an end. In any case, it is occupied by unclean spirits. Jesus' new gathering, however, because of the power of the Holy Spirit, allows for the creation of pure spaces through exorcism.

... Jesus' new spatial practice, ultimately, will be fully consummated, according to Mark, when the Son of man returns, after the centres of civilization, that is, the temple and the city of Jerusalem have been destroyed. (2009: 225)

A summary of Moxnes

Having summarized Stewart I now turn attention to Halvor Moxnes (2003). Moxnes' goal is 'to uncover the spatial dimensions of the historical Jesus' (Moxnes, 2003: 2). The spatial aspect of Moxnes' argument draws largely on the ideas of David Harvey (following Lefebvre) (Moxnes, 2003: 13–14; Harvey: 1989; Lefebvre: 1991). Central to this are three important ideas which Harvey identifies as 'spatial experience' (or material spatial practices), 'perception' (or representations of space—the cultural or ideological level of space) and 'imagination' (or spaces of representation; imagined places) (Moxnes, 2003: 13–14).

Moxnes views place 'not as "fixed" in its identity, as bounded, and as the site of normative authenticity' but rather as 'always unfixed, contested and multiple' (Moxnes, 2003: 12).[8] He states that:

> This perspective has important consequences for the study of Jesus and place. We shall not try and find the right place for Jesus, as if there were only one fixed position and category to put him into. Rather, we will see Jesus and his activity as engaged in a contest over places in Galilee in the first century. These were places of people's lives in production and human interaction, houses and households, village and larger area. People's position in these places also placed them in normative structures that reflected the cosmologies and traditions of Jewish Galilee. (2003: 12)

In focusing on place in the 'earliest Jesus tradition', Moxnes' enquiry draws on three primary sources—those of Q, the Gospel of Thomas and the 'sayings' material of Mark's Gospel (2003: 17). Critical for Moxnes' argument is his understanding that these sources indicate that the 'house' and 'household' were the single most important institution or 'place' for a first-century Galilean; it was the very basis of a person's identity and honor within society. Moxnes draws on Bernhard Scott's place-based reading of the parables, where Scott states that 'in the ancient Mediterranean world everyone had a social map that defined the individual's place in the world. It told people who they were, who they were related to, how to act and behave. At the centre of this map was the family, esp. [sic] the father, then came the village, finally the city and beyond to the ends of the world' (Moxnes, 2003: 43, quoting Scott, 1989: 79–201).

Having identified this significant link between household and identity, Moxnes asserts that Jesus' call to 'follow' represents a dual challenge. On the one hand, to leave the household was to be associated with a radical loss of identity and 'place' within the community; on the other there is no obvious substitutive new place—it is as if Jesus invites followers into 'no-place' (Moxnes, 2003: 49–50).[9] The dual movement of leaving meaningful space and entering 'no-place' causes, in Moxnes' view, a deep anxiety. Edward Casey describes this as 'place-panic' where 'we confront the imminent possibility of there being no place to be or to go. We feel not so much as displaced as *without place*' (Moxnes, 2003: 43, quoting Casey, 1993: ix–x).

Two sayings of Jesus that convey this danger of losing one's place or being excluded from location are in Q 9:57–58 ('foxes have holes . . . but the Son of Man has nowhere') and Mark 6:4 ('a prophet is not without honor except in his home town and among his own relatives and in his own household') (Moxnes, 2003: 49–50). In 'no-place' a person is not only dislocated from a more or less privileged position *in* society, but they are excluded *from* society altogether. Even foxes and birds have a place; the crisis associated with 'no-place' is more fundamental than merely being a vagabond, it is a radical loss of identity (Moxnes, 2003: 50–51).[10]

This movement from household to 'no-place' represents a danger not only for those leaving, but presents a disturbing challenge to the status quo of the wider society. In leaving household-space Jesus, and his young male followers in particular, transgressed the normative social/political/religious landscape of the day—the move was in effect an intentional deviance from 'household-space' and its associated ideology (Moxnes, 2003: 67).

Of fundamental importance to Moxnes' argument is the notion that the first-century Galilean household was essentially characterized as 'male-space'. The household was defined by a male hierarchy centred on the father–son relationship such that 'the normal way of mapping the world started with the household and the father as its head' (Moxnes, 2003: 68). Thus 'male-space' encompassed not only the 'practical social structures of the house and household activities, place in practical terms, but also the ideological and mental structures and the place of men, women and children within that space' (2003: 73). In responding to Jesus' call to follow, young men were in effect abdicating their male responsibilities; in leaving 'male-space' they were in some way experiencing a radical dislocation from male identity, that is, in society's eyes, they were no longer fully men.

Moxnes further explores the significance of leaving male-space through a study of Jesus' eunuch sayings. He notes that Jesus' use of the shocking association of 'eunuch' with 'kingdom' (for example in Matt. 19:12: 'eunuchs for the sake of the kingdom') creates an 'ambiguity over male identity' with a marginalizing effect similar to that experienced by widows and tax collectors (Moxnes, 2003: 89). The ambiguity engendered by the movement of predominantly young men to 'no-place' leads Moxnes to postulate a new kind of place which he describes as 'queer-place'.

By 'queer' Moxnes intends to convey a number of important notions. First, 'queer-place' questions 'settled or fixed categories of identity, not accepting the given orders or structures of the places that people inhabit' (Moxnes, 2003: 5). Perhaps even more strongly, 'queer' 'signals a protest against fixed categories—it thus points out that all categories are historically and socially constructed' (2003: 89). Second, it identifies a new space or social category; one that is defined precisely by Jesus' own presence as an alternative to household. Thus, to follow Jesus is by implication to leave household-space and enter queer-space. Third, to enter this new space was to embrace a 'new set of values, not associated with the previous hegemonic ideal of masculinity' (Moxnes, 2003: 97).[11]

Having thus established a spatial reading of the texts which postulates 'queer-space', Moxnes goes on to discuss the implications or his argument in terms of the way space functions or is 'practiced' within the narrative, particularly with regard to the kingdom of God and exorcisms. By applying Harvey's spatial analysis, Moxnes argues that 'household' functions in early texts as a 'space of representation' or 'imagined place', Harvey's third category of space.[12]

This is seen for example, through the address 'our father' (Q11:2–4) which 'immediately places the petitioner within the "imagined space" of household relations' (Moxnes, 2003: 115). The juxtaposition however of one imagined place denoted by 'father' with another denoted by 'king' (for example, through the phrase 'let your kingdom come', Q11:2) presents the kingdom as taking on the qualities of an ideal household and conversely, that which is imagined as household support now takes place in the kingdom (Moxnes, 2003: 116).[13] Thus the 'combination of kingdom and household sayings makes up an imagined space ... this kingdom is visualised as a household, with God as father and the addressees as his children' (Moxnes, 2003: 118).

That this is referred to as an 'imagined place' does not mean that it is fictitious. It is a fundamental aspect of 'real' space as understood by Harvey, such that 'relations within this imagined place are meant to influence the material practice of the place in which [people] find themselves' (Moxnes, 2003: 118). The first-century Galilean, for example, living under Roman dominance experienced the 'contrast between the small world of household and kinship and large world of politics of empire. In this prayer, these two worlds become one, or a third space. The images of the household and the kingdom are combined. They merge, so to speak, so that the kingdom is characterised by the qualities of the ideal household, and household support takes place in the kingdom' (Moxnes, 2003: 116). Thus 'the kingdom is not presented as a different space, in contrast to the world, rather "it is spread out over the earth". That is, the kingdom and the world are not contrasted but combined. There is not a dualistic view of the world here.' It is not a case of waiting until this 'other space' arrives but of seeing it here and now within the places we occupy—the kingdom is a transformation of the places of the world (Moxnes, 2003: 121).

Reflection and comment on Stewart and Moxnes

The spatial analyses developed by Stewart and Moxnes bring fresh perspectives to the interpretation of Mark's text. It is not my intention here to engage in a critical analysis of their work as a whole, but rather to draw out some key elements which relate to the particular direction of my own research.

By drawing on contemporary spatial theory the authors bring significant depth and sophistication to the interpretation of the geographical and spatial elements of Mark's narrative. They present coherent arguments that geographical and social-spatial references of all kinds are more than mere background or setting against which the main story takes place. They demonstrate how spatial features convey meaning which is essential to the development of the narrative. In particular they develop the plot in terms of power relations by revealing the landscape of power in which the ministry of Jesus is conducted and suggest mechanisms by which that power is expressed.[14] Of interest to my own inquiry is this apparent emphasis by Mark on the locative nature of power. Thus for example, the element of shock or surprise in the demon narratives is not to be found in the fact of demonic manifestation itself but rather that the demons are in the 'wrong' place—demons belong in borderlands or wilderness, not in pure or civilized space. Mark is not presenting an ontological point in relation to the powers (whether the locus of power is spiritual or earthly; supernatural or natural) but is making the point that the powers, that are indeed already a daily part of life, are not in fact all they claim to be.[15]

A critical aspect of this spatial interpretation is to understand the nature of Jesus' own ministry and the kingdom of God in a spatial sense; specifically enquiring about the nature of Jesus' engagement with the landscape of power as presented in Mark. The readings of Mark by Stewart and Moxnes interpret Jesus' ministry in certain helpful but distinctly different ways: in broad terms, for Stewart, Jesus *inverts* space while for Moxnes Jesus, *subverts* space.[16]

Central for Stewart is the notion that Jesus 'gathers' followers around him and in doing so creates a new space of the kingdom of God. Jesus' new movement is founded in the dynamic borderland territories where those gathered experience healing, deliverance and supernatural provision; new spatial practices are adopted especially around food and hospitality. Through Jesus' teaching and deliverance this new space around Jesus is defined as 'pure' space and stands in stark contrast to the Jewish and Roman controlled spaces which Mark has exposed as unclean. Jesus, along with his new community inverts so-called *oikoumene* by invading Jewish and Roman centres of power, such as synagogue and temple, and significant Roman spaces. Jesus moves and acts with impunity so that even on their own turf Jewish and Roman authorities are unable to control this new movement (Stewart, 2009: 219).

For Moxnes, Jesus' spatial engagement has a twofold aspect. On the one hand it is the movement of young men *out* of traditional family structures, which are understood as being predicated on male hierarchy, and on the other it is movement *into* a somewhat ambiguous new space defined by the presence of Jesus as 'brother' and the absence of the father figure. Both aspects of this movement, the 'out of' and 'into' are described by Moxnes as structurally subversive, thus threatening the territorial control of Jewish and Roman authorities.

As Jesus calls young men out of households he seems to threaten the very fabric that holds society together; to break with household was to break with the whole of society—its traditions, values and customs. By identifying the household as the key spatial-structural element of Mark's narrative that Jesus engages with, Moxnes argues for the subversion of space by engaging with power at the micro or local level. Moxnes reinforces this point by defining the new space into which these young men move as 'queer-place' with the specific purpose of defining the new space around Jesus as one that 'questions the settled and fixed categories of identity and is not accepting of the given orders or structures of the places that people inhabit' (Moxnes, 2003:5). For Moxnes, a central part of Mark's spatial strategy is Jesus' creation of 'imagined places' as a mechanism through which the powerless engage with the elite in an attempt to shape their own place. In Jesus' ministry this imagined place of the kingdom is defined through exorcisms, healings, common meals, teachings and parables; it was signified by a non-hierarchical community gathered around Jesus as brother rather than father and where young men share equally with other out-of-place people such as widows.

The need for an alternative spatial model

Underlying the discussion thus far are the somewhat different geographies of space and place upon which Stewart and Moxnes have built their arguments. Foundational for Stewart's argument is that space is socially produced and that space or 'territory' itself replicates and reproduces social power. In establishing this position Stewart draws on Robert Sack who proposes a three-step process for making a space into a territory: classification, communication and control. In contrast Moxnes draws heavily on David Harvey and neo-Marxist thinking about space as structurally produced and maintained. Thus for Moxnes, Mark would understand that power resides in the structures of society so that the subversion of power is about challenging the frameworks and institutions of society and the ideologies embedded and expressed in them.

Critical for my own argument is the need of a geography of space and place that will allow me to engage with the landscape Mark described but also, and importantly, that will be sufficient for engaging with the complexity of contemporary city-space. The theoretical frameworks of 'agency' and 'structure' that run throughout the work of Stewart and Moxnes respectively, while valuable, do not seem to offer sufficient points of connection. Indeed, contemporary analysis of cities draws on a complex range of spatial theories and any development of a spatial theology for cities will need to demonstrate an awareness of this context.[17]

One such geography of place that will move my enquiry in a helpful direction is that presented by Tim Cresswell in his study, *In Place/Out of Place* (1996). Cresswell breaks out of that structure–agency debate by engaging from a cultural-political perspective. Of particular interest for my own research is the methodological basis of Cresswell's proposals. By defining normative landscapes of power in terms of doxa and orthodoxy, Cresswell's method is to investigate the relationship between power and place by studying incidents where doxa is violated. Cresswell refers to these events as points of transgression.

At this point, the limitations of Cresswell should also be noted. The themes that have begun to emerge through engagement with Stewart and Moxnes are in part about the potential for space to be transformed; the notion of 'spaces of imagination' or the representation of place; and the idea of a newly created space being formed by and around Jesus. Cresswell's work offers a critical engagement with these themes, but if they are to be developed other spatial theories must also be considered, not least the ideas of 'third space' discussed by Edward Soja (1996) and Chris Baker (2007/2009) as a way of investigating the 'new space' around Jesus. Cresswell however is an important part of this conversation and I suggest that his approach is the most helpful for advancing the argument at this stage. I offer next then a brief summary of his argument.

A summary of Cresswell

Tim Cresswell develops the thesis that 'place' combines the social with the spatial and that people act 'in place' according to their social standing. In an office for example cleaners, secretaries and executives all act according to their relation to that particular place (Cresswell, 1996: 3). Social space is organized to serve the interest of those at the top of hierarchies; it is thus ideological. Actions or activities which do not conform to the accepted meaning of the place are now seen as deviant or 'out of place'—judgments are not made about actions per se, but about the action's relation to location or place.

A critical aspect of Cresswell's argument is the role of 'common sense as a mechanism of domination' (1996: 18) He draws on Pierre Bourdieu to argue that:

> sophisticated theories of ideology insist that everyday common sense is an essential part of history and power. A group cannot become dominant and rule effectively without claiming common sense as their own. ... People are not simply imposed upon by dominant groups but are convinced that the ideas of dominant groups will also benefit subordinate

groups. Domination thus occurs through common sense. (Cresswell, 1996: 18)

Pierre Bourdieu describes common sense as a 'sense of limits' or as 'doxa'. He argues that in order for an established order to be successful 'it must make its world seem to be the natural world—the commonsense world' (Cresswell, 1996: 18-19). In this established order:

> people must aspire to that which they are meant to aspire to. If the objective position of a person (as worker, woman, and so on) corresponds to his or her 'mental' position ('taken for granted' beliefs about the world), the result is 'ineradicable adherence to the established order. This is because the social world appears as a natural world. (Cresswell, 1996: 19)

In this 'doxic mode of experience there is no conflict', individuals aspire to what their situation allows, but 'if a person's subjective beliefs do not correspond to their objective position, he or she may start to question the legitimacy of the objective limits'. When this happens the established classification of common sense is challenged and 'struggle ensues between the dominated and dominating groups'. 'By revealing what was formerly hidden (the contingent nature of social distinctions) a dominated subject causes the establishment to clarify formally commonsense categories' (Cresswell, 1996: 20). This defines a move from 'doxa' to 'orthodox', where orthodoxy acknowledges the existence of other positions and seeks to establish normative territory not now through common sense, but through notions of 'what is good, just and appropriate' (Cresswell, 1996: 14).[18]

Cresswell's method is 'to examine [these] "crisis points in doxa"—those times and places that were previously unquestioned become questioned and powerful groups seek to defend the order of things against heresies of "deviant" groups. . . . These moments of crisis in the flow of things are referred to here as transgressions' (1996:21). His approach is to investigate 'transgressive acts' and the reactions they prompt in order to understand what was previously hidden from view as natural and common sense. In this way he seeks to use 'transgression' as a tool for identifying and describing ideological landscape.

In summary, Cresswell develops and draws on two central themes to explore this relationship of ideology to place.[19] 'The first is the way in which space and place are used to structure a normative landscape—the way in which ideas about what is right, just and appropriate are transmitted through space and place.' In other words he develops the idea that 'the geographical setting of actions plays a central role in defining our judgment of whether actions are either right or wrong'; that is, actions are either 'in place' or 'out of place' (Cresswell, 1996: 8-9).

Cresswell's second theme is that of 'transgression': 'just as it is the case that space and place are used to structure a normative world, they are also used (intentionally or otherwise) to question that normative world.' In this context Cresswell seeks to 'delineate the construction of otherness through a spatially sensitive analysis of transgression' (1996: 8–9). Ideas then of marginality, difference and otherness are predicated on their relation to specific places—to be 'other' is to transgress the accepted meaning of place.

The central part of Cresswell's work is to describe three in-depth case studies of transgressive events, or in his terms 'heretical geographies' (1996: 31).[20] These studies provide narrative accounts of events that cause crisis in the doxic landscape and the responses of authorities to restore 'normality'.

Reflection on these events raises some further important issues for Cresswell. The first relates to the potential of transgressive events to transform places or the meaning of places. This question relates in particular to the actual nature of place. Cresswell argues that while there might be some transformation in the meaning of a place, 'place' itself is a fundamental category and, as such, it cannot be abolished. Thus: 'to propose a radial transformation is not to propose the abolition of place but to propose transformation in the types of places. Place in a general sense is transhistorical and universal. It is a fundamental element of human existence, a product of the intentional transformation of the natural environment by humans' (1996: 151).

There is an important distinction here. While place and space are vital for ideologies to be established, they are not 'matters of mere ideology'. Rather, they have properties and characteristics that somehow make them 'important and unique'. Indeed 'the reasons space and place are used by powerful groups . . . are reasons internal to the very nature of space and place' (Cresswell, 1996: 151).

By analysing the reactions to 'heretical geographies' Cresswell observes processes involved in the transformation of space and place, in particular noting ways in which ideology may be challenged through place-based transgressive events (or in other words events that are 'out of place') and the transformation of place is at the same time transformative of ideology. The extent to which transgressive events alone can achieve transformation of any depth and permanence is however open to question. This is an issue that I will consider in my theological analysis.

Having explored the nature of the relationship between ideology and place, Cresswell discusses the critical question of how ideology works, and in particular how ideology works in space and place. The first part of the question, 'how ideology works', might be more helpfully reframed as 'what characteristic mechanisms are mobilized in the creation of ideas about what is good and just?' (Cresswell, 1996: 151). In response, he states that it is generally understood that 'ideologies are typically used to classify, differentiate, naturalize and link ideas to action' (1996: 151). The second part of the question, 'how ideology works in space and place', might then be explored by relating each of these categories to characteristics of place. I will briefly outline

Cresswell's approach to this.

In analysing the relationship between place and classification, Cresswell notes that 'space and time are the most fundamental forms of classification. When and where things occur are basic categorizations familiar to all. ... They form the knowledge most fundamental for everyday survival.' Place is 'such a fundamental category of experience that the power to specify the meanings of places and expectations of behavior in them is great indeed.' Cresswell draws on Bourdieu who argues that 'classifications are the site par excellence of struggle'. In particular the primary forms of classifications, he suggests, 'owe their special efficacy to the fact that they function below the level of consciousness and language, beyond the reach of introspective scrutiny or control by the will.' In Cresswell's terms these classifications which remain unarticulated 'add up to doxa'; they are powerful precisely because they remain unstated and 'are not recognised discursively but practically' (Cresswell, 1996: 152).

To take the second ideological mechanism, that of 'differentiation' is to consider especially the nature of 'difference' and its relationship to place. All groups develop identity by creating difference between 'us' and 'them'; the 'more powerful [groups] in any given context will create the distinctions that become most widely accepted'. (Cresswell, 1996: 153). Thus 'the process of differentiation through which "others" are created is a basic ideological mechanism' (1996: 161). Furthermore 'places are fundamental creators of difference' defining who is an 'insider' and who an 'outsider'. An outsider is not just someone from another location, they are people who are 'not to be trusted', they are 'someone who is existentially removed from the milieu of "our" place—someone who doesn't know the rules' (1996: 154).

The third element of ideological strategy is that 'to be effective, [it] must connect thought to action, theory to practice, the abstract to the concrete' (Cresswell, 1996: 161). This is in contrast to popular thought that most often defines ideology in terms of the abstract or narrowly dogmatic. Cresswell draws on Terry Eagleton who states that: 'A successful ideology must work both practically and theoretically, and discover some way of linking these levels. It must extend from an elaborated system of thought to the minutiae of everyday life, from a scholarly treatise to a shout in the street' (Cresswell, 1996: 155, quoting Eagleton, 1991).

As a fundamental category of existence, place is essential for the everyday practices which are necessary for ideology to be successful.

> Places and landscapes are ideas set in stone that, like it or not, we have to act in. Our actions are interpretations of the text of a place that are recognisable to other people and are thus reinforced. ... We are all philosophers because ideas are related to practice by our behavior in a place. Our interpretations of the world are revealed in the way we act. (Cresswell, 1996: 157)

Thus Cresswell concludes that 'place ... contributes to the creation and reproduction of action-orientated (ideological) beliefs' (1996: 161).

The final element of ideological strategy is that place is understood as natural (Cresswell, 1996: 158). 'Ideologies involve the removal of beliefs and actions from their social roots and their placement in the realm of "nature". The materiality of place gives it the aura of "nature". The "nature" of place can thus be offered as justification for particular views of what is good, just and appropriate' (1996: 161).

Cresswell's analysis of place as socially produced and as offering a mechanism for ideological power opens a way for making some initial proposals about how a theology of place might be constructed. I will argue here that a theology of place will have at its core three interrelated aspects: place as newly created, newly imagined and transformative. Before enlarging on these aspects it will be necessary to comment further on Mark's spatial world, but now in the light of Cresswell's analysis.

Cresswell's *In Place/Out of Place* in relation to a spatial reading of Mark

I suggest here that Cresswell's analysis offers the opportunity for a fresh reading of Mark's narrative, namely that it encodes ideological power by defining what is 'normative' on the one hand and 'deviant' on the other. Cresswell defines 'normative' in terms of 'doxa' and 'orthodoxy'; I suggest both these senses are evident in Mark. 'Normative' might be understood in three broad, yet interrelated categories in the gospel: *oikoumene* or civilized space; hegemonic 'male-space'; and 'pure space' as defined by the purity codes.[21] Approaching the text in this way suggests that the narrative recognizes ideological interests and understands that these interests are maintained by preserving and protecting the status quo—that is, maintaining normative landscape or the 'way things are done round here'.

Mark, it seems, plays on this 'common sense' approach to place by 'placing' Jesus in a 'deviant' position. Thus, for example, in Mark 3, Jesus challenges the accepted notions of home-space and family; having 'entered a house' (3:20) Jesus redefines his family in an apparently shocking way as those who were 'in a circle around him' (3:34), while his natural mother and brothers were 'outside' looking for him (3:33). The shock of Jesus' action is that it strikes at the heart of 'the way things are done around here'—it raises questions that were previously inconceivable. The shock is being conveyed not simply through Jesus' teaching *about* an idea, but that he *acted it out* in a way that transgressed the normal rules of the home and thus was seen to dishonor his mother and brothers. Thus, in Cresswell's terms, Jesus provokes a crisis point in doxa, where the previously unquestioned is now questioned.

The portrayal of 'normative landscape' in terms of orthodoxy is more overt within Mark's text and relates for example to laws on purity and Sabbath.

Stewart emphasizes this aspect of maintaining normative space through the enforcement of orthodox practices in his description of the role of scribes and other authority figures as 'spies' or 'enforcers' who operate within synagogues and even homes to oversee the maintenance of purity rules. The important point to remember here is that the defence of orthodox practice is specifically place-based and relates to the maintenance of ideology; orthodox practice in this sense is not solely a matter of religious faith, but is also about protecting the interests of those at the top of hierarchical structures by maintaining their control over the land.

Cresswell's social construction of place offers a distinctly different perspective from that of Stewart or Moxnes on the characteristics of Mark's landscapes. The 'doxic' state of things involves, by definition, that which is mundane, taken for granted and small-scale; it relates to a complex web of social interactions within everyday places. This suggests that while the overarching ideas of *oikoumene*, male-space and pure-space might be essential elements of the spatial framework of Mark's world, in fact the reality plays out in much more intricate and complex ways and the 'smallness' of *all* everyday actions and familiar spaces are in some way understood as the outworking of ideological strategies. We must acknowledge that the cultural and temporal gap between our world and that of Mark means that much of the meaning of these small performances and places will have been largely lost to us. The importance of Stewart and Moxnes is, in part, that they point us to examples of the connections between small performances and ideological strategies, and furthermore they underline the critical role that space and place play in this connection.

Moving towards a theology of place

The basis of a spatial reading of Mark is the understanding that space is a fundamental category of existence. It follows that Mark naturally included spatial categories and spatial caricatures in his narrative of Jesus. By drawing on Stewart, Moxnes and Cresswell I have explored how such a spatial reading might be pursued and I have argued in such a way as to establish grounds for exploring a theology of place which arises from Mark's Gospel.

In this section therefore, I will develop the arguments already presented with the aim of making some provisional proposals about a theology of place. In particular I will argue that the central thought of Mark's spatial narrative is that through Jesus 'new space' is both created and sustained. By engaging with Stewart, Moxnes and Cresswell I will suggest some characteristics of this 'new space' (particularly in terms of imagination) and its relationship to hierarchical or hegemonic space (with particular focus on the transformation of space and place and the questions this raises).

The creation of new space/place[22]

I have established that Mark's spatial narrative sees Jesus engaging with ideological power. I suggest the particular focus of this engagement is the creation of a newly configured space; newly configured in the sense that Jesus defines new meaning (inverting or subverting previous meanings) and new practices to those who are around him. I will argue here that in essence Mark envisages what might be called a 'new space' that is predicated specifically on Jesus' own presence.

In proposing the creation of 'new space' I draw on Stewart's argument that Jesus becomes the new geographic centre of the world by forming a 'gathered' community around himself and exercising 'authority over a new spatial practice' which fulfils all the expectations previously held in the law and Israel's cultic practices (Stewart, 2009: 218–19). Also, Moxnes has postulated some form of new space which he presents in terms of 'queer-space' defined by alternative notions of maleness which are not identified with hierarchal patriarchal structures but are formed by participating in practices of radical equality.

The notion of 'creation' here is critical in that it defines an essential discontinuity with previous categories of space and place. That is to say that this new space is not simply achieved through a progressive development of 'old space' but has about it a uniqueness of substance. Drawing on the idea of 'spaces of imagination', new space embodies a quality that had previously been beyond the realm of imagination or people's ability to conceive. I will develop this thought later.

While discontinuity is an essential quality of new space, so is continuity (here I pick up the familiar eschatological theme of now/not yet). As discussed, space and place are essential categories of being, and there is no suggestion in Mark that Jesus disbands or disregards these categories; on the contrary, the very fact of incarnation, death and bodily resurrection are precisely about relating to categories of existence as they stand.

By drawing on the argument thus far, I suggest that the particular characteristic of 'new space' that makes for discontinuity is the radical inversion of ideological power within 'new space'. This suggests that all previous categories of space and place are in essence embodiments of hierarchical ideologies while Jesus' 'new space' in contrast is in essence both relational and Theo-centric. By relational I mean to describe space in which power is understood and mediated in a wholly different way from hierarchical or ideological space. By Theo-centric I suggest that the essence of new space is sustained through the presence of 'One' who has emptied himself of power and now engages with others in mutuality and solidarity. Such space might be represented as a circle, as centred and as standing in contrast to hierarchical space that would be represented as pyramidal.

'New space' as a space of imagination

Lefebvre and Harvey speak of 'spaces of representation' or 'spaces of imagination' as an essential dimension of space: 'These places represent ways in which new meanings and possibilities for spatial practice, as in the form of utopian plans, can be imagined. They "are mental inventions (codes, signs, 'spatial discourses,' utopian plans, imaginary landscapes, and even material constructs such as symbolic spaces, particular built environments, paintings, museums and the like) that imagine new meanings or possibilities for spatial practices" ' (Moxnes, 2003: 14).

Such 'spaces of imagination' are not simply accounts or descriptions of space as it exists, neither are they merely conceptual imaginings. Rather they are substantial in that they define the way space is formed and the manner in which people perform in particular places. In other words, space and place can exist only in relation to representation or imagination; once the imagination of a space ceases to exist, then the corresponding characteristics of the space itself will likewise cease to exist.

I propose that Mark's Gospel, and by extension the whole of Scripture, functions as a 'space of imagination'. Furthermore, if a spatial reading of Scripture is indeed an authentic reading, then Scripture understood as a 'space of imagination' must be one of its fundamental purposes.

Thus Mark's identification of Jesus as the embodiment of the God of Israel, now self-emptying and cruciform in shape, standing as the central figure in a gathering of relationships of mutuality and solidarity, is itself a 'space of imagination'. This imagination is communicated in Mark through stories of healing, exorcism, feeding, hospitality and service which bring into play imaginations of spaces and practices which would previously have been inconceivable—inconceivable not in the sense that foot-washing, for example, was not already practised in society, but that now for the first time that practice was associated with God himself. Through Jesus, foot-washing is now defined as a characteristic practice of God.[23]

Mark's narrative thus acts as a space of imagination by bringing into play the possibility that people might participate in practices that are alternative to and challenge existing ideologies of power. In short, to 'follow' Jesus is to move from a hierarchical hegemonic space with its associated practices to a new relational/Theo-centric space with its own completely different set of special practices.

The transformation of space and place

Mark's vision of 'new space' opens up a number of key areas for enquiry. Primary among these is the question about how 'new space' and the existing hegemonic hierarchy or 'old space' engage with each other. Does one transform the other or even ultimately replace the other? Can they co-exist in creative tension with each other? By what mechanisms do they engage with each other? In terms of Mark's Gospel, these are, I suggest, questions about the nature of the 'kingdom of God'.

These questions demand a more extensive treatment than I am able to offer here. I will however suggest some ways in which the discussion might be developed. In particular my argument is that Cresswell's notion of normative landscape and transgression are of importance in relating Mark's 'new space' or the 'kingdom of God' to contemporary notions about how space and place are formed and transformed.

Cresswell observes: 'two principal lessons to be learned from [his] analysis of reactions to heretical geographies. One concerns the way place is implicated in the creation and maintenance of ideological beliefs; the other is about the uses and limits of transgression as a way of challenging and transforming these beliefs. The former is a lesson in continuity and the latter a lesson in change' (Cresswell, 1996: 150).

Two points should be briefly noted about the relation of place to ideological belief. First, since place 'in a general sense is transhistorical and universal ... [and] a fundamental element of human existence', it follows that 'to propose radical transformation is not to propose an abolition of place, but to propose transformations in types of places' (Cresswell, 1996: 151). Second, it is the 'very nature of space and place' which implicates them in the 'efficacy of ideological strategies and thus the creation and maintenance of ideological beliefs' (1996: 151, 161). As discussed previously, Cresswell defines four characteristic mechanisms of this ideological strategy: ideologies are typically used to classify, differentiate, naturalize and link ideas to action. He argues that 'each of these can be related to characteristics of place' (1996: 151).

These two assertions frame a way of relating Mark's 'new space' to contemporary 'ideological space'—in other words they suggest a hermeneutical device for a spatial reading of Mark. In particular they invite a fresh reading of Mark through the grid of the four characteristic mechanisms of ideological strategy. Such a reading would suggest ways in which Jesus and his gathered community engage with the normative landscapes of *oikoumene*, male-space and pure-space.

Cresswell's second principal lesson about 'the uses and limits of transgression as a way of challenging and transforming these beliefs' might also offer insights about how to articulate a theology of place. It is based on the understanding that 'the unintended consequence of making space a means of control is to simultaneously make it a site of meaningful resistance' (1996: 163). Thus in seeking to understand the notion of deviance from normative landscape, or 'transgression' Cresswell states that:

> action in space is ... a reading of a text. Because the reading is particularly visible, heretical readings immediately draw attention to

themselves. People acting 'out of place' suggest different interpretations. If enough people follow suit a whole new conception of 'normality' may arise. In effect the 'reading' of people acting in space is also a kind of 'writing' as new meanings are formed. (1996: 165).

Thus deviance or transgression can be considered as tools or mechanisms for the transformation of place. Significantly, in the readings of Mark discussed here, Jesus is characteristically placed in a deviant position with respect to normative landscapes. Important for a theology of place is the concept that such deviance offers an alternative spatial reading and may, if successful, lead to the transformation, or even 'conversion', of the place. Cresswell examines the potentials and limits of such 'misreadings' and asks 'to what degree can "transgression" provide a blueprint—a dress rehearsal—for radical change?' (1996: 165). In considering this, he makes a number of critical observations:

> Transgression, as I have defined it, depends on the pre-existence of some form of spatial ordering. Forms of transgression owe their efficacy to types of space, place and territory. Transgressions do not form their own orders. Boundaries are critiqued, not replaced. This observation is symptomatic of a bigger question—the question of construction versus deconstruction, creation versus critique. . . . Transgression has its limits. Constant transgression is permanent chaos. (Cresswell, 1996: 150)

Again, this second principal of the 'use and limits of transgression' suggests a framework for further development of a spatial reading of Mark and a hermeneutical method for engaging with contemporary space and place. In particular 'transgression' provides a way of understanding Jesus' deviant position in relation to *oikoumene*, male-space and pure-space, and considering the significance of such deviance for the potential transformation of places.

In summary, I argue that the engagement between geographies of space and place and the text of Mark that I have described here suggest an intriguing reading of Mark's Gospel, namely that 'new space' is an important element of Mark's spatial strategy and that critically it is created and defined by Jesus' own presence. Mark's Gospel itself acts as a 'space of imagination', an essential element of space; the text itself becoming an agent of space-creation as it is read and recounted. By engaging with Cresswell's account of ideological strategy and 'transgression', I propose that space and place are transformable and that Cresswell offers a hermeneutic framework between Mark's 'new space' and contemporary space and place. Cresswell's notion of transgression also offers a set of critical questions about the efficacy and extent of transformation that might be achieved through transgression.

Finally there are questions about the 'when' of transformation. I have related the creation of 'new space' to the now/not yet tension of eschatology. This implies that, while new space might be truly 'new' in the sense that it is not in a dependent or parasitic relationship to 'old' hegemonic spaces but is instead self referencing around Jesus, it is perhaps not to be fully established until the eschaton.[24] This would suggest that the kingdom of God is specifically place-related and that through imagination and performance it constantly challenges ideologies of hierarchical power and invites people into alternative, creative and hopeful ways of living. Hierarchical arrangements of space however do not disintegrate until the eschaton when 'new space' is fully and finally established.

Conclusion

The arguments I have presented suggest that 'place' is a fundamentally important category for reading and interpreting Mark (and by implication the gospels in general). By understanding the role of Mark's meaning-filled places within his narrative we gain insight into the world of the powers and we understand that Mark is not telling stories in order to give us insight to the ontological nature of powers (whether they are spiritual or earthly for example, interior or exterior). Rather Mark's narrative connects the reader with a landscape of power, specifically power which is embedded in and manifests through the natural topography, the built environment, and everyday social structures of government, religion and family, and through everyday practices that are performed within these environments. In other words, by telling Jesus' story in terms of encounter with everyday life, Mark exposes to his readers the underlying place-related hegemonies and ideologies which would otherwise not have been apparent. One might argue that Mark uses familiar symbolism and meaning of places in storytelling to show how conflict which is apocalyptic or cosmic in nature might happen through small encounters and actions such as washing feet (see n.23), embracing the unclean and eating meals with 'sinners'.

Mark, I would suggest, directs twenty-first-century readers to the place-based nature of the kingdom of God. The text invites us to exegete our own contemporary landscape—whether small spaces such as the office or factory, city-spaces or spaces of global flow.

I have used Cresswell's notions of 'normative' landscape and 'transgression' as an example of how the 'spatial turn' in social geography might provide us with hermeneutical models as well as practical methodologies for connecting biblical text with the complex spaces and places of our contemporary world.

My enquiry leaves open a number of questions, some of which I have already alluded to. There are however three particular strands of research I have not mentioned. First, the relationship between ideological spaces as discussed and the biblical concept of powers and principalities, particularly as it is presented by the writing of Walter Wink (1984, 1986, 1992). Second, I suggest the development of the concept of 'new space' by engaging with Edward Soja's significant work on 'third space'. And third, I believe there is considerable scope for developing theologically informed ethnographies that would provide practical methodologies for reading urban spaces.

Notes

1 For a concise overview of these developments see Cresswell (2004).
2 See e.g., Amin and Thrift (2002); Soja (2000); Graham and Lowe (2009); Knott (2005); Allen, Massey and Pryke (1999); Massey (2007). Studies are wide-ranging and include areas such as the spatial characteristics of physical and mental health, the impact of globalization in shaping city life and the changing religious landscape of urban areas. A particular focus of my research is the placed-based nature of deprivation and inequality within cities, especially as it relates to the so-called white working-class estates built in the 1930s and 1950s and which are most often found on the physical margins of cities.
3 There other more limited enquiries such as: Brueggemann (1977); Myers (1988); Riches (2000).
4 Greek and Roman literature view borderlands in somewhat different ways (Stewart, 2009: 146–47).
5 Similarly in the Roman territory of the Gerasenes (Mark 5), where the presence of the Legion spirit in the territory exposes as fictitious the notion that the Romans were able to bring 'peace to regions purportedly under their control' (Stewart, 2009: 219). By confronting the demon, Jesus brings peace where Roman legions could not.
6 For 'elite space' and 'city space' see Stewart (2009: 6–7, 184–87).
7 The verb 'to gather' is significant in Mark. It is used seven times including twice in a compound form, Jesus being the object of the verb in all but one case. Provocatively, it is related to the noun 'synagogue' (see Stewart, 2009: 212).
8 Moxnes takes as his starting point that 'identities are located, developed and sustained in place' where 'to be "placed," does not just imply geographical location; we may also, for instance speak of social, ideological and mental places' (2003: 2).
9 For comment on Moxnes' review of all the 'leaving the household' sayings of Jesus in the literature, see Stewart (2009: 27–28).
10 The notions of 'leaving place' and 'no-place' are important to Moxnes' argument (see 2003: 46–71). The thrust of the argument is that, while other categories of people might leave home, they move into alternative meaningful places such as religious communities (e.g., Essenes) or bands of prophets (although prophets lack honor in their home town—see pp. 51–52). As such, Jesus' own situation of 'no-place' and his call to young men to 'leave place' stands in contrast to other familiar categories and groups.
11 The grounds for Moxnes' argument is to recognize a shift from a 'temporal perspective' as the normal interpretive paradigm to a much less familiar 'spatial perspective' (2009: 97) and that such a shift significantly changes the sense of the texts. 'The time perspective [from "before" and "after"] of the story line lends itself to the presentation of male disciples, and the "conversion" or "breakaway," patterns were culturally appropriate to describe male behavior.' Thus, it is easy to imagine for example, 'groups of young men formed for a countercultural purpose, even banditry, but with very conventional expressions of masculinity' (p. 97). 'Moreover, the temporal perspective also lends itself to a modern construction of history-based

progress and change that reinforces male domination' (pp. 97–8). This move from a temporal to spatial perspective of the texts completely changes the sense of the narrative. To leave 'household-space' and enter 'queer space' was to embrace the 'acceptance of a new set of values, not associated with the previous hegemonic ideal of masculinity' (p. 97). Commensurate with this is the observation that 'women ... become more visible' (p. 98) in this reading, with an additional 'insider group' of women among Jesus' followers.

12 Moxnes uses the term 'imagined places' for Harvey's 'spaces of representation'. Perspective of place presented by Harvey and Lefebvre are in three aspects (Moxnes, 2003:109):
    i   material spatial practices—what actually takes place in a location
    ii representations of space—the ideological underpinning under those practices—that represent them as 'neutral' or the 'given order'—this level represents the power of the elite (i.e., Torah in Galilee)
    iii spaces of representation—the perspective from below; the non-privileged position—often as a protest against a practice and ideology of the elite (imagined places).
13 For discussion on use of 'king' and 'father' for God see Moxnes (2003: 115–17).
14 In this sense they add depth to the often discussed symbolic meaning of places (such as mountains, wilderness, temple, cities) and show how this somewhat limited interpretation can now be understood in a broader and more coherent cultural-geographical scheme which includes the small spaces of home and synagogue as well as the macro spaces of civilization and wilderness.
15 This is neither to deny the value of the ontological debate nor to deny the spiritual aspect of the powers. I suggest that this approach to interpreting Mark moves us away from understanding the powers in a dualistic sense (*either* spiritual *or* natural) and towards a more holistic understanding. Mark, it seems, works with a sense of powers as located in territory and engaging with the everyday reality of the world around about him rather than a concept of powers as either/or: heavenly or earthly; spiritual or natural.

    These insights could, I believe, contribute well to Walter Wink's argument (1984, 1986, 1992). Wink focuses on the aspect of powers as both 'interiority' and 'exteriority' but does not develop the locative nature of powers nor the particular mechanisms through which they might be associated to specific places.
16 I am grateful to Professor Paul Cloke for suggesting the phraseology here.
17 See Note 2 for examples of studies in this area.
18 Here Cresswell draws on Goren Therborn's thinking that ideologies work at three levels, defining: a) what exists and does not exist, b) what is good, just and appropriate, c) what is possible and impossible.
19 These two central themes reflect Cresswell's two principal claims. The first is about 'the way place is implicated in the creation and maintenance of ideological beliefs' (a lesson in continuity) and the second is about 'the uses and limits of transgression as a way of challenging and transforming these beliefs (a lesson in change)' (Cresswell, 1996: 150).
20 The case studies were of: graffitists in New York; women peace campaigners at Greenham Common; hippy convoys around Stonehenge.
21 For further discussion about place as defined by purity codes, see e.g., Douglas, (1966, 2002); Sibley (1995).

22 The terms 'space' and 'place' are used to convey a variety of meanings and nuances by different authors; they don't hold consistent meaning across the field. In this paper I do not explore or seek to define the range of meanings used by the authors I have engaged with and have tended to use the terms somewhat interchangeably. Further work on the theology of space/place will require a tighter definition of terms.
23 I acknowledge that foot-washing is not part of Mark's account of Jesus, but use it here as a particularly clear example of how Scripture can invert the meaning of a common practice.
24 In Cresswell's terms, 'social transformation usually implies an end state—a utopian dream. Transgression on the other hand can only play on the ephemeral' (1996: 176).

Bibliography

Allen, J., D. Massey and M. Pryke. *Unsettling Cities*, in series *Understanding Cities* (London/New York: Routledge, 1999).
Amin, A. and N. Thrift. *Cities: Reimagining the Urban* (Cambridge: Polity Press, 2002).
Baker, C. *The Hybrid Church in the City: Third Space Thinking* (London: SCM, 2007/2009).
Brueggemann W. *The Land* (Philadelphia: Fortress Press, 1977).
Casey, E. S. *Getting Back into Place: Toward a Renewed Understanding of the Place-World* (Bloomington and Indianapolis: Indiana University Press, 1993).
Cresswell, T. *In Place/Out of Place* (Minneapolis/London: University of Minnesota Press, 1996).
———. *Place: A Short Introduction* (Malden, MA/Oxford, UK/Victoria, Australia: Blackwell, 2004).
Douglas, M. *Purity and Danger* (London and New York: Routledge, 1966, 2002).
Eagleton, T. *Ideology: An Introduction* (London: Verso, 1991).
Graham, E. and S. Lowe. *What Makes a Good City?: Public Theology and the Urban Church* (London: Darton, Longman & Todd, 2009).
Harvey, D *Condition of Postmodernity* (Oxford: Blackwell, 1989).
Knott, K. *The Location of Religion: A Spatial Analysis* (London/Oakville: Equinox, 2005).
Lefebvre, M. *Production of Space* (Oxford: Blackwell, 1991).
Massey, D. *Thirdspace: Journeys to Los Angeles and Other Real-And-Imagined-Places* (Oxford, UK/Malden, MA: Blackwell, 1996).
———. *World City* (Cambridge: Polity Press, 2007).
Moxnes, H. *Constructing Early Christian Families: Family as Social Reality and Metaphor* (London and New York: Routledge, 1997).
———. *Putting Jesus in His Place: A Radical Vision of Household and Kingdom* (Louisville/London: Westminster John Knox, 2003).
Myers, C. *Binding the Strong Man: A Political Reading of Mark's Story of Jesus* (Maryknoll/New York: Orbis, 1988).
Riches, J. K. *Conflicting Mythologies: Identity Formation in the Gospels of Mark and Matthew*, Scholars' Editions in Biblical Studies (Edinburgh: T. & T. Clark, 2000).

Scott, Bernhard B. *Hear Then the Parable: A Commentary on the Parables of Jesus* (Minneapolis, MN: Fortress, 1989).
Sibley, D. *Geographies of Exclusion* (London and New York: Routledge, 1995).
Soja, E.W. *Postmetropolis: Critical Studies of Cities and Regions* (Oxford: Blackwell, 2000).
———. *Thirdspace: Journeys to Los Angeles and Other Real-And-Imagined-Places* (Oxford, UK/MA, USA: Blackwell, 1996).
Stewart, E. C. *Gathered Around Jesus: An Alternative Spatial Practice in the Gospel of Mark* (Cambridge: Clark & Co., 2009).
Wink, W. *Engaging the Powers: Discernment and Resistance in a World of Domination* (Minneapolis, MN: Fortress Press, 1992).
———. *Naming the Powers: The Language of Power in the New Testament* (Philadelphia: Fortress Press, 1984).
———. *Unmasking the Powers: The Invisible Forces that Determine Human Existence* (Minneapolis, MN: Fortress Press, 1986).

Creator God
> place giver
> peace maker
> pace setter

you gift us with
> belonging spaces
> habitable spaces
> gathering spaces

and when we look
> for the walls
> for the wire
> for the defences

that protect our self-interest
we find that, like the temple curtain,
> they are torn down
> rubbled
> cut through.

When we survey the uncontrollable landscape
> of our lives and of your world
> we see your life bursting through
> in unexpected, beautiful, beckoning ways.
> Give us the eyes to see Jesus,
> ultimate spaciousness,
> who gathers all things, all people,
> walking just ahead,
> hand held out,
> saying

12

'Not Made with Hands':
The Heavenly Temple in Hebrews and Revelation

Stephen Finamore

In the Gospel according to Mark we read one of the accounts, perhaps the earliest to which we have access, of the trial of Jesus before the high priest. The Evangelist tells us that many brought false testimony against the prisoner and that they did not agree among themselves (Mark 14:53–65).[1] Mark regards the content of the accusations as sufficiently interesting to be worth recording. The assembled priests, elders and scribes are told that Jesus had claimed that he would destroy the temple made with hands and in three days build another, not made with hands (ἀχειροποίητον). Mark then tells us that the witnesses could not agree even on this point (Mark 14:56). The intriguing thing is that though the witnesses are described as false, the saying does sound suspiciously like the kind of thing Jesus might have said. Perhaps he is unlikely to have declared that it would be he that destroyed the temple, but the rest rings true. Interestingly, the Matthean parallel has two false witnesses assert that Jesus said he *was able* to do this thing rather than that he *would* do it (Matt. 26:61). Both these Evangelists tell us that when Jesus was crucified passers-by repeated the accusation (Mark 15:29, Matt. 27:40).

In saying that the words of the false witnesses ring true, it is being asserted that the saying is consistent with the presentation of Jesus that we find in the canonical gospels, particularly those sections of them in which the saying is found. It is not necessarily being claimed that the saying is definitively dominical. There are some reconstructions of the historical Jesus with which it would sit uneasily. It might not have come readily from a wandering cynic of the kind imagined by Crossan (1991) nor from the wandering charismatic associated with the books of Vermes (1973, 1983, 1993). However, if, with Sanders (1985), we place Jesus within restoration eschatology,[2] or if we adopt the kind of reconstruction advocated by N. T. Wright (1996), it is plausible that Jesus said this or something like it. The witnesses are then to be understood as false because of their motives in repeating the words or the interpretation that they placed upon them.

There is a similar saying in the fourth Gospel though the context appears to be rather different.[3] Jesus says, 'Destroy this temple, and in three days I will raise it up' (John 2:19). John tells us that Jesus was referring to his body. This link between the temple and the body is one that will be pursued in this paper.

Luke, on the other hand, makes no mention of such a saying in his gospel. Indeed, the accusations against Jesus that he records are rather different (Luke 23:2). The situation in Acts is different again. At Acts 6:14 false witnesses accuse Stephen of saying that Jesus would destroy the temple though no mention is made of its rebuilding. So, while an aspect of this tradition is known to all the Evangelists, the Markan emphasis on something made without hands is distinctive.[4] It is interesting that where the other Evangelists decline to follow Mark, other New Testament texts show an awareness of a tradition about a future temple including the idea that it will be made 'without hands' or 'not made with hands'.[5] These are discussed below, as are similar expressions found outside of the Bible.

Of course, the idea of a renewed temple is not original to Jesus or to the Evangelists. Sanders and others have pointed to a theme within Jewish literature which looks to a new temple seen as the direct creation of God rather than a building constructed by humans. However, Sanders finds no antecedents for the word ἀχειροποίητον. He argues that it is Mark's means of avoiding any implication that Jesus was advocating physical insurrection (Sanders, 1985: 72). In a footnote (1985: 368) he mentions other scholars who agree that the words are a Markan addition, though at least one of them thinks that the referent is the church.

Sanders is not altogether convincing at this point. After all the word is found in 2 Corinthians 5:1, a text generally believed to predate Mark. Furthermore, the use in Hebrews of the words οὐ χειροποιήτου in a context that contrasts an earthly temple with its heavenly counterpart suggests that the expression was known and understood within other strands of primitive Christianity. Furthermore, when Philo contrasts the truest and highest temple, that is the universal world, with the temple in Jerusalem, he refers to the latter as being 'made with hands' implying that the former is not so.[6]

This paper is primarily about the two New Testament texts which may be understood to explore the idea of a heavenly and/or eschatological temple of the kind referred to at the trial of Jesus. These are the letter to the Hebrews and the book of Revelation. Nevertheless, it is hoped that this introduction has demonstrated that the idea of such a temple is also present in both the Synoptic and Pauline traditions of the New Testament.

Messianic texts in the primitive church

While we cannot know how the theological ideas of the primitive church developed, it seems to me to be a reasonable supposition that they were influenced by reflection on remembrances about Jesus of the kind subsequently incorporated into the gospels, on the Hebrew Bible, particularly those texts strongly associated with traditions about Jesus, and on related themes found in some of the intertestamental texts.

Some texts derived from the Hebrew Bible mediated through their Greek translations seem to have been of a special significance to the apostolic writers and they occur within different traditions within the New Testament. One example is Psalm 118:22 which says, 'The stone that the builders rejected has become the chief cornerstone.' This is cited by Jesus at Mark 12 and parallels, at Acts 4:11, Ephesians 2:20 and 1 Peter 2:7. Commentators suggest the psalm was originally spoken by a representative figure and reflects the fortunes of the whole community (Allen, 1983: 123; Anderson, 1972: 797). The apostolic writers, however, understood the text christologically. For them it is a messianic prophecy. The builders are the leaders of Israel and Christ is the stone which they reject. However, in the purposes of God, the rejected stone becomes the capstone. The image seems to be drawn from temple building and so, for the New Testament writers, may carry the idea that Christ is the key part of the new temple (Beale, 2004: 216).

The most frequently cited text from the Hebrew Bible in the New Testament is Psalm 110:1, 'The LORD says to my lord, "Sit at my right hand until I make your enemies your footstool." ' The text may originally have been associated with the coronation of a king or even a priest–king. It seems probable it was understood in messianic terms within Second Temple Judaism but whether or not this was the case, it is certainly treated as a christological prophecy by the New Testament writers. God is understood to address his Messiah, the writer's Lord. As a result, the words are understood to be those spoken by the Father to Jesus on his ascension into heaven.[7]

The text is cited in the gospels (Matt. 22:44 and parallels), in Acts 2:34, in the Pauline letters (1 Cor. 15:25, Eph. 1:20), in Hebrews 1:3,13, which can be read as an extended reflection on its words, and it probably lies behind the idea expressed at Revelation 3:21. Indeed some scholars (Caird, 1984: 78–79; Craddock, 1986) have argued that Revelation as a whole can, indeed should, be read as an explication of the way that God will bring about the thing promised in this verse.

The Hebrew text of much of the rest of the psalm, especially verse 3, is corrupt. If one were skeptical one might wonder if Christian propaganda based on the psalm did not encourage those who transmitted the Hebrew text to add a number of glosses or even make alterations. It is conceivable that the Septuagint is a more reliable guide to the original than is the Masoretic text. In any event, a Christian writer might well think that if verse 1 applies to Christ, then so might the rest of the psalm. This certainly seems to be the logic of Hebrews which applies verse 4 to Jesus. The standard translation of the LXX of verse 3 reads, 'With thee is dominion in the day of thy power, in the splendours of thy saints: I have begotten thee from the womb before the morning.' This involves translating ἐν ταῖς λαμπρότησιν τῶν ἁγίων as 'in the splendours of thy saints' but in the context of a coronation liturgy 'in the splendours of your sanctuary' seems to be at least as likely. The psalm might be read to teach that the Messiah, who we learn in verse 4 is a priest forever of the order of Melchizedek, was begotten in the heavenly Holy of Holies. The christological interpretation of Psalm 110, along with other related texts, could well have led to a number of conclusions, some of which may have affected the way the doctrine of the Trinity subsequently developed.

Potential implications of the messianic use of these psalms for primitive Christian belief

Firstly, Psalm 110:1 suggests an understanding of the Father as one who is enthroned. If heaven is a way of speaking about the place of the Father's presence then one of the primary ways that this will be articulated and, presumably, imagined and envisaged, is as a throne room. Heaven would then be depicted as a palace or as a temple. If this were so then one would expect that other traditions which regard heaven in such terms would be influential.

Secondly, the same verse suggests that Jesus, as God's Messiah, shares the Father's enthronement; he is seated at God's side. Interestingly, at Acts 7:55, Jesus is seen by the martyr Stephen standing, rather than sitting, at the right hand of God. Perhaps he is going to be Stephen's advocate, perhaps he is preparing to make the martyr welcome. In any event, the work of Jesus is now complete. His parousia will merely confirm on earth what is already established in heaven.

Next, God's Messiah, though enthroned, has enemies. There remain beings who are opposed to his rule and his status. Their eventual fate is certain; they will be placed under the feet of the Messiah. This suggests that though they are already defeated they remain active until that defeat is fully actualized. The realm of their activity is unlikely to be heaven where the Messiah is now enthroned and so, if we assume a three-tier universe, it must be either the earth or the region under the earth.

Then, the christological use of Psalm 8 would suggest that it is not simply the Messiah's enemies who are subject to him. Rather, all of creation is under his feet. This would be taken to include all things, both visible and invisible. There are a number of texts found in different traditions within the New Testament which articulate this idea. They include Ephesians 1:20–23, Philippians 2:9–11, Hebrews 1:3–4 and Revelation 5:13.

Next, the use of Psalm 118.22 as a proof text would suggest that Jesus is the key part of a new temple. This might lead to speculation that the community around him constitutes the rest of the building, an idea we find a various places in the New Testament, and to the idea that he constitutes the renewed temple, as suggested in John 2:19.

Finally, as suggested above, anyone reading through the rest of Psalm 110, whether or not they made anything of verse 3, would conclude that the person addressed is a priest forever according to the order of Melchizedek. Priestly activities would include prayer for others and the offering of sacrifices. The context for such activities is most likely to be a temple.

These observations might provide an appropriate conceptual background for the interpretation of Hebrews and Revelation.

The temple and the early church

There is plenty of evidence that the early church retained a strong interest in the temple even after it had been destroyed by the Romans. One way in which this gets manifested is in the traditions which developed about James the brother of the Lord. Eusebius and his sources tell us that James was the first to be elected to the episcopal throne of the Jerusalem church and that he had strong links with the temple, being permitted to enter the Holy Place and even the sanctuary itself.[8] Given that these are well-known to be the privileges of the descendants of Aaron alone, something intriguing is going on. Jerome makes it clear that he believed that James entered the Holy of Holies. Robert van Voorst, in his contribution on James to the *New Interpreters' Dictionary of the Bible*, says that this demonstrates how unaware Jerome and his sources were of the most basic Jewish priestly practice. However, it seems unlikely that Jerome could have been quite so ignorant given that the letter to the Hebrews quite clearly states at 9:7 that only the high priest may enter the sanctuary and he only once each year. Was Jerome really unaware of this text? Or of the verses in Leviticus which spell this out? Or was something else understood by them? Or was it imagined that James entered some other temple?

Of course, there is no way of knowing the extent to which rules about entering the Holy of Holies were ever enforced. Or even if, in the form in which we know them, they predate the Second Temple period; 2 Kings 19 suggests that King Hezekiah entered the Holy of Holies and the author of Isaiah 6 was familiar with its layout. Then again, perhaps it was believed that James was considered to be the (or a) high priest. And it is not to James alone that such traditions can be traced. There are some late traditions discussed by Bauckham (2004) that John wore the high priestly petalon.

There are hints elsewhere in early Christian literature that church leaders were understood to relate to Christian people in the same way that the priests and the high priest related to the Jewish people. It is by no means clear that all such language was intended to be understood metaphorically.[9]

The key New Testament texts

With all this in mind, we turn first to the letter to the Hebrews and then to the book of Revelation. I do not intend to enter discussions about the original recipients of the texts nor about whether the Jerusalem temple still stood when the texts were written. I confess to being drawn to an early date for each but nothing in my argument depends on it. In both cases I find it hard to conceive that an event such as the temple's destruction would not have more obviously influenced the argument or the narrative. I can still hear my old tutors telling me that this is an argument from silence but it has always struck me as an extraordinarily eloquent silence. Of course, I recognize that the temple itself is not mentioned in Hebrews but the discussions of the tabernacle raise the same or very similar issues.

Hebrews

In Chapter 2 of Hebrews we are told that the topic of the discussions is the world to come, τὴν οἰκουμένην τὴν μέλλουσαν. It is that coming world which is subject to Jesus who is already crowned with glory and honor. In the author's mind there is a clear connection between the world to come and heaven, the place to which Jesus is ascended. One is the anticipation of the other. The corollary of this is that heaven has changed. At a point in the past no human reigned there but now one does.

The theme of Jesus's priesthood and the making of a sacrifice of atonement for sin is mentioned in this chapter but, unless the references to God's house in Hebrews 3 should be interpreted that way, there is no specific mention of the heavenly temple until Chapter 6.[10] There we are told that the hearers of the letter have a hope that enters the sanctuary behind the veil. In other words they may hope to enter the Holy of Holies, the presence of God, the place to which Jesus has already gone.

So, Jesus is in the presence of God as both Messiah and priest. The roles are not always separated so that at the start of Chapter 8 we read that we have a high priest who is seated at the right hand of the throne and yet who ministers in the sanctuary, the true tent set up by the Lord.

It is very important to the writer to the Hebrews that the earthly tabernacle is closely related to the heavenly. He understands the former as a sketch or a shadow of the latter. Exodus 25:40 is cited to argue that Moses was told to build the earthly shrine as a copy of the real one that he had seen on the mountain. This was not a position devised for the convenience of the writer's argument. Similar views are found in Philo where the tabernacle is understood to be 'an imitation perceptible by the outward senses of an archetypal sketch and pattern'.[11]

We have seen that one of the tasks of a priest is to offer sacrifices in a shrine. The earthly priests kill their victims and then offer them at the altar (see

Marshall, 2009). The sanctuary itself was entered only in order that a sacrifice might be offered. At Hebrews 9:11 we read that Jesus has passed through the temple not made with hands, that is, of a different order of creation, and has gone into the Holy of Holies. Jesus has entered, we surmise, in order to offer his sacrifice; there is no other reason to enter.

According to the writer to the Hebrews, one of the primary deficiencies of sacrifices under the old covenant is their inability to address the conscience of the believer (9:9). The blood of animal sacrifices functioned to purify the flesh of those who had been defiled but no more than that (9:13). The sacrifice of Jesus, on the other hand, is able to purify the conscience. The connection between the sacrifice of Jesus and the heart and mind is also brought out in Hebrews 10:14–16 where there is reference to the impact of the new covenant on hearts and minds.

The blood of the animal sacrifices was sprinkled around the tabernacle in order to purify it. The corollary of this for the writer to the Hebrews is that Christ cleansed the heavenly temple. He did this by means of his better sacrifice (9:23). As Marshall puts it, 'the work of atonement was not completed until something had been done in heaven that ratified what has been done on the cross; at that point the sacrifice is complete' (2009: 271).

The reader may wonder why the heavenly temple needed to be cleansed. One answer is that the rites of the two shrines must be parallel to one another. But can the argument depend on this alone? It seems there is also the matter of a link in the writer's mind between the human conscience, or perhaps the human will, and the heavenly sanctuary.

Certainly, in Chapter 10 the writer to the Hebrews argues that Christ's sacrifice is essentially one of the will (10:5–10). How might the heavenly sanctuary and the human soul be related? There may be hints of an answer elsewhere in the New Testament and within Philo and other Jewish texts.

Body–temple–Spirit language in other parts of the New Testament

First of all, we know that the Apostle Paul, in addition to applying temple language to the church, occasionally applies it to the Christian believer. He describes the body of a believer as a temple of the Holy Spirit (1 Cor. 6:19). Similarly, the argument in 2 Corinthians 5 seems to depend on the idea that language associated with the heavenly temple may be applied to both the earthly life and to the after-life or the resurrection experience of the believer. Paul speaks of the destruction of the οἰκία τοῦ σκήνους which is contrasted with the anticipated building not made with hands (2 Cor. 5:1). In Hebrews 9:11 the writer refers to the greater and more perfect σκηνῆς οὐ χειροποιήτου.

These writers are not alone in referring to the temple in this way. As we have seen, the evangelist John insists that Jesus's resurrection body is the, or a, temple.

Body–temple typology in Philo

Philo too uses this kind of language. Hayward states that in Philo's thought 'the cosmos, which is the macrocosm, finds its microcosm in human beings, who themselves may function as a temple' (1996: 111).[12] In discussing the creation of the body of Adam from the most excellent clay of all the earth, he refers to it as a 'sacred temple for a reasonable soul'.[13] This is not an isolated idea. Elsewhere he refers to the human head as the temple of reason.[14] Furthermore, he claims to have borrowed this idea from other writers.

Of course, Philo also understands the whole of creation as the highest and truest temple and refers to the angels as priests in this context. Here he is in line with the ideas of Josephus and others.[15] He emphasizes this double interpretation when he writes that 'there are, as it seems, two temples belonging to God; one being this world, in which the high priest is the divine word, his own first-born son. The other is the rational soul, the priest of whom is the real true man, the copy of whom, perceptible to the senses, is he who performs his paternal vows and sacrifices'.[16] Here Philo seems to be asserting that the Holy of Holies in the temple in Jerusalem in which the high priest ministers is a representation of the rational soul. Elsewhere he insists that 'a man who was not of the family consecrated to the priesthood, but who was a lover of God and beloved by God, though standing without the holy shrine, was nevertheless, in reality, in its inmost parts'.[17] Elsewhere, he compares the tabernacle with the idea of incorporeal virtue.[18] Finally, when discussing the image of God, he argues that the human mind with its six senses (he includes voice) and undivided mind is a reflection of the heavens with its six planets and an outermost sphere devoid of motion. He writes, 'for I imagine the heaven is in the world the same thing that the soul is in the human being.'[19]

Body–temple typology in other Jewish texts

Philo is not alone among Jewish writers in thinking of the temple in these terms. According to Simon Goldhill, the Babylonian Talmud states that 'The temple corresponds to the whole world and to the creation of man who is a small world' (2004: 106–7)[20] and that 'Each element of the temple ... corresponds to the world ... and also corresponds to a part of man—so the golden altar corresponds to the soul of man and the brass altar to the body of man'(2004: 106).

Furthermore, there is evidence for the persistence of these ideas in other Jewish sources. Goldsmith states:

> In an ancient Jewish legend, Yahweh orders Moses to build him the Tabernacle. 'But how shall I know how to make it?' Moses asks. Yahweh answers:

> Do not get frightened ... just as I created the world and your body, even so will you make the Tabernacle. ... You find in the Tabernacle that the beams were fixed into the sockets, and in the body the ribs are fixed into the vertebra, and so in the world the mountains are fixed into the fundaments of the Earth. In the Tabernacle there were bolts in the beams to keep them uptight, and in the body limbs and sinews are drawn to keep man upright, and in the world trees and grass are drawn in the earth. In the Tabernacle there were hangings to cover its top and both its sides, and in the body the skin of man covers his limbs, and his ribs on both his sides, and in the world the heavens cover the Earth on both its sides. In the Tabernacle the veil divided between the Holy Place and the Holy of Holies, and in the body the diaphragm divides the heart from the stomach, and in the world it is the firmament which divides between the upper waters and the lower waters.'[21]

Some of the evidence is reviewed by Patai who, having discussed cosmos-temple typology, writes: 'Another interesting comparison, carried through in every detail, is that between the human body and the world. ... We have already seen that the two pillars Jachin and Boaz were by Jewish legend regarded as symbolic of the sun and moon. The same source makes these two column correspond also to the eyes of the human body.' He goes on to cite a number of texts which explore this typology. The details vary. One of them states that 'The soul is within the body corresponding to the altar of incense which is within the Tabernacle' (Patai, 1947: 113–15).

Finkel cites the talmudic evidence for understanding the human as 'a small world' (1995: 115). He writes of the eleventh-century Torah commentator Ibn Ezra that 'He sees both man and the Sanctuary and its furnishings as a reflection of a higher world' (1995: 1–17). On the basis of the evidence he has gathered Finkel argues that:

> The Holy of Holies parallels the world of angels and celestial beings. Its counterpart in man is the head, the seat of his intellect and the power of speech. ... The outer chamber of the Tabernacle ... is indicative of the universe, filled with countless orbiting heavenly bodies that declare the glory of God. In man it conforms to the life force that is concentrated in the heart, the central organ that radiates vitality to all parts of the body.

The third part of the Tabernacle is the Outer Enclosure. ... It is symbolic of our lowly world. ... It parallels the natural functions of man ... .

This, the spiritual realm, the universe, and man are all reflected in the Tabernacle. (1995: 15)

> Elsewhere Finkel cites a rabbi who teaches that 'you should consider your body as the Holy of Holies. ... The brain of man can be compared to the

Ark and the Two Tablets of the Covenant. It is the noblest part of man' (1995: 16).

Some of these texts are undoubtedly late. However, Philo is broadly contemporaneous with the New Testament writers and claims to be citing ideas which he has drawn from other writers. We may conclude that there was a stream of thought within Judaism and its adherents which understood the temple in terms of the human body and that within that stream were some thinkers who identified the Holy of Holies with the human mind, soul or will. I recognize that such an understanding of the temple may not have been common and that the links between Philo and Hebrews have been a matter of dispute for some years. Nevertheless, it seems to me unlikely that Philo, who was a senior figure among Alexandrian Jews, could have been wholly a maverick thinker. It is more likely that many diaspora Jews, and perhaps some Palestinian Jews, of the period shared at least some of his ideas. The references to other Jewish texts, even if they are later and dependent on Philo, support this. Perhaps common ideas lie behind Philo and Hebrews on this point if not on others.

The temple in Hebrews

It seems possible that such ideas or something similar to them can give us some insights into the thinking that lies behind the images being used in Hebrews. The temple is a macrocosm of the human being. The way this might be expressed is difficult to summarize because our anthropology is so different from that of the ancients. However, we might understand the outer courts as the body, the holy place as the mind and the holy of holies as the secret, the invisible, the most mysterious of places; the soul or the will. This is the part, both in heaven and in humanity, that could not be cleansed by the sacrifices of the old covenant but which is impacted by the sacrifice of Jesus in the new one. The link between the sanctuary and the body seems also to be made at 9:9–10 where we are told that in the earthly sanctuary sacrifices are offered that cannot cleanse the conscience but deal with regulations for the body.

There is a further intriguing argument within Hebrews which may be related to these ideas. At 10:19–20 we are told that Jesus has opened a way to God for us; he has gone through the veil into the Holiest Place and we may hope to follow him. The writer says that the way is opened διὰ τοῦ καταπετάσματος, τοῦτ' ἔστιν τῆς σαρκὸς αὐτοῦ; through the veil, this is his flesh.

Exegetes disagree about the interpretation of these words. Some read the word 'through' to apply to Jesus' flesh so that they can understand that a believer may enter heaven by means of Jesus' flesh. Some support this reading by claiming a parallel with verse 19 where we are told that we enter the sanctuary ἐν τῷ αἵματι Ἰησοῦ; in or by the blood of Jesus. However, others have found an identification in the author's thought between the flesh of the high priest and the temple veil. This view might be supported if the link between heavenly temple and the human will is regarded as having been established. Jesus' flesh is likened to a veil which hides from sight his perfect will whose sacrifice cleanses the heavenly holy of holies.

Bruce summarizes his own position when he writes:

> The veil which, from one point of view, kept God and mankind apart, can be thought of, from another point of view, as bringing them together; for it was one and the same veil which on one side was in contact with the glory of God and on the other side with the need of men and women. So in our Lord Godhead and manhood were brought together. . . . And by his death, it could be added, the 'veil' of his flesh was rent asunder and the new way consecrated through it by which human beings may come to God. (1990: 252)

Chapter 12 of Hebrews is also full of temple imagery and stresses the heavenly destination of the faithful readers. The writer speaks of judgment in terms of a shaking of the cosmos so that only the unshakeable remains. The created has gone and what is left is that which is found beyond the veil in the temple. That which is not made by hands.

Occasionally when reference is made to the heavenly temple, objections are made on the basis that a cosmology of the kind implied in this argument is not found elsewhere in the New Testament (e.g., Peterson, 1982: 143). For the reasons I have given, I am not convinced that this is the case. Language of ascension and exaltation is very significant in nearly all strands of the New Testament (John 20:17; Acts 2:33–35; Rom. 8:34; 1 Cor. 15:24–5; Eph. 1:20–22; Phil. 2:9–11; 1 Tim. 3:16; 1 Pet. 3:22). Many of the texts include references to angels and powers being made subject to Jesus. There may not be considered by some to be an explicit reference to a heavenly temple, but the link to the idea found in Psalm 110 makes its presence implicit.

The heavenly temple in the book of Revelation

Of course, the New Testament text which speaks most clearly of the heavenly temple is the book of Revelation. The opening vision is of the exalted Jesus, his face shining like that of one who has just been in the presence of God (the experience of Moses at Exod. 34:29). Notwithstanding the absence of a turban, the long robe and sash suggest that Jesus is dressed as a priest and his location in the midst of the seven golden lampstands suggests that he is standing among the lights of the menorah. Is it possible that we are supposed to imagine a heavenly version of the ceremony held on the Day of Atonement, the high priest having emerged from the Holy of Holies which he can have entered only in order to offer the sacrifice of atonement?[23] Given that the other major text from the primitive church that focuses on the heavenly temple suggests such a ritual, an interpretation of this kind must be at least possible. This would give a connection worth exploring between the thought of Hebrews and that of Revelation.

The implication of this is that the seer has been standing in the Holy Place, the inner court of the temple. The same voice which told him to write later, at 4:1, summons him into the Holy of Holies itself where he sees, as one would expect, a throne. Astonishingly, what he does not see, but what one would surely expect of any Christian vision of heaven, is Christ seated at the right hand of God.[24] This must be deliberate. Instead the author sees, among other things, elders wearing symbols of authority and the cherubim who seem to constitute the living throne of God. John hears a promise, and for this part of the argument to work it is important to recognize that the verbs of 4:10 are not present continuous, as nearly every English translation implies, but future, that the crowns, the elders' symbols of sovereignty, *will* be cast before the throne.

Scholarship has reached no firm conclusions about the identity of these elders or why there should be 24 of them. Most popular commentaries associate them with the 12 tribes and the 12 apostles.[25] This seems reasonable but it is unclear why the apostles should be present when Christ is, as yet, absent. If we take the temple context of the vision seriously, it seems far more likely that the number 24 derives from 1 Chronicles 24.1–19 where we are told about the heads of the 24 courses of priests who 'had as their appointed duty in their service to enter the house of the LORD according to the procedure established for them by their ancestor Aaron, as the LORD God of Israel had commanded him' (1 Chr. 24:19). These heavenly counterparts of the priests of the old covenant might be expected to hand over their responsibilities when a new kind of priest was appointed. If the thought world has parallels with that of Hebrews, this will happen at the exaltation of Christ or, to put it another way, when the heavenly version of the Day of Atonement ritual takes place. It may be this that is witnessed or affirmed in the second part of the vision, recorded in Chapter 5, when the Lamb appears and the elders fall before him. The true priest, the one whose blood has ransomed saints from every nation, has been appointed and has carried out the necessary ritual; the one referred to in Hebrews 9 and 10.

John then witnesses the seals of a scroll being broken and the consequences of this action impacting the Earth. Temple imagery persists throughout the sequence, being explicit in the events associated with the fifth and seventh seals and with the interlude between the sixth and seventh seals.

The heavenly temple remains the key locus of the action described in the text. This motif culminates in the closing visions of the book. The New Jerusalem is an enormous cube (Rev. 21:16) and is of course the heavenly Holy of Holies. Lots of the imagery associated with it is derived from stories about Eden and yet there is something more. The stones which adorn the city are those associated with the breastplate of the high priest (Exod. 28:17–20). There they may well represent the stars of the heavens which must be passed through to reach the dwelling-place of God. But now the heavens which once stood between the earth and the invisible realm of God's dwelling have been bypassed for this heavenly sanctuary has descended to earth. At this point we are told that there is no temple in the city (Rev. 21:21) but it might be better to say that there is nothing redeemed which is not the temple. Furthermore, the jewels of the breastplate which once enclosed a human body now hold all that is redeemed.

It might be wiser not to press these points, but there are suggestions of body–temple typology in these chapters. First of all, the New Jerusalem is referred to as a bride at 21:2,9 suggesting that one way it may be understood is in terms of a human person. The imagery of a wedding feast has already been introduced into the text at 19:9. Furthermore, given that the jewels that adorn the foundations of the wall of the city are those of the high priest's breastplate, there may be a hint that the walls may be understood, among other things, as garment around a human body.

That everything redeemed should be pictured as the Holy of Holies and that this should be expressed in terms of the garments of the high priest seems to me to be consistent with the logic of the great narrative of the whole Bible. Eden itself included a garden but it is clearly described in terms of the later temple and Adam and Eve are its priests (Wenham, 1987: 41–67; Beale, 2004: 66–80; Barker, 1991: 57–103). The commission they are given to fill the earth may be understood as extending the temple grounds until the whole earth is subdued or, to put it in terms of later prophecy, until all the earth is filled with the knowledge of the glory of the Lord as the waters cover the sea (Hab. 2:14). So, the culmination of all things is aptly described in terms of all that is redeemed, or of all that is redeemable, finding itself part of a city which is also a shrine, with the suggestion that the whole may be compared to a body.[26]

Conclusions

The idea of a heavenly and/or eschatological temple is known to Second Temple Judaism and is present in strands of the Jesus tradition. It has found its way into the thinking of Paul and is at least implicitly present in Christian interpretation of the Old Testament texts most frequently cited in the New Testament. Hebrews and Revelation are both concerned with this heavenly and eschatological temple and with the place of the exalted Christ within that temple. They present this in rather different ways but actually have a surprising amount in common. They may both be understood as reflections on the same or on a similar theme. They may well include references to the same event. Perhaps further comparative work would enhance our understanding of both texts.

In Revelation, though body typology is not entirely absent, the focus seems to be on the temple as a representation of creation and indeed as the goal of creation. In Hebrews, while a cosmos–temple typology is present, there is also evidence of a body–temple typology. The writer of Hebrews understood that the temple could stand for the human being and that a sacrifice of the human will of the kind he outlines would be efficacious to cleanse the heavenly sanctuary which was taken to represent the human soul or will or conscience.

Notes

1 The biblical quotations in English are from the *New Revised Standard Edition*. Those in Greek are from the 1979 edition of Rahlffs for the Old Testament and from the Nestle-Aland 27th edition for the New.
2 A key element of restoration eschatology is its focus on the idea of a new or eschatological temple.
3 The context must differ because the writer places the story at the beginning of Jesus's public ministry.
4 The Lukan Paul tells the Athenians at Acts 1724 that God does not live in shrines made by hand.
5 In addition, the words have provided inspiration to hymn-writers of different kinds. There is a bluegrass song, 'I am a pilgrim', recorded by the Byrds which speaks of a heavenly destination 'not made with hands'. Then, in a rather different style, there is the recording of a song called 'Not made with hands' by the Thomas Sisters. Finally, there is a hymn in a more classical tradition by Michael Bruce which begins with the lines:

Where high the heavenly temple stands, the house of God not made with hands,
a great High Priest our nature wears, the Guardian of mankind appears.

Furthermore, in the orthodox tradition, the word *acheiropoieton* is used for an icon alleged to have come miraculously into existence. Examples include the Veil of Veronica and the Turin Shroud.

6 *The Special Laws* 1.67.
7 Ps. 8, though without explicit temple imagery, is also significant. When read christologically it sees all things as being subject to Christ. It is sometimes read in conjunction with Ps. 110 as in 1 Cor. 15:25–27 and perhaps Heb. 1:13—2:9.
8 2.23.
9 Barker (2003, 2004, 2007) offers intriguing insights into, if not always totally convincing reconstructions of, the place of the temple within the early church.
10 It could be argued that the words used of the ministry of angels in Hebrews 1 strongly suggest a liturgical and hence a temple context.
11 *On the Life of Moses* 2.74. *Exod.R.* 35.6 suggests that similar ideas existed within other Jewish traditions.
12 Elsewhere he points out that 'the cosmos and the rational element in human beings are brought together in Philo's exposition of this ancient oracle' (Hayward, 1996: 115).

13 *On the Creation* 137.
14 *Questions and Answers on Genesis* 1.5. See also *On the Virtues* 187–88, *On Dreams* 1.149.
15 *The Special Laws* 1.66. Josephus *Antiquities* 3.7.7. See the work of Beale and Barker.
16 *On Dreams* 1.125.
17 *Who is the Heir?* 82. Elsewhere Philo compares the design of the tabernacle to the human mind. *Life of Moses* 2.80–82, 96. At 134 Philo argues that the high priest may himself become 'a little world'. In *Migration of Abraham* 102 he identifies the great high priest with reason.
18 *On Drunkenness* 134–36.
19 *Who is the Heir?* 233. See *The Worse Attacks the Better* 84–85.
20 Edward Goldsmith ascribes the same words to the Midrash Tanhuma <http://www.edwardgoldsmith.org/page58.html> (accessed 14 June 2010). See Midrash Tanhuma-Yelammedenu 3.
21 <http://www.edwardgoldsmith.org/page58.html> (accessed 14 June 2010). See *Bereshith Rabbati ad* Exod. 26:33.
22 *Bereshith Rabbati*, ed. Albeck.32.
23 This argument is made in a far more elaborate and speculative form by Barker (2000: 84–6).
24 For the view that this scene includes no specifically Christian elements, see Rowland (1982: 222).
25 See e.g., Buis (1974: 27). The interpretative options are discussed by Feuillet (1958).
26 Perhaps there is Adamic imagery at work.

Bibliography

Allen, Leslie C. *Psalms 101–150*, Word Biblical Commentary, vol. 21 (Milton Keynes, UK: Word, 1983).

Anderson A. A. *The Book of Psalms*, New Century Bible Commentary, vol. 2 (Grand Rapids: Eerdmans, 1972)

Barker, Margaret. *The Gate of Heaven: The History and Symbolism of the Temple in Jerusalem* (London: SPCK, 1991).

———. *The Great High Priest: The Temple Roots of Christian Liturgy* (Edinburgh: T. & T. Clark, 2003).

———. *The Revelation of Jesus Christ; Which God Gave to Him to Show to His Servants What Must Soon Take Place* (Edinburgh: T. & T. Clark, 2000).

———. *Temple Themes in Christian Worship* (Edinburgh: T. & T. Clark, 2007).

———. *Temple Theology; An Introduction* (London: SPCK, 2004).

Bauckham, Richard. *Jude and the Relatives of Jesus* (Edinburgh: T. & T. Clark, 2004).

Beale, G. K. *The Temple and the Church's Mission: A Biblical Theology of the Dwelling Place of God* (Leicester: Apollos, 2004).

Bruce, F. F. *Hebrews* (Grand Rapids: Eerdmans, 1990).

Buis, Harry. *The Book of Revelation; A Simplified Commentary* (Philadelphia, PA: Presbyterian and Reformed Publishing, 1974).

Caird, G. B. *A Commentary on the Revelation of St John the Divine*. Black's New Testament Commentaries (London: A. & C. Black, 2nd edn, 1984).
Craddock, Fred B. 'Preaching the Book of Revelation'. *Interpretation* 40 (1986), pp. 270–82.
Crossan, John Dominic. *The Historical Jesus: The Life of a Mediterranean Jewish Peasant* (Edinburgh: T. & T. Clark, 1991).
Eusebius. *The History of the Church from Christ to Constantine* (trans. G.A. Williamson; Harmondsworth: Penguin, 1965).
Feuillet, André. 'Les vingt-quatre veillards de l'Apocalypse'. *Revue Biblique* 65 (1958), pp. 5–32.
Finkel, Avraham Yaakov. *In My Flesh I See God: A Treasury of Rabbinic Insights about the Human Anatomy* (Northvale, NJ: Jason Aronson, 1995).
Goldhill, Simon. *The Temple of Jerusalem* (London: Profile, 2004).
Hayward, C. T. R. *The Jewish Temple; A Non-Biblical Sourcebook* (London: Routledge, 1996).
Marshall, I. H. 'Soteriology in Hebrews' in *The Epistle to the Hebrews and Christian Theology* (ed. Richard Bauckham et al.; Grand Rapids: Eerdmans, 2009) pp. 253–77.
Patai, Raphael. *Man and Temple in Ancient Jewish Myth and Ritual* (London: Thomas Nelson, 1947).
Peterson, David. *Hebrews and Perfection: An Examination of the Concept of Perfection in the Epistle to the Hebrews* (Cambridge: Cambridge University Press, 1982).
Rowland, Christopher C. *The Open Heaven: A Study of Apocalyptic in Judaism and Early Christianity* (London: SPCK, 1982).
Sanders, E. P. *Jesus and Judaism* (London: SCM Press, 1985)
Van Voorst, Robert E. 'James' in *The New Interpreter's Dictionary of the Bible* Vol. 1 (ed. Sakenfeld, Katharine Doob et al; Nashville, TN: Abingdon, 2008), pp. 183–88.
Vermes, Geza. *Jesus and the World of Judaism* (London: SCM Press, 1983).
———. *Jesus the Jew; A Historian's Reading of the Gospels* (London: Fontana, 1973).
———. *The Religion of Jesus the Jew* (London: SCM Press, 1993).
Wenham, Gordon. *Genesis 1–15* (Milton Keynes: Word,1991).
Wright, N. T. *Jesus and the Victory of God* (London: SPCK, 1996).
Yonge C. D. trans. *The Works of Philo Complete and Unabridged: New Updated Edition* (Peabody, MA: Hendrickson, 1993).

God of awesome presence,
Creator of time and space
    of beyond time and beyond space
    of cosmos and kronos
    of heaven and earth.

We seek you in holy places
    needing repair and redemption
    clutching our consciences
    with calloused hands
    held before you in confession.

Cleanse us with waters that
    cascade through creation,
baptize us with waters that
    bring new birth,
that in time or out of time
    in heaven and on earth
we are united with you
    divine life
    embodied love
    swirling agent
    in whom we find our rest
    our adored one

PART FOUR

... and Cricket

13

'Play Up! Play Up! And Play the Game!' Cricket and Our Place in the World

Robert Ellis

While football has a justifiable claim to be the national sport of the English (a claim which might be based on numbers participating and watching, media coverage, etc.), it could equally be argued that no game is more quintessentially English than cricket. The game on the village green is part of the English rural idyll, a certain kind of English vision of paradise. It is appropriate, therefore, that cricket be a subject for some theological reflection—and very appropriate that such reflection be part of our honoring of a theologian who is also an ardent cricket fan.

In this essay I want to engage in theological reflection on cricket and what it tells us about our place in the world. I will do that in five interrelated sections. First I will consider some objections to sport in general and cricket in particular, including those which can be traced back to the Puritans who have been influential in the Baptist tradition in which both Ernest Lucas and I stand. More positively, I will turn to consider some cricketing aesthetics and use this as a route into discussing cricket as a phenomenon which may be said to bear some religious characteristics. Then I will attend to various issues relating to cricket and our place in the social world by examining cricket and class, before going on to consider how cricket might be said to create or express its own system of values and its own way of looking at the world. Finally I will identify three clues for a theological interpretation of cricket, elements, in effect, of a theology of sport—our place in God's world.

Taking guard: the Puritans and sport, accentuating the negative

The origins of cricket as such are not the subject of this chapter, but it is worth pausing for a moment to consider some aspects of the game's beginnings,[1] and do that in the context of the beginnings of sport more generally. The relation of sport to religion is a complex subject. If we look to the ancient world it would appear that what we might call 'sport' is intimately connected with religious ritual and may be itself a means of manipulating deity or re-enacting sacred story: certainly the meso-American ball game,[2] and the early Olympics (see Baker, 1988: 14ff.) can be thought of in these ways. Christianity has had a more complex and conflicted relationship with sport. While churches often sponsored or used games for financial and social purposes, official pronouncements were generally negative—certainly until the middle of the nineteenth century. One of the concerns expressed by churchmen from the outset was not only about what competition did to the individual who otherwise cultivated eirenic virtues, but also about what happens to the spectators who are drawn into the unfolding drama. In this regard it is worth contrasting to more or less contemporary accounts from antiquity. Tertullian wrote this of the admittedly bloody Roman games around AD 200:

> See the people coming to [the circus] already under strong emotion, already tumultuous, already passion-blind, already agitated about their bets. The praetor is too slow for them: their eyes are ever rolling as though along with the lots in his urn; then they hang all eager on the signal; there is the united shout of a common madness. Observe how 'out of themselves' they are by their foolish speeches.[3]

By contrast the pagan writer Lucian, in the second century after Christ, puts these words into the mouth of the wise Solon, who is trying to explain the appeal of watching the games amid the other more 'serious' pursuits of life:

> By seeing what was going on you would be able to appreciate that we are quite justified in expending so much ardour on the spectacles. I cannot find words to give you an idea of the pleasure that you would have if you were seated in the middle of the anxious spectators, watching the courage of the athletes, the beauty of their bodies, their splendid poses, their extraordinary suppleness, their tireless energy, their audacity, their sense of competition, their unconquerable courage, their unceasing efforts to win a victory. I am sure that he would not cease to overwhelm them with praise, to show it again and again, to applaud. (1905 edn)

Tertullian appears here to anticipate the kind of Puritan opposition to sports which would be heard again in Europe more than a millennium later—an opposition not based simply on a killjoy instinct, as is sometimes suggested, but upon a range of concerns about the use of time, the opportunities for vice (such as the gambling Tertullian feared) presented in an atmosphere of leisure and drink, and so on. Lucian's words suggest not only the thrill of competition but a delight in the aesthetics of sport. Such delight might have concerned the Puritans too, and be seen as a slippery slope ending in all kinds of lasciviousness—this joy in bodies and poses—and even the courage might have seemed a misplaced valour.

In 1611 James I of England published his *Book of Sports*. Sport historians find this a useful insight into sporting pastimes of the early seventeenth century, though it is unlikely to have provided a complete list. Cricket does not feature in James' book, suggesting that if it existed it was limited in its geographical and social appeal. The word 'cricket' is probably derived from French, perhaps indicating a Norman origin. But if so, it is unlikely to have been played by the higher social classes at first (the various lists we have of sports usually reflect the pastimes of the elite) or to have involved either large numbers watching or playing (also likely to have been reflected in contemporary records). In Elizabethan times the word begins to appear to describe a bat and ball game, and it appears in an Italian–English dictionary of 1598 compiled by John Florio (Birley, 1999: 5). However, also in 1611 two men are prosecuted in Sussex for playing cricket instead of going to church. A few years later, in the same county, six men are arraigned for playing cricket—and for breaking church windows with the ball (Birley, 1999: 7). Despite these infractions against Sunday observance, cricket does not really figure in the accounts of the Puritan crusade against sport. References only really begin to come thicker and faster after the Restoration in 1660 (see Brailsford, 1992: 44ff.).

Though cricket itself largely escaped Puritan censure, many of the Puritan concerns would have been brought to bear upon it if it had been a more significant phenomenon in the early seventeenth century. The Puritan concerns about sport can be summarized briefly. It is worth noticing that these objections are less to do with the games themselves and much more to do with the potentially formative effect of participation in games.

The first area of concern involved when the games were played—on Sundays and saints' days (the only days that working people had time off to play games). The connection with saints' days, however, brought an association with 'popery', and games were thus under suspicion because of this association, however oblique. There may have been an economic dimension to this objection too. Puritans were often members of the rising middle class. The many saints' days were days off for their workers, and so also unproductive days (Hill, 1964: 153ff.). Puritan masters defended their right (and that of their employees!) to work six days each week without interruption from saints' days—and after six days' hard work, rest was an appropriate way to spend the Sabbath. As for the Sabbath, when our Sussex men were 'caught' playing cricket, it was a day for listening to God's Word in sermons, marvelling at the Creator and his creation, and for resting. It followed that it was not a day for playing any kind of game, which could be seen only as a distraction from more worthy pursuits. Sabbath observance was already on the statute book, and the Puritans wanted the existing laws enforced. As their influence grew the court records show that they managed to ensure this in a patchy way across the country.

A second area of concern relates to types of behavior which often accompanied games. According to Phillip Stubbes' *The Anatomie of Abuses*, a major Puritan tract on the subject published in 1583 (1972b), it was permissible for Christians to play cards or bowls together provided no gambling took place. However, those who took money at gambling were basically robbers, taking money that they had not earned (Stubbes, 1972a). And Stubbes could also call bowls 'brothel bowls' and complain that it leads to swearing, blaspheming, and 'Whordome, Thefte, Robberie, Deceipt, Fraude, Cosenage, fighting Quareling, and Sometymes Murder . . . drinking, beggerye' (Stubbes, 1972a).

Third, like Tertullian centuries before, Puritans were also exercised by the violence of sport. Here football attracts particular censure as one of those practices which lure participants into sin. He describes it as 'a freendly kinde of fight. . . . A bloody and murthering practice', and we have various records of deaths occurring in these primitive and often violent football-like games (Sharp, 2000: 14ff.).

Finally, one specific consequence to which any of these recreations could be thought to lead was idleness. Time was a precious gift from God for the Puritans, and had to be invested carefully and with an eye to its productive outcome—whether for the soul or the pocket. George Herbert reflects this fear of idleness among the wealthier in his pastoral theology, *The Country Parson*, written in the early 1630s. The Puritans' fear of idleness did not refer just to the lazing around during playing, but the inculcating of a frame of mind which is easily distracted by the ephemeral and tends not to concentrate on things of real value. The Puritans regarded games as trivial—they could not see their 'point'. Later I hope to sketch a more positive theological appraisal of sport—and of cricket.

It is not difficult to imagine what the Puritans might have said to the cricketers if the rise of the game had come a hundred years or so earlier. Some Christians may still have reservations about Sunday sport, but sports of all kinds are now such a part of Sunday life in the UK and elsewhere it is difficult to remember how recent a phenomenon this is. The sport-free Sunday was a legacy of the Puritan campaigns of the seventeenth century. Some sports did allow Sunday play, and these were typically those played by the middle and upper classes in exclusive private clubs, such as golf and tennis (Brailsford, 1992: 115).[4] In both of the World Wars restrictions were lifted for workers at home, needing some let up after an arduous and long working week, and for troops overseas (Brailsford, 1992: 122). After the Great War cricket began to be played more often on Sunday. Many amateur football clubs found the move to Sunday matches in World War II so congenial (Rippon, 2007; 37) that they never went back to Saturday, despite an FA rule forbidding Sunday matches (Brailsford, 1992: 123). The government began a consultation exercise in 1961 on whether and how to relax the Sunday observance laws in regard to sport, and cricket was the first major sport to change its practice at the elite level. Afternoon charity games led to a series of televised 'all-star' charity games beginning in 1966, and then to a Sunday League in 1969, in a much shortened form of the game. The image of cricket as associated with elite social groups, as being bucolic and gentle may well have helped its move to Sundays. But the Puritans would have considered it an illegitimate way to spend the Lord's Day.[5]

Of modern sports, cricket was among the first to codify its rules.[6] The reason that rules were important in cricket before the age of organized competitions was so that gamblers could be clear with one another about what constituted a favorable result, and the proper means to obtain one. It is certain, of course, that wherever gambling plays a formative part in sport there will also be some abuse of the agreed rules, and as in other sports there have frequently been accusations of matches being thrown, and so on. It is salutary to bear this in mind with the recent furore about betting irregularities in cricket which resulted in three Pakistan international players being given jail sentences in 2011.

Recent years have seen a new, more raucous, kind of cricket fan. Matches in the twenty-first century often have large numbers of mainly young supporters who can be loud and alcohol-fuelled, though usually good-humoured. This type of behavior would not have surprised the Puritans. From early days commercial cricket matches were sponsored by public house landlords and seen as an opportunity to make money through sales of alcoholic drinks, so there is not much new in this behavior. However, put alongside the culture of various types of betting, the sales of merchandise and general air of consumerism which surrounds cricket and all other major sports, one can see there may be at least pause for thought here. Could such habits 'form' cricket's adherents in ways considered undesirable?

When it comes to violence, cricket might appear at first to have a benign reputation befitting a leisurely gentleman's pursuit. Who can become too overwrought about winning when a game can last five days and end in a draw? However, 'chin music' is a term used to describe the fast ball, steeply bouncing up to and around the batsmen's face. It is difficult to play well for all kinds of geometric reasons, but these deliveries can cross a line between fair play and physical intimidation. The practice of sledging involves (usually) fielders speaking to batsmen in an attempt to distract or enrage them. Some of the most frequently quoted examples are hilarious, but others are nasty and even vicious—again forming a pattern of intimidation. We might say, rather blandly, that competition does things to people, and not all of the things that it does to people are nice.

The complaint about idleness might seem particularly apt when levelled against a relatively sedentary (though not at elite level) sport such as cricket. But the heart of the complaint is nothing to do with how quick or slow a game is to play or watch but how distracting from more worthwhile things it can become. It is difficult to argue that the avid test match enthusiast is not at least somewhat distracted over a five-day period, but the Puritan assault kicks in when distraction makes us less effective in devotion or production: time is a gift of God, we would still say (with due qualifications no doubt), and should be properly accounted for. However we are also very much aware of the need for balance in life. Some 'distractions' can be healthy, we argue, and 'downtime' is as important as time spent in work or worship. We might even go so far as to argue that proper leisure could be a form of worship.

The Puritan critique of sport was not directed to cricket but it is possible to see how it might have been. Their concerns—about Sundays; about drinking, gambling and similar activities; about violence and competition; about the use of time and the dangers of obsessive distractions—still need to be taken seriously, however, as we consider the nature of our engagement with even the most cherished sporting activity, and even with cricket. Once more, of course, cricket is here reflecting the world. It is fashionable to disparage the Puritans, but with a little more discernment we will begin to see that they identified real dangers.

'Beautiful ball, Warney!'
From the beauty of cricket to worship and religion

Cricket aficionados tend to have a strong sense of the *beauty* of their game. C. L. R. James devotes a chapter to cricket as art (1994: 195–211). He discusses it in relation to aesthetic theory, and for James the artistic beauty of cricket is about its form and movement, and their peculiar integration in the game. The recognition of this beauty may be acknowledged by even the casual observer, but a refined and knowledgeable appreciation may be required for its finer points. James offers John Arlott's description of a bowling action and his own reflections on batting and fielding as illustrative evidence of the 'art' of cricket (1994).

When I undertook a survey of local cricketers, part of a much larger survey of sports players and spectators in order to understand how those who engage in sports understand their activity and how it relates to the things that they value in life, I found ample evidence of this sense of 'art'. Some answers, and these were a notable feature of the cricket responses, noted the aesthetic appeal of the setting of the game itself: players in whites on a ground surrounded by trees, for instance. But players also reported pleasure in the well-timed shot and the well-taken catch. One of my colleagues delights to replay on YouTube the ball which announced the arrival of the Australian bowler Shane Warne in England. The delivery spins dramatically to dismiss an astounded English batsman, and my colleague marvels in it as a thing of remarkable beauty.[7] Among cricket players and supporters his reaction is not untypical.

An appreciation of the 'beauty' of Shane Warne's leg break, or of David Gower's flashing cover drive, or of the tableau created by flannelled players under a blue sky in some scenic rural outpost (or perhaps a quasi-rural haven amid an urban sprawl) could lead us in a number of directions. The first of these would be to connect aesthetics with worship, and thence to consider cricket as a 'religious' activity. We might see in the admiration or even awe for excellent play, something like the experience at the heart of much religious experience and practice. According to Allen Guttmann, 'many sports spectators experience something akin to worship' (1986: 177). The wonder which is akin to worship may derive from a player's sense of just how hard it is to do what he or she has just seen; or there may be a 'purer' delight in what Lucian called 'their splendid poses, their extraordinary suppleness, their tireless energy, their audacity, their sense of competition, their unconquerable courage', or in what James celebrated as the wonder-ful integration of form and movement. A cover drive might be enjoyed in the same way as a *pas-de-deux* or the more static integration of form and movement in a painting. This wonder is evoked sensually; it is a response to what is seen primarily, though the various noises of cricket (swoosh, clip, clunk, etc.) and even the smell of the game may not be irrelevant. Christians nurtured in a non-conformist tradition where worship is predominantly verbal may not be used to the sensual prompts which stimulate the processes of worship. In more liturgical traditions the awe and wonder at the heart of worship is excited by such things as stained glass, incense, vestments, elaborate ritual, and other elements which may assist the worshipper.

If the jump from the cricket square to worship seems far-fetched we might consider the highly ritualized aspects of the game even at the most junior level. Michael Novak argues that all sports are 'organised and dramatised in a religious way' (1994: 19). He notes the rituals and vestments which usually accompany sport, and which can certainly be seen in cricket. Ninian Smart suggests that 'religions' can be analyzed as a matrix of interacting characteristics: they each have, to a greater or lesser extent, six dimensions—ritual, mythological, doctrinal, ethical, social, and experiential. Worship may figure in the first and last of these: its outer aspects as ritual and its inner as experience (though it will also contain the other four). Cricket is replete with ritual. From the moment players enter the field of play (and, indeed, before they do) there are expected patterns of behavior which are followed in strict sequence. From the tossing of the coin to the batsman's acknowledging applause for an innings, from the fielder's appeal to the umpire to the taking of guard at the stumps, and from the umpire's raising a finger in dismissal (rather like Caesar deciding the fate of a gladiator with his thumb) to his signalling of a boundary—and in the stands, from the Barmy Army's[8] liturgical responses to the crowd's polite applause to a rival batsman's century—ritual is everywhere. Of course, such ritual is not of itself a sure sign of any *religious* or quasi-religious intent or motivation, but it is an interesting coincidence how modern sports (with their attendant and growing spectator element) have developed since the middle of the nineteenth century when churchgoing reached its post-industrial peak, and has since been in decline (see Gill, 2003: 212). A question which seems worthy of some reflection is whether modern sport in some sense fulfils something of the function previously fulfilled by religion—particularly in England, of course, by Christianity.[9]

This sense of ritual cricket shares with modern sports in general, but it is a fine exemplar of them. As Novak remarks, religions begin with ceremonies which are often performed by surrogates wearing sacred vestments (one thinks of the fuss in some quarters when 'colored vestments' were introduced not so long ago for one-day games), and the action is highly formalized—movement and sound and silence, concentration and intensity. Novak recalls that *ascesis* is important in religion. Our word 'ascetic', applied to particular kinds of austere spirituality, derives from the Greek word used to describe the disciplines that the athletes imposed upon themselves so that their wills might control their bodies. Novak goes further than this, arguing that religions channel the sense that most humans have of danger and fate: religion puts us in the presence of powers greater than ourselves and its rituals give these powers shape, making explicit the common dreads of human life such as ageing and dying, cowardice and betrayal, failure and guilt (1994: 30).

Religion is universal in scope but also has a special place for particularity in terms of place and time. It makes certain days and hours special, and lifts its sacred time out of everyday routine creating a time within which one forgets ordinary time. For the cricketer (and the ardent fan) it's not 12.30 p.m. but half an hour before lunch, and not Friday but the second day of the test match. Cricket generates its own 'sacred' time. In the sacred time and space of sport (at the MCG, perhaps, as the first ball of an Ashes series is delivered) the players are not merely entertainers. Rather, argues Novak: 'people identify with them in a much more priestly way' as they exemplify the meaning of the sports various symbols and rituals—and the central struggle at the heart of sport, its drama, rather like the struggle between life and death itself—as we shall consider later. These superstar players no longer belong entirely to themselves and are no longer treated as ordinary run-of-the-mill human beings: 'their exploits and their failures have great power to exult - or to depress' (Novak, 1994: 32). Cricket would seem to have certain (quasi-) religious characteristics, which is all the more interesting given changes in religious practice and expression in our contemporary world.

'Who's that at third man?' Cricket, class, and our place in the world

Talk of awe and beauty can also point in another direction—toward sentimentality and nostalgia. John Simons begins an article on cricket's 'Englishness' by asserting that 'the game of cricket has become almost synonymous with all that is English' (1996). The cricketer, he argues, has a place in the national consciousness akin to a primal swain. Its antiquity is played upon (and perhaps overdone), and the idealization of the game feeds the notion of England as an 'essentially rural society' (Simons, 1996: 41) and also, we might add, of classless activity in which all groups participate as equals.

Cricket has no obvious myth of origin in the way that baseball and rugby, for instance, have told stories about the beginnings of their sports which are dubious but which enshrine certain values and also mark off possession or control. Rugby Union's story of William Webb Ellis picking up the ball and running while playing football at Rugby School has an extremely slender basis and is almost certainly untrue. But in 1896 when the story was 'discovered' it served a useful purpose in the propaganda war for the ownership of rugby at the time when the northern clubs were breaking away over the payment of players. Cricket has no such story, though it has its iconic clubs (Hambledon, MCC) and players (W. G. Grace).

Cricket may have developed among farm laborers in the sixteenth and early seventeenth century, but it soon became annexed by the ruling classes. For those obsessed with gambling, and with long leisure hours, cricket became an ideal pastime. Huge sums were wagered on the outcomes of games between assembled teams, and before long members of the aristocracy were employing professionals to play for their teams often through some sinecure on their estates. With winning came prestige, but also the opportunity to win large sums. The games were no less lucrative for the players who were handsomely rewarded. A typical division of labor saw the leisured classes specialize in batting, while the laborers added the sweaty hard graft of bowling.

It is often remarked that cricket has always been a game in which the social classes have mixed as equals, and there is some truth in that. Indeed, in the 2012 BBC Radio 4 series, *Sport and the British*, it is suggested that this is the reason why the British aristocracy suffered no uprising akin to the revolution which rocked France.[10] However, while it is true that cricket did enjoy a unique degree of social mixing and that on the pitch there was a certain equality to this (though umpires were not beyond being swayed in decision-making if their own livelihoods depended upon the 'right' call when the squire was at the crease), this remains a superficial appearance—it was the mixing of oil and water. The classes mixed to play but their distinctions were evident as they played (through the division of sporting labor) and before and after too (in the power relationships which maintained the game as a growing social phenomenon) (see Birley, 1999: 47).

The most obvious way in which social distinction was maintained until 1963 was in distinguishing 'gentlemen' (i.e., amateurs) from 'players' (i.e., professionals). The county professionals who comprised the backbone of late-nineteenth-century county sides evolved from the early professionals on country estates and the jobbing cricketers who, like mercenaries, could be hired by the game or the season—often earning huge sums by the standards of the day. Counties such as Kent had clubs which were dominated by 'gentlemen' in off-the-field matters and professionals on the field (Birley, 1999: 76ff.). Considerable social status was at stake in the distinction which accounts for W. G. Grace's insistence on being regarded as a 'gentleman', while at the same time claiming huge 'expenses' in excess of what any professional earned

(Horne et al., 1999: 55f.). The social distinctions were maintained and expressed in various ways: often 'gentlemen' and 'players' used separate dressing-rooms and even separate gates to the wicket; amateurs were known as 'Mr' or 'Esq.', whereas professionals were known by their initials—or amateurs' initials were printed before their name on the scorecard and professionals' printed after their name. In one oft-repeated incident, the home debut of a young player who would go on to have a distinguished international career was marked on the PA system at Lord's in 1950 by an apology for a mistake on the printed scorecard circulated at the ground. The announcer intoned that 'F. J. Titmus should read Titmus, F. J.' (Birley, 1999: 184ff., 271). In the last twenty years the MCC has surrendered its governing functions to an international body but it remains a symbol of the establishment and an exclusive social group.

It should not surprise us that all sports, including cricket, give clues about social relationships in the communities where they are played. Cricket is a social phenomenon and the way it is organized and played will inevitably reflect the culture in which the game exists. As cricket became more organized and 'institutionalized' through clubs and governing bodies it was probably inevitable (given the conservative nature of most institutions, especially those dominated by the elite social groups who have a vested interest in the status quo) that the game would be behind the cutting edge of social developments in wider society. It is probably true to say that social distinctions, even prejudices, have remained ingrained in aspects of cricket even though many of the old attitudes have been discarded.

Cricket reflects our place in the social world, and vigilance is required in devotion to it. Uncritically accepting the version of the world which cricket embodies and reflects back to us in its practices and values *may* lead to a distorting of values which Christian theologians and believers would want to promote for other reasons. In this, cricket is like any other sport, or indeed, like any other social practice, and the matter should not be overstated. We would not want to go to the lengths of the Puritans in their almost complete disparagement of sport. The Puritans may, however have something to teach us in realizing that sporting practices are not neutral but support and suggest other values. Christian living in the world requires an attempt at 'distance',[11] and sport must not be given a free pass from this on an assumption of its innocence or neutrality.

'Play up! Play up!' Cricket as a lens for the world

We turn now to the question of values and, more broadly, at beliefs and ways of experiencing the world. Earlier, I noted Ninian Smart's suggestion about religion having six interacting dimensions, which included the doctrinal and the ethical. It may seem at first far-fetched to think of cricket as having these quasi-religious dimensions, but consider first this recollection of cricket in a Trinidadian school in the first part of the twentieth century from C. L. R. James. James is recalling hearing the Labor politician Aneurin Bevan say that he did not so much join the Labor Party as be brought up in it. He likens this to the way he, James, imbibed certain values for life at his school, and primarily through cricket there. He likens this to receiving a doctrinal deposit from the masters (all Oxbridge men). While inside the classroom the code seemed to have less effect, and was outweighed by the effects of upbringing or temperament; on the cricket field it took its grip.

> But as soon as we stepped onto the cricket or football field, more particularly the cricket field, all was changed. We were a motley crew. The children of some white officials and white businessmen, middle-class blacks and mulattos, Chinese boys some of whose parents still spoke broken English, Indian boys some of whose parents could speak no English at all, and some poor black boys who had won exhibitions or whose parents had starved and toiled on plots of agricultural land and were spending their hard earned money on giving the eldest boy an education. Yet rapidly we learned to obey the umpire's decision without question, however irrational it was. We learned to play with the team, which meant subordinating your personal inclinations, and even interests, to the good of the whole. We kept a stiff upper lip in that we did not complain about ill fortune. We did not denounce failures, but 'Well tried' or 'Hard luck' came easily to our lips. We were generous to opponents and congratulated them on victories, even when we knew they did not deserve it. We lived in two worlds. Inside the classroom the heterogeneous jumble of Trinidad was battered and jostled and shaken down into some sort of order. On the playing field we did what ought to be done. (James, 1994: p. 25f.)

James recalls that he came to develop, in a relatively short time exposed to this cricketing value-system, a kind of Puritan discipline.

> I never cheated, I never appealed for a decision unless I thought the batsmen was out, I never argued with the umpire, I never jeered at a defeated opponent, I never gave to a friend a vote or a place which by any stretch of imagination could be seen as belonging to an enemy or to a stranger. My defeats and disappointments I took as stoically as I could. If I caught myself complaining or making excuses I pulled up. If afterwards I remembered doing it I took an inward decision to try not to do it again. From the eight years of school life this code became the moral framework of my existence. It has never left me. I learnt it as a boy, I have obeyed it as a man and now I can no longer laugh at it. I failed to live up to it at times, but when I did I knew and that is what matters. (James, 1994: p. 26)

From the colonies we hear about a very 'English' ethic which points clearly to a system of values which is embedded in traditional forms of cricket at least. Cricket, as with most other modern sports, was (re-) moulded in part by its place in the elite school system of nineteenth-century England, as well as by connected notions of Olympism and amateurism, and laden with these values was exported around the empire. It is no coincidence that the most serious cricket-playing nations are former British colonies. Cricket is not just a symbol of a certain sort of Englishness; it is also a game with a peculiar connection to imperialism. The ruling elite in the colonies had both the leisure time and the power patronage required to sustain long games over several days. James' reflections suggest that the spirit of 'fair play', of playing for the team, and so on, shape the persons playing cricket as they play. In the same way that Christians would argue that participation in a worshipping community, or that sharing in other practices of a Christian congregation *form* the persons as Christian disciples, so cricket is a formative activity. All the more reason, of course, to engage with cricket in a critical and reflective way.

James' description of the formative effects of cricket is rooted in school experience, but would not be limited to it. However, if we go back a little further in time we will discover another 'testimony' from school life which suggests something about the 'doctrinal' element of cricket. The Victorian poem 'Vitai Lampada' by Henry Newbolt connects cricket at Clifton College in Bristol[12] with the exploits of the British Army in the Sudan in 1885. The refrain of this poem, 'Play up! Play up! And play the game!' evocatively roots it in the Clifton cricket experience, but the poem is written after the heroism of the British at Abu Klea in an unsuccessful attempt to reinforce Khartoum—explicitly referred to in the central stanza.

Vitai Lampada by Sir Henry Newbolt (1862–1938)

('They Pass on the Torch of Life')

There's a breathless hush in the Close to-night –
Ten to make and the match to win –
A bumping pitch and a blinding light,
An hour to play and the last man in.
And it's not for the sake of a ribboned coat,
Or the selfish hope of a season's fame,
But his Captain's hand on his shoulder smote –
'Play up! play up! and play the game!'

The sand of the desert is sodden red, –
Red with the wreck of a square that broke; –
The Gatling's jammed and the Colonel dead,

And the regiment blind with dust and smoke.
The river of death has brimmed his banks,
And England's far, and Honour a name,
But the voice of a schoolboy rallies the ranks:
'Play up! play up! and play the game!'

This is the word that year by year,
While in her place the School is set,
Every one of her sons must hear,
And none that hears it dare forget.
This they all with a joyful mind
Bear through life like a torch in flame,
And falling fling to the host behind –
'Play up! play up! and play the game!'

This poem is fine testimony to the way in which sports in general, and here cricket in particular, begin to bear ideological freight in the elite schools of the period. The poem also suggests that sport has begun to generate, or at least express, a whole way of looking at life and the world as it shows us how playing a sport can shape the way that life in general is viewed—as a 'game' in some sense, and so the same virtues noticed and nurtured on the cricket pitch are to be valued in battle and in every sphere of life. The code of ethics is not so explicit as in James' account, but Newbolt is giving us an instance of the ethical code, James reflecting consciously upon it. In any case, Newbolt's poem is rather more than an opportunistic use of sporting imagery. Cricket, in a complex way, is first bearing an ideology brought to it from outside but then also shaping it in particular ways, with notions such as fair play, courage, selfless sacrifice, and service. It is no surprise that phrases such as 'it's just not cricket' have become part of everyday speech. Such expressions illustrate the way in which cricket has served and shaped an ideology, a British way of looking at the world. This being so, it is no wonder that the Puritans, and other churchmen before them, have been wary of the power of sport, and its shaping work.

End of play: some theological clues in cricket

It would, I am sure, be possible to write a full-blown theology of cricket. Elsewhere I attempt to sketch a fuller theology of sport (Ellis, 2012a,b), but here I will conclude by touching on three aspects of cricket which may seem fruitful for a theological interpretation of cricket.

Cricket and the creation narrative

In Genesis 1:26 the biblical narrator tells us that God determines to make humankind in God's image. There is no consensus on the meaning of the *imago Dei* texts in Scripture, but creativity is often regarded as an aspect of God's image in humanity (cf. Novak, 1994: 24). God the Creator creates creative creatures. It may be appropriate to speak of God's 'play' in creation: among biblical texts Proverbs 8:22ff. comes to mind. 'The creative God plays with his potentialities and creates out of nothing what is his good pleasure' according to Moltmann (1985: 311). In the face of the terrible uncertainties of life, human persons can understand their relationship with God as a game God plays with them, just as through evolution creation is a game played with God, says Moltmann. When we play we share in God's play, are caught up within it, and so, potentially at any rate, within God.

When human beings play they 'create a world'—cricket, for instance is a world with its own rules, boundaries (literally), and conventions. To be immersed within it can be to become unaware of the other, 'real' world beyond. Time is measured in a new way in the game, and within a repertoire of established moves cricketers improvise (create) and express themselves. Here again we see the particularity of cricket with its individual/team dynamic which gives individuals the special opportunity to create within the context of the work of the team as a whole.[13]

It is possible to think of all sports, including cricket, in particular ways, as a means by which human beings express the creativity which God has given to us in making us in *imago Dei*. Or to put it more forcefully, we might say that in playing cricket we participate in the creativity of God in creation. But the creation narrative does not reach its climax in the creation of humankind in God's image; its climax is in the Sabbath, the resting of God which lays down a pattern for the resting of human persons too. For the Puritans Sabbath/Sunday observance meant a discipline which seems to most of us austere and unnecessary. It will seem to many now that the Puritans' understanding of 'rest' was far too restrictive. Genesis 2:2f. does not tell us *why* God rested from his work of creation on the seventh day. Human rest from work seems sensible to us because we might become tired and jaded, but we would not normally think of God's rest in this way. Creating the universe had not worn God out. Instead the impression is given, considering the repeated 'and it was good' that acts as a refrain through the narrative, that God rests in order to enjoy creation.

The pattern is set: God rests, we rest. In our case it must be connected with our weariness. But in common with God's rest our Sabbath can also be an opportunity to enjoy creation. As Lucian suggested, albeit from the spectator's viewpoint, we might enjoy our bodies in sport—not a thought which would readily have occurred to the Puritans. But the opportunity to have fun, to do something which has no productive value (unless, of course, we earn our living from it—another story) and which serves no other end. Whatever else can be said about our play, it is not work. It is rest, and re-creative at that—it is a Sabbath experience.

It isn't only a game—it's life and death

In common with all modern sports, cricket arouses great passion, generates considerable suspense (if you are not a fan you might have to take my word for this), and brings with it a sense of exhilaration in success and despair in failure. Psychologically, this is probably a product of intensity of concentration, but also arises because of the way players and spectators identify their fortunes (or their team's fortunes) with the action in the game. According to Michael Novak this can be expressed more dramatically:

> the underlying metaphysic of sports entails overcoming the fear of death. In every contest, one side is defeated. . . . Defeat is too like death. Defeat hurts like death. It can put one almost in a coma, slow up all of one's reactions, make the tongue cleave to the mouth, exhaust every fount of life and joy, make one wish one were dead, so as to be attuned to one's feelings. (1994: 47f.)

The cricket fan and the cricket player will know something of the truth of this, even if this seems rather overstated. The dismissive 'it's only a game' does not work—it is not only a game, somehow something more is at stake. Every game, every *contest*, says Novak, is conducted in the view of the gods like some ancient Olympian spectacle. 'Each time one enters the contest, one's unseen antagonist is death' (Novak, 1994: 48). In my empirical survey I found plenty of evidence for such sentiments. It seems possible that the sporting experience of playing competitively is one way in which human beings test themselves in an ultimate way, push themselves to the limit and go, as it were, to the edge of the abyss which is defeat. It is a commonplace (again with ample evidence in my survey) that playing sports is considered to be a way of learning to deal with adversity. But it may be something rather more profoundly metaphysical than that: to contemplate defeat is to look into the abyss.

In cricket, with its peculiar tension between individual and team, this takes on an extra dimension. Cricket became preoccupied by, and its discourse became shaped by, statistics at a chronologically earlier stage than was the case with most other sports. It is now common to have a footballer's individual statistics (distance run during the game, passes successfully completed, etc.) displayed during TV coverage. But in cricket, the basics of batting and bowling averages, and fielding statistics have been collected and studied for generations. More recently they have been developed further—a batsman's 'strike rate' for instance is considered alongside his average score. These statistics point up the tension between cricket as a team game and cricket as a game of individual performance, because there are also many statistics relating to the team rather than the individual. Players win and lose as teams, and the individual represents the team in each phase of play when batting, bowling or fielding—however lonely their activity might seem at that moment. Cricket comprises a series of highly personal duals between this player and that in a way that is not true of nearly every other sport.[14] Cricketers, in other words, have a particular opportunity to feel this sense of exhilaration and despair, this opportunity to explore their own mortality through sport.

Cricket and transcendence

When players compete, really compete, try to be the best they can and determine to win if they can, they find themselves engaged in a quest for perfection. It is, despite the commentator's hyperbole, a quest which is doomed to fail—or at least be realized only fleetingly and provisionally. Here again the cricketer shares the drive common to all sports. The Olympic motto captures this well: 'Faster, higher, stronger'. When an athlete sets a new record for the 1500 metres, when a jogger sets a new personal best for the lap around the local park, all they have done is established another target to beat. The best performance always lies in front. It's positively eschatological.

Cricket corresponds to this pattern. The bowlers look for their best figures each time they run to the crease; the batsman looks to improve his highest score; collectively, the team seek wins, then trophies, then (for the old cliché says it is much harder to win them a second time) to retain them. Faster, higher, stronger. It appears that in truly competitive sport continuous reaching after improvement is like a restless spirit coursing through the players. The batsman wants to time the ball perfectly and hit the middle of the bat, dissect the field placing, and for a moment realize perfection. The bowler aims for the line and length which is just right for the surface and the conditions, and to make the ball move away in the air, or spin wickedly off the pitch, and will toil for hours for the one ball that is right—always lured on by this ideal of perfection.

Competition can have a negative effect on players, but the continual desire to play better seems more positive, and can be characterized as a movement towards self-transcendence. It seems to be an essential element of all serious sport: players train for it and spectators wait for it and celebrate it. It is connected to the recognition of moments of beauty which we discussed earlier, and which I suggested had some kind of religious overtone.[15]

In terms of theological anthropology we are helped here by John Macquarrie's account of Heidegger's view of the human person as 'something that reaches beyond itself' (1982: 32)—a view which Macquarrie argues is rooted in the Christian view of creation and the *imago dei*. Humanity in the *imago Dei* is a dynamic creature of potential, reaching beyond itself to God. Here part of the human restlessness, a striving for better, is named as a striving after God. We recall Augustine's famous statement from the beginning of his *Confessions*, 'for You have formed us for Yourself, and our hearts are restless till they find rest in You.'[16] The atheist existentialist Jean-Paul Sartre interpreted this human restlessness or dissatisfaction as a sign of the futility of human life, representing a futile attempt to control, to *be* God rather than to *reach* God. But for Gabriel Marcel the reaching outward and upward which characterizes human life is instead always a reaching outward and upward to God (2001; 46). We can paraphrase Marcel to say that the experience of human transcendence always tends towards an experience of *the* transcendent—God. Our experience of restless striving, of wanting to be better—of improving our average or finally beating the opponents who seem always to get the better of us—is a sign of reaching for the Creator who made us so that we restlessly reach for him.[17] Sport is always a contest, against oneself, against an opponent, and so always involves this effort at transcendence, this reaching to the transcendent. Lest this sound far too Pelagian we recall that our creative play in sport is a participation in the very play of God. God makes us restless, but our restless play is a sharing in the very life and creativity of God, and a reaching out to God.

Notes

1 For an account of the origins of cricket see Birley (1999), Major (2007) and more popularly Hughes (2009). For cricket in a broader context, see Brailsford (1992).
2 This game, which resembles modern basketball or volleyball in certain respects, appears to have been tied to aspects of the cult in its courtly form. It is likely that the losers were sacrificed. See Goldblatt (2006: 9ff.).
3 Tertullian, *On Spectacles*, XVI. Online at <http://www.earlychristianwritings.com/text/tertullian03.html> (accessed 9 June 2010).
4 A concrete example is found in Horne et al. (1999: 59).
5 A professional Christian cricketer who refused to play on Sunday would not last long, one feels. By contrast, the attitude of Scottish international rugby union player Euan Murray, who refuses to play for club or country on a Sunday, feels rather like an echo from a bygone, Puritan, age. See: <http://www.guardian.co.uk/sport/2010/feb/04/six-nations-scotland-euan-murray-interview> (accessed 29 March 2012).
6 The earliest extant rules date from 1727, though there must have been earlier versions. We know that St Alban's had a club as early as 1660. See Brailsford (1969: 209f.).
7 It can still be viewed on YouTube, in several variations of presentation. This is among the most straightforward: <http://www.youtube.com/watch?v=jrdV1jXIMDQ>. This delivery may be a good example of needing to know something about the game to know just how 'good' and therefore how 'beautiful' it is, though slow motion helps: see <http://www.youtube.com/watch?v=rnyQFWJTvQI> (both accessed 27 March 2012).
8 The England team's supporters, especially abroad, are known by this (mainly) affectionate name.

9   I examine this thesis in somewhat more detail, and also consider how Smart's other 'dimensions' of religion may be understood with reference to sport in Ellis (2012).
10 The second programme in the series, entitled 'A Level Playing Field', begins with the presenter Clare Balding suggesting: 'Now here's a theory: the French Revolution might never have happened if the French had played cricket.'
11 Rom. 12:2. One thinks also of the way Barth insists that Christ the Word stands over and against every human institution (including the church—and the MCC and ICC).
12 Ernest Lucas may almost have been able to hear the contemporary matches from his office.
13 'Each player is in the limelight long enough for aspects of character to register indelibly on other players and spectators' (James, 1994: 199).
14 'One individual batsman faces one individual bowler. But each represents his side. [Indeed,] for that moment, to all intents and purposes, he is his side. This relation of the One and the Many, Individual and Social, Individual and Universal, leaders and followers, representative and ranks, the part and the whole, is structurally imposed on the players of cricket' (James, 1994: 196f.).
15 A study by Oxford psychologists among rowers reported that team sports seem to offer increased levels of satisfaction when these moments of self-transcendence are co-ordinated, allowing team members to endure higher levels of pain and hardship because of their sense of achievement. See Cohen et al. (2010: 106–8).
16 Augustine, *Confessions*, Book 1, ch. 1: online at <http://www.newadvent.org/fathers/110101.htm> (accessed 30 March 2012).
17 Sometimes the personal pronoun seems inevitable, though not, perhaps, inevitably masculine. I note in passing that the MCC admitted women into membership in 1998.

Bibliography

Baker, William J. *Sports in the Western World* (Urbana: University of Illinois, rev. edn, 1988).

Birley, Derek. *A Social History of English Cricket* (London: Aurum, 1999).

Brailsford, Denis. *British Sport: A Social History* (Cambridge: Lutterworth, 1992).

———. *Sport and Society* (London: Routledge & Kegan Paul, 1969).

Cohen, Emma E.A., Robin Ejsmond-Frey, Nicola Knight and R.I.M. Dunbar, 'Rowers' High: Behavioral Synchrony is Correlated with Elevated Pain Thresholds'. *Biology Letters* 6/1 (2010), pp. 106–8.

Ellis, Robert. ' "Faster, Higher, Stronger"—Sport and the Point of It All'. *Anvil* 28:1 (2012a).

———. *The Games People Play: Theology, Religion and Sport* (Eugene, OR: Wipf & Stock, 2012b).

Gill, Robin. *The 'Empty Church' Revisited* (Aldershot: Ashgate, 2003).

Goldblatt, David. *The Ball is Round: A Global History of Football* (London: Viking, 2006).

Guttmann, Allen. *Sports Spectators* (New York: Columbia, 1986).

Herbert, George. *A Priest to the Temple, or, The Country Parson, His Character and Rule of Holy Life* (London: T. Garthwait, 1652).

Hill, Christopher. *Society and Puritanism in Pre-Revolutionary England* (London:

Secker & Warburg, 1964).

Horne, John, Alan Tomlinson and Gary Whannel, *Understanding Sport: An Introduction to the Sociological and Cultural Analysis of Sport* (London: E. & F. N. Spon, 1999).

Hughes, Simon. *And God Created Cricket* (London: Doubleday, 2009).

James, C. L. R. *Beyond a Boundary* (London: Serpent's Tail, 1994), first published in 1963.

Lucian, *Anacharsis: A Discussion of Physical Training*, in *The Works of Lucian of Samosata*, trans. H.W. Fowler and F.G. Fowler (Oxford: Oxford University Press, 1905), vol III.

Macquarrie, John. *In Search of Humanity: A Theological and Philosophical Approach* (London: SCM Press, 1982).

Major, John. *More than a Game* (London: Harper Sport, 2007).

Marcel, Gabriel. *The Mystery of Being* (South Bend, IN: St Augustine's Press, 2001).

Moltmann, Jürgen. *God in Creation: An Ecological Doctrine of Creation* (London: SCM Press, 1985).

Newbolt, Henry. *Selected Poems of Henry Newbolt* (London: Thomas Nelson, 1940).

———. 'Vitae Lampada'. In Newbolt, *Selected Poems*, 87.

Novak, Michael *The Joy of Sports* (Lanham, MD: Madison, rev. edn 1994).

Rippon, Anton. *Gas Masks for Goal Posts: Football in Britain During the Second World War* (Stroud: Sutton, 2007).

Sharp, James. *The Bewitching of Anne Gunter: A Horrible and True Story of Football, Witchcraft, Murder, and the King of England* (London: Profile, 2000).

Simons, John.'The Englishness of Cricket'. *Journal of Popular Culture* 29:4 (Spring 1996), pp. 41–50.

Smart, Ninian. *The Religious Experience* (Upper Saddle River, NJ: Prentice-Hall, 5th Edn, 1996).

———. *The World's Religions* (Cambridge: CUP, 2nd Edn, 1998).

Stubbes, Phillip. 'Cards, Dice, Tables, Tennisse, Bowles, and Other Exercises, Used Unlawfully in Aligna'. In *The Anatomie of Abuses* (Amsterdam: Da Capo Press, 1972a—a facsimile of the Bodleain Library ms), no page numbers.

——— 'The Manner of Sanctifying the Sabaoth in Aligna'. In *The Anatomie of Abuses* (Amsterdam: Da Capo Press, 1972b—a facsimile of the Bodleain Library ms), no page numbers.

Our God
>   Creator of pleasure and playfulness
>   blender of beauty and batting
>   and bowling and fielding
>   bound together in intricate webs
>   of written rules and unspoken ways.

> We thank you for cricket
>   for the drawn-out Tests
>   a triumph of the long play
>   countercultural waiting
>   hour upon hour
>   lived in hope and anticipation;
>   and for the immediacy of 20/20
>   floodlit, fast, frenzied
>   over giving way to over
>   run to run
>   not long now.

> We thank you
>   for disciplined working together
>   and for individual brilliance
>   for hallowed time
>   spent in shared suspense
>   for quickening reflexes
>   and the umpire's hawkeye.

> And all the people said,

Select Bibliography of Works by Ernest Lucas

Our World (with Hazel Lucas) (Lion, 1986).
Some Scientific Issues Related to the Understanding of Genesis 1–3 (UCCF, 1987).
Being Transformed (with M. Eden) (Marshall Pickering, 1988).
Akkadian Prophecies Omens and Myths as Background for Daniel Chapters 7–12, PhD thesis, University of Liverpool, 1989.
'The Origin of Daniel's Four Empire Scheme Re-Examined', *Tyndale Bulletin* 40.2 (1989), pp. 185–202.
'God, GUTS and Gurus: The New Physics and New Age Ideology', *Themelios* 16.3 (1991), pp. 4–7.
A Short Introduction to the New Age Movement (Regents, 1992).
'Sacrifice in the Prophets'. Pages 59–74 in R. T. Beckwith and M. J. Selman (eds), *Sacrifice in the Bible* (Baker, 1995).
Science and the New Age Challenge (Apollos, 1996).
Christian Healing; What Can We Believe? (ed.) (Lynx, 1997).
'Science, Wisdom, Eschatology and the Cosmic Christ'. Pages 279–300 in K. E. Brower and M. W. Elliot (eds), *The Reader Must Understand: Eschatology in Bible and Theology* (Apollos, 1997).
'The New Testament Teaching on the Environment', *Transformation: An International Journal of Holistic Mission Studies* 16.3 (1999), pp. 93–9.
Decoding Daniel: Reclaiming the Visions of Daniel 7–11 (Grove Books, 2000).
'Daniel: Resolving the Enigma', *Vetus Testamentum* 50.1 (2000), pp. 66–80.
Can We Believe Genesis Today? The Bible and Questions of Science (IVP, 2001).
Daniel (Apollos, 2002).
Ezekiel (Bible Reading Fellowship, 2002).
Exploring the Old Testament Vol. 3: The Psalms and Wisdom Literature (SPCK, 2003).
'A Statue, a Fiery Furnace and a Dismal Swamp: A Reflection on Some Issues in Biblical Hermeneutics', *Evangelical Quarterly* 77.4 (2005), pp. 291–307.
'Science and the Bible: Are They Incompatible?', *Science and Christian Belief* 17.2 (2005), pp. 137–54.
'A Biblical Basis for the Scientific Enterprise'. Pages 49–68 in D. Alexander (ed.), *Can We Be Sure about Anything? Science, Faith and Postmodernism* (IVP, 2005).
'Interpreting Genesis in the 21st Century', *Faraday Papers*, Faraday Institute for Science and Religion 11 (2007).
'Poetics, Terminology of'. Pages 520–25 in T. Longman III and P. Enns (eds), *Dictionary of the Old Testament: Wisdom, Poetry and Writings* (IVP, 2008).
'Wisdom Theology'. Pages 901–12 in T. Longman III and P. Enns (eds),

Dictionary of the Old Testament: Wisdom, Poetry and Writings (IVP, 2008).
Think God, Think Science (with Michael Pfunder) (Paternoster, 2008).
'Daniel'. Pages 518–71 in J. H. Walton (ed.), *Illustrated Bible Backgrounds Commentary Vol 4* (Zondervan, 2009).
'Infallibility and Inerrancy of the Bible'. Pages 260–61 in J. H. Y. Briggs (ed.), *A Dictionary of European Baptist Life and Thought* (Paternoster, 2009).
'Inspiration of the Bible'. Pages 264–5 in J. H. Y. Briggs (ed.), *A Dictionary of European Baptist Life and Thought* (Paternoster, 2009).
'Statue et fournais ardente', *Hokhma*, 95 (2009), pp. 60–83.
'Interpreting Genesis 1–3 in the Twenty-First Century', *The Bible in Transmission*, (Spring 2009), pp. 13–15.
'Preaching Apocalyptic'. Pages 179–96 in G. J. R. Kent, P. J. Kissling and L. A. Turner (eds), *'He Began with Moses ...': Preaching the Old Testament Today* (IVP, 2010).
'God and "Natural Evil" ', *Faith and Thought* 50 (2011), pp. 16–26.
'Daniel, Book of'. Pages 110–23 in M. J. Boda and J. G. McConville (eds), *Dictionary of the Old Testament Prophets* (IVP, 2012).

www.ingramcontent.com/pod-product-compliance
Lightning Source LLC
Chambersburg PA
CBHW071246230426
43668CB00011B/1606